ChristWise

Leader's Guide for Juniors, Teens, and Youth

To order additional copies of *ChristWise: Leader's Guide for Juniors, Teens, and Youth,* by Troy Fitzgerald, call 1-800-765-6955.

Visit us at www.reviewandherald.com for information on other Review and Herald® products.

ChristWise

Leader's Guide for Juniors, Teens, and Youth

Troy Fitzgerald

REVIEW AND HERALD® PUBLISHING ASSOCIATION
HAGERSTOWN, MD 21740

The author assumes full responsibility for the accuracy of all facts and quotations as cited in this book.

Unless otherwise indicated, all Scripture texts are from the *Holy Bible, New International Version.* Copyright © 1973, 1978, 1984, International Bible Society. Used by permission.

This book was
Edited by Gerald Wheeler
Copyedited by Delma Miller and James Cavil
Designed by Tina M. Ivany
Electronic makeup by Shirley M. Bolivar
Cover art by PhotoDisc
Typeset: 12/16 Veljovic Book

PRINTED IN U.S.A.

06 05 04 03 02   5 4 3 2 1

R&H Cataloging Service
Fitzgerald, Troy, 1968-
    ChristWise

    1. Baptism—Handbooks, manuals, etc.   2. Seventh-day Adventists—Doctrinal and controversial works.   3. Baptism—Examinations, questions, etc.   I. Title.

                              265.13

ISBN 0-8280-1713-1

Dedication

To Mom and Dad, who by their faithful example taught me
the joy of the Adventist message.

Contents

Statement of Philosophy

The *Leader's Guide* is a simple resource tool for those who study the *ChristWise* lessons with young people. It contains basic ideas about the way this study has been designed as well as instructions and suggestions on how to make the lessons most effective. The *Leader's Guide* includes all the material of the student editions, plus instructional and background information, teaching commentary, and annotated suggestions for each lesson.

Introduction

ChristWise is a journey through the life of Christ with the purpose of preparing young people for baptism. Our use of the life of Christ is more than a series of stories that teach truths about God. It is a chance to cooperate with the Savior in guiding young people to an understanding of Seventh-day Adventism. The goal of the journey is to know Christ personally and therefore unite with Him in a relationship that not only shapes the character of young people, but significantly affects the world they live in. My prayer is that this experience will enable young people to enter into both baptism and the church with a sense of purpose and active participation in spreading the good news of Jesus Christ.

1
Background on Religious Education

One of the missing elements in our culture today is what I call "the Grand Narrative." While our world is becoming more and more busy and information-packed, the story of humanity and of God—the story that defines people—is fading. Eugene Peterson comments:

"We live in a world impoverished of story. Words in our culture are a form of currency used mostly to provide information. By the time we have completed our assigned years in the classroom, we have far more information than we will ever be able to put to use. . . . There is no discovery, no relationship, no personal attentiveness in them (words). For that we need story and storytellers."*

Throughout the centuries God has used stories to foster His relationship with people. God reminded Israel of their role as His children through stories. A story narrated by the prophet Nathan led David to yield his life to God with unwavering fidelity. God clarified His commitment to His children through the story of Hosea and Gomer. In Scripture God is the great storyteller of "the Grand Narrative."

At the heart of God's course description for passing on the faith to His children is a challenge to find ways to constantly keep that faith before them:

"These commandments that I give you today are to be upon your hearts. Impress them on your children. Talk about them when you sit at home and when you walk along the road, when you lie down and when you get up. Tie them as symbols on your hands and bind them on your foreheads. Write them on the doorframes of your houses and on your gates" (Deut. 6:6-9).

This text displays the ultimate goals of religious education:

1. "These commandments that I give you today are to be upon your hearts." Children can intuitively sense someone who is genuine. It is no surprise that those who are effective teachers will inspire children with their sincere expression. Somehow, the greatness and goodness of God is in the heart of the teacher. The teacher tells the stories with passion and conviction. Such stories leap to life most easily for children when they are already alive in the heart of the storyteller. The first goal for teachers using this study guide should be to deepen their own understanding and experience. Inevitably, "who we are" will teach as much as, if not more than, anything we say. This study seeks to transfer more than information—it is driven by the notion that the heart of the teacher (parent, fellow student, pastor, leader) motivates the student to strive to understand God's Word.

2. "Impress them on your children." At one time, parents served as the major source of knowledge about God. While others in the communities were helpful, Mom and Dad were the primary teachers. Today the family often relies on the local church, church school teachers, and others to help engage young people in a committed relationship to God. Whether the teacher is a family member, a pastor, a teacher, neighbor, or a dedicated young person in the church, the task is the same: Impress the truth of God on young people. Teaching (Impress) in this context is more than doling out dry data. Studying, memorizing, serving, creating, and sharing are all part of the learning journey. Many young people know what happens to the body when a person dies. They recognize that Saturday is the Sabbath of the Bible. And they understand that Jesus will come in the clouds literally, personally, and visibly. But something is still missing. The word "impress" carries a sense of impact and permanence that goes beyond passing on a list of facts. Real education is built on the idea that we share honestly and openly in a growing relationship.

3. "Talk about them when you sit at home and when you walk along the road, when you lie down and when you get up." The key focus of the third goal is that we grow spirtually as we live in the cycle of daily routine. Because of our hectic pace of life, it is crucial to learn to integrate the discovery of God's love and goodness. In ancient times children spent all day with their parents, who could tell them stories, share experiences, and teach songs as they worked, played, and lived. Today, school, lessons, and sports divide the day. Our fractured lives call for teaching structured in such a way that it becomes part of the everyday experience.

4. "Tie them as symbols on your hands and bind them on your foreheads." Children are inherently creative. When it comes to religious education, what we hear someone else say has only a minimal lasting effect on our minds and hearts. But when young people create and construct the lessons of the Christian life, the impact is everlasting. We call it active learning. As young people learn by doing and creating, shaping and refining, they move beyond a completed lesson to a new way of living. In short, they make it real by living it.

5. "Write them on the doorframes of your houses and on your gates." Learning is most effective when we can fix the lessons into our memories with symbols, stories, and significant markers that in one look, one glance, one thought, connect the mind and the heart to a moment when God's power and presence were real to us. This is the purpose of rituals and reminders. The more we remember the things we have done, the deeper we sense the power of our learning. We especially tend to remember what we write. The process of writing things down crystallizes and clarifies important experiences.

Children usually choose baptism when they are young. As they grow, their experience of faith changes. Their concrete understanding of the facts about God and His Word shifts to abstract "wonderings" that search for links to their daily lives. We need to understand that at the point of conversion and baptism their education is only beginning. Young people will ask questions about their faith—count on it. Such questions come in many forms, both verbal and behavioral. God knows the way we develop, and in Deuteronomy 6 He gives parents and teachers one of the greatest answers to the challenges of teaching spiritual truths to kids:

"In the future, when your son asks you, 'What is the meaning of the stipulations, decrees and laws the Lord our God has commanded you?' tell him: 'We were slaves of Pharaoh in Egypt, but the Lord brought us out of Egypt with a mighty hand. Before our eyes the Lord sent miraculous signs and wonders—great and terrible—upon Egypt and Pharaoh and his whole household. But he brought us out from there to bring us in and give us the land that he promised on oath to our forefathers'" (verses 20-23).

God's leading and blessing, His discipline and supernatural power, all find their perfect medium in the story. Be assured, though—the *Bible* is more than "just a bunch of stories." The wonderful narratives of Scripture provide direct instruction, truthful sayings, and statements about people, life, and God's unfailing love for people.

Ultimately, the Bible is a story about God and people, and we find our faith in the living God by weaving our own stories into the fabric of the continuum of God's Word.

Against the backdrop of this "Great Story," the goal of *ChristWise* is to grow young people firmly into an experience with Christ that demonstrates a commitment to His church and a certainty of God's purpose for their life here on earth and in the world to come.

---

* Eugene Peterson, *The Stories of Jesus,* p. 8.

2
Philosophy of
ChristWise

What response do we give children when they ask to get baptized? How do we approach the task of preparing them to walk fully in the grace of God's Son? What resources do we use to make sure that young people are ready for baptism? How can we be sure that they really understand what they are doing? What all do they need to know before their baptism? What's the best age? How long should they wait? The joy of the child's decision can fade as we hesitate to jump in too soon or do not respond quickly enough to a fleeting window of opportunity. Many young people maintain that "they didn't know what they were doing" when they were baptized as a child. Others recall wanting to be baptized, asking to be baptized, but ultimately losing interest when no one paid any attention.

Clearly, we need a thoughtful approach for relating to, preparing, and developing the youth of our church. The very core of this study is the hope that each person who uses this model will become united with Jesus confidently and permanently.

ChristWise is a journey in which young people prepare for baptism by starting and ending with the person of Christ. "What about 'the truth,' the whole truth?" many ask. The truth (the myriad of doctrinal teachings) is incomplete if Christ is not present and central to each idea. The idea is not a new one to Adventist education:

"Christ's favorite theme was the paternal tenderness and abundant grace of God; He dwelt much upon the holiness of His character and His law; He presented Himself to the people as the Way, the Truth, and the Life. Let these be the themes of Christ's ministers. Present *the truth as it is in Jesus.* Make plain the requirements of the law and the gospel. Tell the people of Christ's life of self-denial and sacrifice; of His humiliation and death; of His resurrection and ascension; of His intercession for them in the courts of God; of His promise, 'I will come again, and receive you unto myself' (John 14:3)" (*Christ's Object Lessons,* p. 40; italics supplied).

"If we teach the truth as it is in Jesus, religion will not be regarded as drudgery, but as a delight. Let the teachers bring sunshine, gratitude, and hearts full of tenderness and Christlike compassion, into their work, and leaven the hearts of their scholars with the spirit of unselfish love; for this is the spirit that pervades heaven" (*Counsels on Sabbath School Work,* p. 107).

"The love of the truth as it is in Jesus means the love of all that is comprised in the truth Christ taught. Let our teachers strive to follow His example, to cherish His spirit of tender sympathy. Let none leave the love of Christ out of their labors, but let each ask himself the questions, Is my life a consistent life? Am I guided by the Holy Spirit? It is the privilege of every teacher to reveal the power of a pure, consistent, Christ-loving workman. The spiritual-minded teacher will never have an uncertain religion. If he truly loves the service of Christ, he will have spiritual discernment and spiritual life" (*Counsels to Parents, Teachers, and Students,* p. 362).

"The Truth as It Is in Jesus.—Teach the simple lessons given by Christ. Tell the story of His life of self-denial and sacrifice, His humiliation and death, His resurrection and ascension, His intercession for sinners in the courts above. In every congregation there are souls upon whom the Spirit of the Lord is moving. Help them to understand what is truth; break the bread of life to them; call their attention to vital questions" (*Evangelism,* p. 188).

"The truth as it is in Jesus can be experienced, but never explained. Its height and breadth and depth pass our knowledge. We may task our imagination to the utmost, and then we shall see only dimly the outlines of a love that is unexplainable, that is as high as heaven, but that stooped to the earth to stamp the image of God on all mankind" (*Christ's Object Lessons,* p. 129).

This study guide seeks to present opportunities for young people to discover every "truth as it is in Jesus." John, the disciple of Jesus, would agree: "Now this is eternal life: that they may know you, the only true God, and Jesus Christ, whom you have sent" (John 17:3).

The major features of this study all emphasize a journey toward Christ-centered truth. It is:

Built on stories. The most effective way to teach children how to follow Christ is through stories. Stories mean different things to kids at different stages of development. With young people who are junior age (9-12), the facts contained in the stories make them meaningful. As young people grow into their early adolescence stage (13-15), the characters in the story become the highlight for them. They are trying to figure out "who they are," and identification with other people helps this process. Youth (16-18 and up) tend to wonder what the meaning of the story might be in light of their own experience. The stories of Christ's life are the perfect way to shape young hearts and minds. Furthermore, when students connect their stories to the experiences of Christ, it deepens the certainty of their faith more than if they were to simply recall "the old story." Curriculum for faith development must be narrative-driven.

Christ-centered. The Bible is clear about focusing on Christ first and foremost as we teach: "You diligently study the Scriptures because you think that by them you possess eternal life. These are the Scriptures that testify about me, yet you refuse to come to me to have life" (John 5:39, 40). Everything in the Bible seeks to draw our attention to Christ. The book of Revelation describes itself as the "revelation of Jesus Christ" (Rev. 1:1). Hebrews adds: "In the past God spoke to our forefathers through the prophets at many times and in various ways, but in these last days he has spoken to us by his Son, whom he appointed heir of all things, and through whom he made the universe" (Heb. 1:1, 2). Ellen White writes that Christ is the center of knowledge—"the truth as it is in Jesus." The bottom line is that every doctrine (the state of the dead, the Sabbath, the sanctuary) is meaningless without Christ. The study of these doctrines as they appear in the daily life of Jesus adds color and meaning to those beliefs that Adventists have embraced for years.

Doctrinally integrated. The Seventh-day Adventist Church holds a cluster of 27 major teachings that it considers to be foundational. Rooted in Scripture, they are wonderful descriptions of God and His love for people. But if these teachings are presented separately, one by one, it is difficult to see the big story, the story of God and you.

The beautiful truths of the Seventh-day Adventist Church need to be understood in the context of the story of Jesus. Looking at the doctrines individually is like staring at a painting with your nose an inch away. It is hard to see the big picture because you can see only one small part at a time. But examining the life of Christ is like stepping back and viewing the whole picture at once. While you can focus on the different colors, the special parts of the picture, it all makes sense only when you can see those details as they are in Christ.

You will see the *great controversy* in the temptations of Jesus.

You will see *the Trinity* at the baptism of Jesus.

You will see *the law of God* written out, not on blocks of stone, but by the hand of Jesus on the hearts and lives of people.

You will see *the Sabbath* as Jesus kept it, and how we might experience the joy of that rest.

You will hear Jesus make promises about the *Second Coming*, at which He will end the old story and start a new one.

You will see a remnant, a group of people who are faithful to Jesus when others turn away.

You will see a young girl come back to life again, and view the smile on Jesus' face as He talks about *the resurrection.*

You will break bread with Jesus and the disciples and sense the renewal that comes at *the Lord's Supper.*

You will hear the sound of the Temple curtain torn in two in *the sanctuary* when Jesus turns ritual into reality.

As the disciples go out to use their *spiritual gifts,* you will be wondering what God is calling you to do.

When you see a widow give all she has to God, you too will experience the joy of *Christian stewardship.*

As Jesus uses clay to restore blind eyes, you will remember that at *Creation* He originated those eyes. You will hear Jesus say that He was around before Abraham, even before the world began. While that may be hard to fathom, again and again He will demonstrate in His life that He is the Creator and Re-creator of our lives.

You will see people racing to the riverside, eager to start a brand-new life with God in *baptism.*

You will be surprised as the failures of Jesus' most devoted friends reveal the true *nature of humanity.*

When Jesus speaks of the way *marriage and family* used to be, you will open your eyes to God's incredible plan for people in this world.

You will notice that when Jesus talks about *Christian behavior,* His expectations are so great that you will have to trust Him for help to be what He wants you to be.

When Jesus talks about *the church,* you won't see buildings, but people living and loving the way He did.

When Jesus reminds the church leaders about the way they treated the prophets of old, you will learn to listen to the *gift of prophecy* that we still have today.

When Jesus quotes from the *Holy Scriptures,* will you see another rule-book or will you see the story about God and you?

Active Learning (methods). Jesus was the master teacher, and learning the way He taught is the ultimate teaching goal. The methods He used are simple, yet profoundly powerful. His widely varied teaching strategies include:

1. *Parables (stories).* Jesus would paint the truth on the canvas of the hearts and minds of people through stories. The lessons buried in the story were life-changing—because at their heart, stories are relational. They have to do with real people, with real problems, with the nitty-gritty of everyday life. Parables and stories also allow learners/listeners to discover the truth on their own. This study will seek to create opportunities for just such discoveries.

2. *Thoughtful Questions.* The questions we ask and the way we formulate them have everything to do with effective learning. For example, a teacher can easily ask, "What does John 3:16 say God did for us?" The answer is just as effortless: "He gave His only Son." Not only is the response obvious, but arriving at the answer doesn't require the learner to think, feel, or experience anything other than the process of reading the words. But look at the kind of questions Jesus asked:

- "If the salt loses its saltiness, how will it become salty again?"
- "If you love those who love you, what reward do you have? Don't the tax collectors do the same?"
- "Why are you worried about clothing?"
- "Which is easier to say, 'Your sins are forgiven,' or 'get up and walk'?"
- "Why are you afraid?"
- "Do you believe that I am able to do this?"
- "Who do you think I am?"
- "Have you not read what David did when he was hungry?"
- "What is written in the Law—how does it read to you?"
- "Which of these three proved to be the neighbor?"
- "What do you want Me to do for you?"
- "Who is greater, the one who reclines at the table or the one who serves?"

The questions Jesus asked don't simply seek to gain the correct response—they pulled the learner into an experience—a struggle. We must seek to ask good questions, ones that make the student think, feel, experience, and respond.

3. *Action.* When the lawyer discovered what mercy was, Jesus said, "Go and do likewise." To do it. Try it. Experience it. Live it. Furthermore, He compelled those He touched to talk about their experience as well. He gave the disciples power and authority to cast out demons, heal the sick, and raise the dead—He gave them the gift of experience. Jesus said to Peter, "Drop your nets and come learn what it means to be a fisher of men." Similarly, He also pointed the man He had healed of a demon toward personal action: "Go and tell everyone in your village how God has had mercy on you." Part of this journey is doing what Jesus does (example) and what He says to do (instruction). Active learning is simply learning by doing. You can know that forgiveness is important and that God forgives everyone who asks, but you "really know" forgiveness when you experience what it is like to forgive someone who has wronged you. Jesus told the story of the two foundations: "Everyone who hears My words and does them is like the man who built his house on the rock." What strengthens the faith experience of young people, what provides it with a solid foundation, is the active expression of their faith.

4. *Reflection.* The reflective portion of every study is also vital. Journaling and reflecting are significant exercises that deepen faith and strengthen our understanding. Some recommended journal promptings appear toward the end of every study and sometimes at the beginning. Many of the writers of religious education curriculum know that the exercise of journaling is helpful, but their curriculum leaves little room for it. The suggestion to young people is obvious: if there is no room, you must not want me to say much. *ChristWise* leaves space for the thoughts and experiences of the learner in each study.

The People Who Teach

ChristWise is designed for pastors, teachers, youth leaders, Sabbath school teachers—for anyone committed to mentoring young people in their walk with Christ. However, my experience is that this study works best when done in pairs. Pairs are more personal than a classroom full of students. Honesty and accountability increase in smaller groups and decrease as groups become larger. High school and college students often are the most effective at leading young people in this study because of the mentoring element that grows out of the experience. High school and college students are usually the first to admit that they don't know it all, which makes the journey more cooperative and less directive. Clearly, young people grow best when they sense they are learning *with* their teachers as well as learning *from* them. Bible studies that are predominantly question and answer, explanation and quizzing, stating and repeating, tend to fail at really engaging young people to live more fully in a relationship with Christ. *ChristWise* seeks to have those involved share experiences and responses back and forth as they proceed through the studies. It assumes that no matter their age or identity, two people can learn from and with each other.

3
The Different Age Groups:
Juniors, Teens, Youth—Who They Are and How They Learn

Juniors (9-12)

Who They Are. I'm fascinated with how long people can keep their eyes open without blinking. Without a doubt, some of the junior-age children I observe seem to think that if they blink during a riveting story they will miss the best part. Probably one of the most exciting and most crucial moments in faith development happens between the ages of 9 and 12. If we understand the wide-eyed nature of juniors and meet it with appropriate action and activities, the potential for shaping their faith experience is unlimited.

In order to provide meaningful religious education for the junior-age child it is important to note some key characteristics about them. While many leaders of faith development have created models for distinguishing the various stages of faith, the characteristics and suggestions for teaching remain similar. A specific model, Gillespie's *Experience of Faith,* however, includes a more thorough understanding of the field and a working knowledge of how Adventist churches and schools present religious education. The junior-age group is more or less a transition between middle childhood and early adolescence.

One of the core tendencies of early adolescence is the powerful role people play in children's lives. Children at this stage begin to strive for independence as they become more aware of their own individuality. The process of growing as an individual occurs simultaneously with a search for people whom they can identify with and model their lives after. Mothers and fathers, close relatives, those who interact regularly with children, such as teachers, and older heroes become significant role players in the way they come to know God. Juniors are building the structure of their own faith on the one hand, while on the other measuring the people they want that structure to represent.

Children at this stage tend to move "from concrete thinking to a more intuitive thought."[1] It is important to note that even while they are beginning to employ abstract thinking, the development of meaningful faith experiences depends on whether they have enough hooks to hang their ideas on. In other words, as each child develops intellectually and acquires new experiences and information, his or her ability to connect abstractions to reality will also increase.

Children learn actively and enthusiastically at this stage. Given the fact that juniors accumulate information and intentionally organize it while at the same time formulating their values, they are constantly willing to experience new ways to perceive and describe God. It is no wonder that during this stage many young people make the choice to surrender their life to God and show it by baptism. Their concern about how such decisions will appear to their peers will emerge later in their adolescent journey. But for now they are responding in ways that beg for churches to build upon their thirst for newness and ingenuity.

How They Learn. The most powerful tool in teaching juniors is friendship. As juniors develop a sense of who they want to grow into, their relationships with significant spiritual role models become foundational. As we seek to lead young people closer Christ, it becomes vitally important to understand that the friendships of pastors, teachers, and parents will shape these children's lives more than a clear and in-depth awareness of John 3:16. The most powerful demonstration is how these loved and admired people relate to the truths found in John 3:16. Another word for this is "modeling."

The story is another mode through which juniors acquire a knowledge of God. Stories that feature people who demonstrate heroic faith in the midst of challenging circumstances move juniors to adopt the values of the characters they read or hear about. Indisputably, stories are the oldest and most powerful teaching method, regardless of age or developmental stage. Inherent in the fabric of stories is the most sacred learning moment—the opportunity for discovery. The parable leaves the listeners to sort out the meaning and apply the message to their life. Stories are human and timeless, connecting the imagination with reality and providing lasting memories. Thus stories are powerful, personal, and unforgettable.

The lessons that teach faith work best through active experimentation. Here is where even stories fall short of a complete learning experience. We can define compassion by colorful language, animate it through accounts of heroic action by compassionate people, but nothing teaches the full meaning of compassion as well as the experience of feeding the homeless or holding the hand of a dying cancer patient. Ultimately, it is the collaboration of many methods that deepens the religious experience of children growing up in—or toward—the church. Understanding who they are and how they learn enables those entrusted with their teaching to be more effective.

Teens (ages 13-15)

Who They Are. Without a doubt, teen speakers are the hardest to find for camp meetings. And there is a good reason. What is happening to young people during the ages of 13-15 (junior high) is phenomenal—and also fearful. Instead of the wide-eyed receptivity of juniors, the teen displays a faith development as fragile as it is significant. Parents will nod in agreement as Gillespie explains, "Adolescents have begun to discover that they are finally their own person. At last, they can decide their fate and their future. They really don't have to take 'it' anymore."[2] The best way to describe the faith experience of junior high youth is that their faith is now extremely personal.

Faith development can become a war between a personal desire for a spiritual experience and the competing values of a culture that strongly appeals to teens. Advertisers market hard for this age group. Yet these same young people desire an authentic spiritual life. Since teens don't think much about the future, they strive to experience God's presence right now. Religious education must seize every opportunity to build faith. The phrase "You'll get it when you are older" will not sit well with them. They demand an experiential connection with the world of spiritual things, never doubting that they are ready for such an experience.

We can also characterize young teens by their struggle for freedom. As independent beings teens demand the right to make decisions about their relationships, their lifestyle, their behavior, and their religion. Any hint of coercion instantly short-circuits the process of faith development. That is not to say that we should mindlessly turn them loose to their own inventions. But when it comes to the spiritual life and the acceptance of a faith system that works for them, the task is not as much to guide their behavior as it is to give them tools to enable them to develop their own worldview. When we entrust them with the power of making their own choices, they can truly embrace a faith experience based on the notion of freedom.

In the whirlwind of such an uncertain process, though, the self-esteem of the typical teen is extremely fragile. The journals of young people in their teens testify that the smallest thing can either crush or strengthen their egos and sense of self. We can sum up the task of religious education and ministry to this age group in a few brief goals: actively experiencing the spiritual life disciplines with them, deepening their faith experience by allowing them to choose wisely from the information available, and honestly affirming them in their journey. If we meet these goals, they will acquire deep personal faith.

How They Learn. Effective teachers understand their learners. If nothing else, their characteristics and attitudes may at least suggest what not to do. In the case of teens, a few helpful suggestions will help you guide them to a real faith.

Have meaningful conversations about what is real and right. Teens are struggling to construct their theories of personal ethics, and you can use the experiences they see in the world around them to help them formulate a Christian response. Empower students for significant ministries. Their faith will then grow as a result of their own response to needs and opportunities. The fact that we have asked and expected them to function as adults is not only affirming but also sobering.

When teens read Bible stories it is important that they see their cultural context and situation. Studying Scripture without understanding its context lessens its true relevance.

As teens, students will affirm their own faith simply by communicating their ideas, beliefs, and values. In many ways this experience is true to all age groups—our faith deepens when we share it.

Stories of real people doing things, feeling similar feelings, and struggling with issues seem to be the most powerful narratives for the teen.

Youth (16-18)

Who They Are. The journey of personalizing faith in the teens continues into the later youth stage. One difference is the fact that while teens focus on the immediate here and now, youth tend to become more reflective and thoughtful about the future. Realities such as relationships, college, marriage, careers, and the meaning of life will awaken more philosophical musings in later youth. Ultimately, older youth (high school and up through college) have a strong desire to rediscover what they believe and the reasons they believe it. This comes from a desire for meaning and an awareness of their own significance as a person.

Another quality of the religious experience of youth is their wholistic approach to life. They want to integrate all beliefs, activities, and ideas in order to make them fully authentic. This may seem contradictory when youth often behave surprisingly contrary to their beliefs. But the experience of faith is a process, and often the discovery of how all this "stuff" fits together will suddenly happen through an event or an experience, perhaps even through a serendipitous thought that dawns on them. Either way, their relationship with God is an emotional experience as well as a cognitive discovery. "Religious faith is more than a feeling. It is a commitment to a life which includes God in all its activities."[3] I find that youth who are sensitive to spiritual growth want a faith that not only meets their emotional needs but also makes sense in the world they live in.

Arguably, relationships are the most valuable part of youth culture. The need for relationships makes sense as youth become independent from their parents and more aware of their own sense of self. It is in this moment of life that the idea of the church becomes either increasingly important or rapidly irrelevant. Church communities that do not demonstrate an authentic concern for the things that youth value will drive them away from the life of the church. On the other hand, when the church community creates a sense of belonging and purpose, it becomes not only a safe place for them to grow but also provides a viable opportunity for them to actively participate in the mission of the church. Even more, a church that demonstrates that it needs youth fosters a remarkable connection in the lives of young people. Roger Dudley, in his 10-year research project *Why Our Teenagers Leave the Church,* estimates that about 50 percent of Adventist teenagers leave the church by their 20s.[4] The research doesn't indicate that they abandon their faith, but it does show that youth won't participate in church if they do not feel wanted.

How They Learn. Youth learn well in communities. While they strive to make their faith their own, they often reach this experience in concert with friends who share the same goal. Small groups provide the perfect learning environment for youth by providing vital interaction and support.

Even for youth the power of a story is unquestionable. Stories allow them to momentarily inhabit the world of others who experience life as they themselves want to. Stories that describe the human condition and the way that grace can restore people are powerful tools for developing a youth-friendly faith system. Those that are thoughtful as well as emotional are the hardest to forget. As important as the story is, however, the question of how the story relates to them personally, and how they might live differently because of it, especially demands an answer. Any story worth telling invites active response.

Because youth seek to discover their faith firsthand, active experimentation in faith-developing situations is crucial for spiritual growth. Challenging young people to forgive the way Christ compels His followers to forgive can be a terribly difficult but life-changing experience. Inviting youth to practice secret goodness builds a selfless spirit and instills the value of service to others. James's advice is particularly relevant for youth today: "Do not merely listen to the word, and so deceive yourselves" (James 1:22). Youth who participate in short-term missions acquire a faith maturity that results from serving. This should be no surprise—their active experimentation in service builds a solid foundation for their relationship with God and their world.

The next section offers a summary of the detailed components of *ChristWise* lessons and an outline of the studies. In addition to this brief introduction, this study contains a how-to section and some examples that have proved effective.

---

[1] Bailey Gillespie, *The Experience of Faith.*
[2] *Ibid.,* p. 126.
[3] *Ibid.,* p. 156.
[4] Roger Dudley, *Why Teenagers Leave the Church,* p. 35.

4
Introduction to Teaching With *ChristWise*

Teaching spiritual truths that shape the mind and forever change the lives of children has to be one of the greatest experiences possible. Many focus on mastering teaching techniques, assuming that the secret of good instruction is simply a set of skills. But the *ChristWise* lessons rest on the premise that "who the teacher is" has a greater impact on the student than their ability to describe, illustrate, or explain concepts and ideas.

"Good teaching cannot be reduced to technique; good teaching comes from the identity and integrity of the teacher." *

Even Christ, the Master Teacher, characterizes the result of real teaching: "A student is not above his teacher, but everyone who is fully trained will be like his teacher" (Luke 6:40).

ChristWise was developed with techniques and exercises that can assist anyone seeking to teach young people the timeless truths of Scripture. Most of the impact occurs because of the character and disposition of those who guide young people. As you endeavor to share in this journey with a young person, keep some of the following attributes of successful Bible studies in mind.

Attribute Number One. Successful teachers share a genuine love for young people. It is not enough to know the Bible, the truth, or even a lot of creative teaching tricks. Rather, to lead young people to Christ we must truly love them and have a passion to see them grow. Young people need affirmation: "That is really insightful, Janet! I have never even thought of that." Nothing will destroy the learning experience as quickly as fear. Prevent such fear through warm and positive reinforcement. When students feel safe about sharing, they will share more freely.

Attribute Number Two. The mentor should attempt to strike a sensitive balance between active coaching and simple listening and learning. When Jesus called the disciples to follow Him, the word "follow" did not mean to tag along behind, but to "accompany alongside." Christ invited them to work alongside Him, not to trail passively behind. This brand of true involvement breeds response. One of the most incredible experiences a young person will have is being able to inspire and help someone older than they are. What an affirming, faith-building moment when a child senses that they have taught an adult something. These moments enable young people to be thinkers and leaders, and not just the recipients of our knowledge.

Attribute Number Three. Be consistent in your example as a teacher. The journey is most effective if your meetings take place weekly, without skipped sessions or changing times. When a study session meets consistently despite our busy schedules, it emphasizes the value of such study to the young person. That is why I encourage laypeople, parents, friends—anyone who can carve out the time—to do it regularly.

Attribute Number Four. The journey of discovery is most effective when both teacher and student prepare the lesson faithfully beforehand. Although the students may not be used to the discipline of doing the work on their own, they can learn it—in fact, they *need* to learn it! Such learning will first develop from your own example. Later, the consistent encouragement and accountability you show from week to week will help to sustain it. If a young person says to me, "I just forgot to do it," I would say, "I know exactly how you feel. There is always a lot going on, isn't there? Would it be helpful if I reminded you with a note or a phone call?" It is perfectly appropriate to admit to students that Bible study is not always exciting work at first, but as they push forward, they will see why it can be a great experience.

Attribute Number Five. Probably the greatest rule in effective Bible studies is to be sure to allow the student to discover and share as much as possible. Teaching is not telling, explaining, or illustrating. Rather, it has to do with engaging the student to learn by thinking and sharing. Look at Jesus as the Master Teacher:

"On one occasion an expert in the law stood up to test Jesus. 'Teacher,' he asked, 'what must I do to inherit eternal life?' 'What is written in the Law?' he replied. 'How do you read it?' He answered: '"Love the Lord your God with all your heart and with all your soul and with all your strength and with all your mind"; and, "Love your neighbor as yourself."' 'You have answered correctly,' Jesus replied. 'Do this and you will live.' But he wanted to justify himself, so he asked Jesus, 'And who is my neighbor?' In reply Jesus said: 'A man was going down from Jerusalem to Jericho, when he fell into the hands of robbers . . . Which of these three do you think was a neighbor to the man who fell into the hands of robbers?' The expert in the law replied, 'The one who had mercy on him.' Jesus told him, 'Go and do likewise'" (Luke 10:25-37).

Jesus never did the thinking for the student. Holding back our own answers takes patience and persistence, but it is necessary. Students learn by thinking for themselves and by sharing their own thoughts and ideas.

When the more quiet ones in classrooms share something—it is thoughtful and usually complete. Others think with their mouths open. They talk their thoughts out loud in order to make sense out of them. Although they often contradict themselves in the process, that's all right. It is a process, and if students don't have the opportunity to share openly, their ideas rarely turn into understanding. Be patient with the quiet ones and give them time to respond without anxiety. Keep the loud ones talking but help them by paraphrasing their statements, questioning, "Is that what you are saying?" Ultimately, knowing the student and how they learn best is the first order of the teacher.

The following sections will equip you with tools to do the lessons effectively. More than anything else, the most powerful tool is your personal commitment to Christ and the relationship you have with that particular young person. Youth will not remember every story or insight gained during your time together. But they will remember you—your honesty and compassion, your hopeful and positive affirmation, and, most of all, the confidence you have that they will become like Jesus.

---

* Parker Palmer, *The Courage to Teach,* p. 10.

5
The Components of *ChristWise* and How Each Exercise Works

Opening Story

Anecdotes that depict the realities of life offer a meaningful way to begin any study. Stories and "real life" scenarios have a way of capturing attention while simultaneously creating a thoughtful bridge to the topic of study. The class can read the story at the beginning of the study as a way for everyone to move into the topic together, or the students can read the opening story before they arrive and simply be ready to share with their study partners.

Open-ended/Value Questions

A thoughtful open-ended question elicits an experience instead of a one-word response. For example: "When in your life have you sensed God's closeness the most? When has He seemed most distant?"

The goal is to engage the learner's experience. In order to respond to this question the students have to dig back into their own lives and answer with a personal story. Even if they don't say anything out loud, the process of thinking through the question is still meaningful. But you should avoid a very similar form of question: "Has God ever been close to you? Does God ever seem far away?" This type isn't helpful, because it elicits only a positive or negative response: "Yes, of course God is close to me" or "Yes, God sometimes seems very far away." A person can answer such questions automatically without ever thoughtfully personalizing them.

A value question requires students to think about what they already believe or know about an issue. We have derived the style of value questions from Bailey Gillespie's *Teaching Values*. *ChristWise* utilizes exercises such as voting, ranking things on a continuum, and either/or decisions to challenge young people to think about what they already know and believe about a certain topic. Here are some sample value questions:

Voting (agree or disagree): "God will save everyone who believes that He is our Savior from sin."

Continuum (where are you on the spectrum?): My closest friends know me as:

Someone who stands for what they believe				Someone who keeps their beliefs to themselves
1	2	3	4	5

Either/or (which is more likely to be true for you?): "The heart of the Christian life is about—serving or believing.

Ranking in the order of importance to you (1—most important; 5—important):
Communication with God is mostly about:

_____ Listening to Christian music

_____ Praying

_____ Studying the Bible

_____ Talking about spiritual things with others
_____ Being alone in nature

Value questions can foster some great discussions. An appropriate and necessary response to what young people might say is "Why did you answer that way?" or "Why do you believe this way?"

The opening anecdote and value questions segue into the Scripture. It is essential to use them as transitions only; otherwise they can easily become the unintentional focus of the study.

Life of Christ

Stories from the life of Christ demonstrate faith in a human form. His experiences of life and death, purpose versus emptiness, and befriending and betrayal are all experiences students can relate to. The stories of the life of Christ are powerful and, most of all, human. Followed up with questions that move the story to their relevance today and to a particular doctrine, Christ-centered Gospel stories build between our experience, Jesus, and the truths that grow out of God's Word.

We Believe

Each topic has a reference to one of the 27 fundamental beliefs. The statements are thorough and yet succinct enough paragraphs to read out loud together. Have the students underline or circle any words or phrases that they don't understand or want to comment on. The following is a sample statement:

The Law of God. "The great principles of God's law are embodied in the Ten Commandments and exemplified in the life of Christ. They express God's love, will, and purposes concerning human conduct and relationships and are binding upon all people in every age. These precepts are the basis of God's covenant with His people and the standard in God's judgment. Through the agency of the Holy Spirit they point out sin and awaken a sense of need for a Saviour. Salvation is all of grace and not of works, but its fruitage is obedience to the Commandments. This obedience develops Christian character and results in a sense of well-being. It is an evidence of our love for the Lord and our concern for our fellow men. The obedience of faith demonstrates the power of Christ to transform lives, and therefore strengthens Christian witness." *

This component contains three exercises: paraphrasing, chain-referencing, and synthesis or personal statement of what the students believe about a particular doctrine. Some lessons offer a verse to memorize or to apply to the students' personal lives.

Paraphrasing. As the students read the passage, they need to be thinking, *What does this mean?* Have the students write a brief paraphrase of each verse. The initial tendency will likely be just to rearrange the words in the verse: "God loved the world, so He gave His Son so we could have eternal life." That rendering employs the same words, adding or subtracting only a few incidentals. The goal is to have them process the verse personally, using their own language and their own expression. While it is essential that you are affirming, you can say, "I noticed that you used the same words in the verse, and that's good, but I want you to think about how you yourself would say this. Try to use different words. I want this to sound like it is coming from you." They may need a couple of examples from you or from a modern paraphrase, but practice the exercise and be faithful to it. The more they paraphrase, the more they have to think about what they read—and the more the words of Scripture will become real and stay with them.

Chain-referencing. The lesson lists the verses for study in order so that the students can mark their Bibles in a chain-reference format. Many like to do this because it gives them a more tangible way to share their beliefs with their friends with confidence and authority. I have asked many youth, "What do you think happens when you die?" They typically answer, "You sleep until Jesus comes."

"Good," I reply. "Can you show me in your Bible that this is true?"

Their response is often, "No, but I know it's in there." The point is that young people want to be more literate in Scripture but haven't really discovered a mechanism to enable them.

Young people should mark their Bibles for three good reasons. The act of underlining and writing, of physically responding to the text, creates a special connection with its words and ideas. Having a simple system helps students find the passages that they "know are in there" and become familiar with their Bibles. Most of all, the experience of being able to share answers and ideas from Scripture with another person independent of a pastor or teacher or parent is a faith-building experience.

One of the kids in my church struggled with the idea of Bible marking because it took too much time. Then one day he burst into my office five minutes early for his study with me and said, "I'm so the man!" (Well, at certain moments you trade a little humility for confidence.) "I gave a Bible study to my cousin on the phone last night. He started asking me all these questions, and I used my own Bible to show him what was up. Like I said, I'm so the man!" I was excited for him. I can't think of anything I would rather a young person get overconfident about than sharing the words of Scripture with someone else. The cousin joined us in the study, and both were baptized in a nearby river.

A chain-reference is a simple way to connect several verses of a similar topic together in order that you might use them in a Bible study when needed.

Step 1: Write the topic of the study in the front of your Bible with the first verse in the study next to it: "'4—The Experience of Salvation' a. John 3:16."

The number 4 refers to the lesson/topic being studied ("The Experience of Salvation" is the fourth *ChristWise* lesson), and the first passage of the study is "a. John 3:16."

Some ask, "Why not put all the verses in the front of the Bible?" The blank pages will fill up quickly. Also, you would have to refer continually to the front of your Bible for the next verse, which might be awkward.

Step 2: Look up the first passage (John 3:16) and read, underline/highlight, and write the next verse of the study in the margin. Here's an example:

16 For God so loved the world that he gave his one and only Son, that whoever believes in him shall not perish but have eternal life. 4b—Romans 3:21.

The next verse of the study is at the end of the verse or in the margin (4b—Romans 3:21). You know it is study number 4, "The Experience of Salvation," and the second verse of the study is indicated by the letter "b." Continue to the next verse, Romans 3:21, and read, underline/highlight, and write the third verse of the study at the end in the margin, thus:

21 But now a righteousness from God, apart from law, has been made known, to which the Law and the Prophets testify. 4c—2 Corinthians 5:17-21.

Continue the study until you complete the list of verses. At the end of the last verse (Romans 12:2), write: 4x end.

This marks the last verse of "The Experience of Salvation" study in your Bible. Go back to the front of your Bible and write "4x end Romans 12:2."

Now you have the whole study in your Bible. This process may seem a bit tedious, but for some students it will be the most lasting learning experience of the entire study. By the end of this journey, their Bibles will be filled with markings, and they will have a way to witness or to review personally.

Summary, or Synthesis

The act of pulling their thoughts together after they have thoroughly studied the lesson empowers students to make a belief their own. They can say it their own way, using their own words to state what they believe about the Bible, the Second Coming, baptism, or anything else. Teenagers react negatively to beliefs seemingly imposed by well-intentioned pastors, teachers, and leaders. This exercise allows them to flesh out their own thoughts on the matter with freedom. I have had students (especially youth) write what they believe and what they still have questions or struggle with. Either way, it is important to have them say something about what they believe.

Way to Pray

This section challenges students to manifest their faith in their daily lives. It encourages them to pray about opportunities, God's will, His revelation of Himself, the courage to make good decisions, and an unselfish mind-set. The nurturing quality of the discipline of personal prayer is powerful at this stage of their development. Their lives are becoming more hectic and hurried in a way that threatens to squeeze out moments of intimate prayer with the Savior. **Way to Pray** is a way to focus their prayer life in a variety of directions. Some lessons focus more on the inward experience, and others more on the outward opportunities to serve.

More Than Words

This activity permits youth to interview others for their views, experience, and advice in a nonthreatening format. Listening to others tell their stories of faith is a powerful learning experience. Not only is it a fresh perspective, the interview enables many others in the church to participate as teachers. The student might ask, for example, "I'm preparing for baptism, and I was wondering if I could interview you with a few questions about the state of the dead?" The exciting part of this exercise is that no matter what age or developmental stage a young person is at, the stories and ideas of others can shape the way the student grows. As the student and mentor return to the study, they can share their stories and insights. It is an excellent way to review the last lesson in a conversational format.

In the Mirror

Here students reflect on how the current study shapes the way they want to live their lives. Thoughtful reflection deepens the significance of the study in their heart. But it is not always easy, nor is it a normal activity for students at first. The masses of information flooding the world today overwhelm many young people. We must foster the discipline of simply thinking and reflecting if we want them to be thoughtful adults. But more than any other reason, such reflection provides an opportunity to extend the learning to deeper levels of experience.

---

* *Seventh-day Adventists Believe*, p. 232.

6
The Role of the Mentor and the Power of Relationships

We have created *ChristWise* so that anyone can become a teacher. Society has popularized the term *mentor*, but it is an important concept to understand in religious education. A mentor is someone who can be "a guide, a coach, a model, an adviser." The student is looking for someone who knows about life. In essence, they are seeking a *mentor*.

"When the Greek warrior, Odysseus, went off to fight in the Trojan War, he left his young son, Telemachus, in the care of a trusted guardian, Mentor. The siege of Troy lasted 10 years, and it took Odysseus another 10 years to make his way home. When he arrived, he found that the boy Telemachus had grown into a man—thanks to Mentor's wise tutelage." *

Youth and young adults can mentor children with tremendous success. Many high school students are giving these studies to elementary and junior high school students, because they are excited by the powerful influence they can have on younger children. Anyone who loves and wants to work with young people can use *ChristWise*. Often, teachers, parents, and pastors are ready and willing to do this task and are well equipped, but consider what might happen to your youth in the church if we integrate them into the service of the church by their doing the work of preparing children for baptism. Present this opportunity to the youth and to young adults and give them the first shot at fulfilling a promise Ellen White gave long ago: "With such an army of workers as our youth, rightly trained, might furnish, how soon the message of a crucified, risen, and soon-coming Saviour might be carried to the whole world!" (*Education*, p. 271).

But whatever age you are or whatever relationship you have with the student, the key to being an effective mentor has to do with your vision and commitment to that young person you are working with. Paul explains this to Timothy: "Don't let anyone look down on you because you are young, but set an example for the believers in speech, in life, in love, in faith and in purity. Until I come, devote yourself to the public reading of Scripture, to preaching and to teaching" (1 Tim. 4:12, 13).

The apostle encourages Timothy to take charge, to set the tone and the tenor for both old and young believers in the church. Besides stressing the importance of right living, Paul also advises Timothy on the importance of teaching those principles to others. "You then, my son, be strong in the grace that is in Christ Jesus. And the things you have heard me say in the presence of many witnesses entrust to reliable men who will also be qualified to teach others" (2 Tim. 2:1, 2).

Thus Paul tells Timothy to continue the tradition of mentoring, encouraging him to instruct new teachers. Be an example. Be a mentor. Teach others to mentor as well, he urges.

As I was giving the *ChristWise* lessons to a seventh grader, I mentioned close to the end of the series, "You know, Nikolas, I'm going to want you to do this for someone else. Do you think you would be willing to give these studies to a younger person in the future?"

He looked at me with a mix of shock and amazement. But when we entrust young people with big tasks, they become big workers.

---

* Howard and William Hendricks, *As Iron Sharpens Iron*, pp. 17, 18.

7
Baptism and Baptismal Studies

It is essential that the parents know exactly what is happening and have a role to play in their children's preparation. The decision to follow Christ is most likely a result of Christian parenting, and the parents need to continue to be part of the process. If their parents are not active in a church, it is also imperative to have a conversation with them. It is not unusual for secular parents to involve their children in church school, Pathfinders, summer camp, or events such as Vacation Bible School. Children attend, but the homes are religiously inactive or secular. In this case, be sensitive yet positive about the young person's choice as you approach the parents.

When young people indicate their desire to be baptized, the first step in the journey is a conversation that joyfully affirms their choice. Nothing can do more damage (other than ignoring their choice) than questioning their readiness to be baptized. From a theological perspective, what makes anyone ready for baptism? Knowledge? The Great Commission in Matthew suggests that we are to "go and make disciples of all nations, baptizing them in the name of the Father and of the Son and of the Holy Spirit, and teaching them to obey everything I have commanded you" (Matt. 28:19, 20). The teaching is continual. We could phrase it: "And continue teaching them to obey everything."

What makes young people ready for baptism? Conversion. When our children sense God's Spirit pulling at their hearts and they feel the conviction to surrender their lives to Jesus—that is God's grace at work. Affirm their decision with joy and sincerity:

"Melissa, I can't tell you how proud I am of you right now."

"God must really be speaking to your heart right now."

"I want to affirm you for your decision."

"You have to know how God loves to hear you say that."

Sadly, adults sometimes speculate about the motivation of some kids. It is important never to question the sincerity of young people when it comes to their decision for baptism (or anyone else for that matter). If they have mixed motives or selfish intentions, that is not for us to determine or to rectify. Our role is to affirm, guide, instruct, and share in the experience of learning to follow Jesus with them. We need to hold the experience of baptism with the utmost sacredness, and an affirming, joyful response does more to honor the rite of baptism than defensive suspicion ever could.

Make an appointment with them to talk about preparing for baptism. It is appropriate to ask the students to share with you what has been going on in their hearts and minds that has led them to this choice. Listen and affirm them with a prayer to God for their decision for baptism and their future work in the church. As you leave, you need to make sure they have the lessons, the date and time of the study, and the instructions for the first lesson clear in their minds.

Giving the Bible Studies

The best way to approach the components of this study is to have the students come to the study having already read the opening story and thought about and answered the opening question. The two of you (or the group) will be ready to discuss the story and the thought-provoking question as you start. It is easier to talk about a story than to dive right into a Bible study. Another reason to have them read the story ahead of time is that it's easy. Sometimes students are so busy that they may not have had time to do a lesson, and thus they arrive embarrassed or discouraged. They can read the story and the question in five minutes, making coming prepared easier for busy kids.

The next step is to read the story in the **Life of Christ** section and make the connections to the specific doctrine. The leader's guide will provide some questions to discuss the significance of Christ's life to the doctrine. The key to making this section meaningful is to create a relational link from the **Opening Story** to the **Life of Christ.** The leader's guide will provide a question to transition to the **We Believe** section.

The students will spend the bulk of their study time in paraphrasing and making a chain-reference in their Bible. They can write what they think the verse is saying in their *ChristWise* book as they mark their Bible. When you are done with this part of the study, review the next three sections with them so you both know what to expect in the coming week.

The sections entitled **Way to Pray, More Than Words,** and **In the Mirror** offer personal activities to experience during the week. It is appropriate to share and discuss them together at the next meeting or during the week as you might see them. Do some of the **More Than Words** activities together, if you can.

You can modify this process however you think it will work best. Some may like to paraphrase and chain-reference at home while doing the other activities together. The idea is to find a pattern that works and be consistent with it. I have had some kids do the whole study before we meet, and then we talk and pray about the things they have experienced and discovered as well as the questions they have about the study. Everyone is different, as is every pair or group. We have designed the components of *ChristWise* to be flexible, so make it work for you. Remember the power is in the Spirit-filled relationship and not in the step-by-step process of the book. Be consistent. But follow a format that enables you to know each other as well as know God more intimately.

8
The Variety of Settings in Which *ChristWise* Can Be Experienced

Person-to-Person Format

The most recommended setting is two people studying and working together. This can involve a parent, a pastor, a grandparent, a Sabbath school teacher, a young adult, or an older youth. A partner approach allows two people to interact, to share, and to hold each other accountable much more easily than a group of 10 could. With larger numbers, fewer get a chance to talk and express their experiences.

I once watched an academy sophomore study with a fifth grader in the youth room after school. As they conversed back and forth, I didn't remember ever seeing the fifth grader talk so much in class when I would visit her school. From an interactive standpoint, the level of activity increases monumentally when the interaction is between two people. Also, there is a sense of comfort and confidentiality with two that is more difficult to experience with a small group or a classroom. While the beginning stages of the study may be a little awkward, it reaches a level of intimacy and openness much more quickly than in a larger group. This study succeeds because of good student-mentor relationships. Because most of us can give quality time to only a small number of young people, it is much more realistic to disciple one or two people than 10 or 20.

Small Group Format

ChristWise will work in a small group format if the leader understands the purpose of the lessons. Small groups thrive on interaction and accountability. In a small group format the leader could use the opening story or question as a warm-up and then refer to the small group questions to guide the students through their study of the life of Christ. The group can also do the doctrinal portion, but with so many verses to unpack, time might be a factor. Once again, the key is to look at the components carefully and decide what you think would work well. The bottom line with small groups is to engage everyone in the study and involve everyone in the application. For the sections entitled **Way to Pray, More Than Words,** and **In the Mirror,** you can have the group members pair up to do these activities together during the week. When the group meets again, have them share their experiences.

Classroom Format

If you plan to use *ChristWise* in a classroom setting, please attempt a cooperative approach to learning that allows students opportunities to share their insights, questions, comments, and discoveries in a warm and open environment. Using pair-share, small group methods is really the best way to approach this exercise. Here's how I have done it:

Divide the class into small groups of no more than four. (They need to have their notebooks, Bibles, and pencils, etc. ready.)

Read the opening story/illustration from the front and introduce the lesson. Invite the various groups to answer the open-ended question among themselves and share their responses with each other. (If you have time, ask the groups to share responses out loud so all the students can hear what the other groups think.)

The teacher makes the transition from the story/illustration to the **Life of Christ.** Have the students in groups respond to the question: How is this glimpse into the life of Christ connected to that particular doctrine?

Students can do the chain-reference and summaries in groups, each sharing their personal summaries of the verse. The students will still need reminders and examples of good paraphrases (not using exact words but communicating the basic idea). They can (if time permits) search for one basic statement that they agree on.

The Summary. Students compose their own statement of belief and share it with the rest of the class. You may even write out the key words or phrases that are essential to the doctrine.

The application sections **(Way to Pray, More Than Words, In the Mirror)** can be done as they fit your class personality, but remember that *ChristWise* is designed primarily with a personal format, and sometimes that is difficult in classrooms. Be flexible. Maybe this part is something that the students can turn in as a journal or even not at all.

Keep track of the great statements, insights, and discoveries that individual students make. Make a list of those moments and mention them in public as a way to affirm the students for their work and also to solidify their understanding.

E-mail

Because of the hectic nature of our lives, some people just can't make the appointments. I have been interacting via e-mail with several high school students as we journey through the lessons together. It is a little awkward, but it can work. I share the insights I gained from the study, and they write back their thoughts about what I said and about what they think as well. We can share our prayers and experiences in this format, and when we see each other we can connect and affirm what we have already been writing about. It may seem a little impersonal, but I have found that sometimes people will write things in e-mail that they might not say in person. Once again, different people with different learning styles require different methods. We have to find ways to share the gospel and grow together, and the Internet may not be a bad idea.

My prayer is that as you journey through the *ChristWise* lessons, you will discover new ways to love the Seventh-day Adventist message and also find meaningful ways to work for His church. More than anything else, I pray that you and your students will be so securely fastened to Christ that His grace will pour out of your lives into the desert of our world.

9
ChristWise Introduction

If this book belongs to you, then it may be because you have made the decision to be baptized or are seriously thinking about it. Congratulations! There are several truths about baptism and preparing for baptism that are important to understand. Know first and foremost that while many people may be proud of you for taking this step, no one is more excited about your decision to follow Christ in baptism than the Father in heaven. Baptism represents the following wonderful things.

1. It signifies a desire to be born again (John 3:1-6; John 1:10-12).
2. It is a confession and asking for forgiveness of sins (Acts 2:38; Mark 1:5-9).
3. Through it the Father announces that we rightfully belong to Him (Mark 1:10-12).
4. It indicates death to the old self and the embrace of a new life (Romans 6:1-6).
5. We become part of a church family (1 Corinthians 12:13).
6. All heaven rejoices (Luke 15:7).

Repentance and baptism. Repentance simply means to "change your mind and turn your steps the other direction." People who want to be baptized usually have experienced a heartfelt desire to surrender their life to Christ and live fully for Him. As you continue to grow in God's grace it is my sincere hope that you will learn the great truths of Scripture and live in the certainty and joy of a relationship with the Savior.

ChristWise is a journey through the teachings of the Seventh-day Adventist Church as portrayed in the life of Christ. It is our belief that Christ is the source and center of all of Scripture and that the doctrines describe the many ways God's character and His love permeate this world of sin. The lessons rest on several building blocks.

1. Christ wants us to know Him personally, not just facts about the Bible. To know what day the Sabbath is or what happens to a person's body at death is only important as it emerges from the person of Jesus. Adventist faith involves a deep abiding knowledge and walk with Jesus.

2. Young people can actively study, experience, and live in ways that serve as examples to other believers. Since we learn best by doing, we have designed the lessons so that you can learn together with a partner as well as experience the Christian life individually.

3. Other people are important in the learning process. The *ChristWise* approach seeks to integrate young people with those who can serve not just as teachers, but as mentors—friends who join the journey of discipleship with you. The experiences and ideas of others in your congregation are significant tools for learning as well.

ChristWise **will** engage your heart and mind in a variety of ways:

Open Question: It includes questions that seek to get us thinking. Questions that prompt more than a yes or no from us. They encourage us to take a stand, to tell a story, and to make a choice. An open question fosters good thinking.

Opening Story: The lessons contain a short story or illustration that opens up the topic by getting to the heart of the issue. Such stories can make us laugh, cry, or even get mad. The opening story launches you into the study in which you can then approach the Word with a thoughtful mind.

Life of Christ: A section from Christ's teachings or a story from His life creates the perfect backdrop for the teachings of the Adventist faith. The lessons have as their goal discovering the many ways in which He tried to portray God's great plan for humanity.

We Believe: A statement of faith rooted in Scripture, it seeks to deepen your understanding and your knowledge of the Bible by encouraging you to mark up your Bible in a way that will help you to witness to someone else.

Way to Pray: Praying to God is like breathing. The lessons will prepare you to move beyond clichés to enable you to pray to God with power and sincerity. You will learn to pray about things that you never talked to God about before.

More Than Words: Take time to listen to people tell their stories. They will share their insights and ideas as you interview them with questions that will probe to the heart of the matter.

In the Mirror: Honestly looking inside our hearts and minds is a good way to grow up in Christ. Reflecting on how you have learned and what you think makes you morally and spiritually strong.

A few final tips before you start the journey:

Communicate clearly with your partner about the meeting time, expectations, and the things each of you need to bring.

Make this study a priority for you. Sometimes you may be tempted to sleep or watch TV instead of doing the work in this book. Commit yourself and your partner to remain faithful.

Don't breeze over any of the parts of this study. If you fall behind, save it for later. It is better to do just a little and do it thoughtfully than to rush through the whole study without letting it get into your heart and mind.

Be thinking about how you might become someone who is a leader/teacher or a mentor for someone else in the future.

ChristWise: Juniors
Lesson 1
The Scriptures

Objective: Students will discover the authority of God's Word and the power it has to shape an individual's life. The first study is always a little awkward, and the key to getting a good start is to pay attention to their comfort level.

Opening Story and the **Life of Christ.** The message in the opening story involves trusting what people say about themselves. Many find themselves duped and deceived by lies. At the end of this story, ask the students: "Have you ever met someone who said things about themselves that you had a hard time believing? Why?" Jesus announces that He is the fulfillment of the prophecy in Isaiah, but the people don't believe Him.

As a precursor to the coming exercises it is a good idea to build a foundation of evidence that the Bible demonstrates its own authority. For example, what the Bible says will happen has happened!

You might draw the students' attention to other forms of apparent truth: "Have you seen the ads for fortune-tellers and psychics? If even half of their predictions or mind readings were true, would you have confidence in them?"

The purpose of the Old Testament/New Testament prophecy exercise is to build the students' confidence that God's Word has been true and reliable for centuries. Go through the exercise with them. You may want to look up the Old Testament passages while they search for the New Testament passages. When you finish, ask them: "Do you think this kind of evidence would convince most people that the Bible is God's reliable word for us?"

Opening Story

When I was a kid, the TV show *To Tell the Truth* ranked right up there in my estimation with ice cream, football, and firecrackers. I loved it because picking the genuine from the fakes came easy for me because lots of pranksters practiced on me. That meant lots of time trying to guess whom I could trust.

As one of the youngest kids on the block, I was the target for tricks of all types. I got to guess whether the brown stuff in Judy's gift to me was really chocolate pudding, or whether Fred would *really* give me a dollar for spending the whole day in a tree, or who had filled my bathtub with slugs.

To Tell the Truth tested my skills of perception. The game featured three contestants. Each told stories about themselves, answered questions, and gave away secrets. In the end, though, only one of them was telling the truth—and the object was to figure out who. Did the man with glasses and a greasy mustache really escape killer sharks and survive for weeks on a deserted island? Did the quiet woman really live a secret life as a world-famous spy? With practice, I developed the following tools to help me determine who was telling the truth.

Tool 1—Was there reasonable evidence for the claims the contestants made?
Tool 2—Did the person seem believable?
Tool 3—Over the course of the game, did a contestant's answer ever contradict information that they had given before?

These tips helped me ace the game "to tell the truth," both on TV and in the real-life chocolate pudding version.

But life is not always a game. Many years ago I was sitting in the church lobby daydreaming out the window. Suddenly a flash of red ended my daydream. A man in a red shirt and torn blue jeans hurtled over the fence and bolted toward the back door of the church. Bursting through the doors, he shouted, "Get me a pastor. I need a pastor, right now!"

After the secretary coaxed him to have a seat and catch his breath, he told his story. "I was a key player in a mob family," he began. He then described his conversion to Christianity and his resolve to abandon his gangster connections. Killing, selling drugs, gambling, and prostitution didn't really fit with following Jesus, he decided. The man explained how his decision had made the mobsters suspicious that he was an informant. "My life is in danger," he sighed. "I came to the first church that I saw for help."

I had heard many stories before, and this one was perfect—perfect for the game "to tell the truth." But this was no game. If the story was true and the man was a real mobster, I could be in serious danger. I began to test my skills at "to tell the truth." Was his story too outrageous? Was it simple, real, and possible? One thing that I had learned was that some of the most outrageous stories often turn out to be true—but so did the simple ones. I, the biggest fan of "to tell the truth," was stumped.

As it turned out, the man disappeared on a Greyhound headed to Dayton. To this day I wonder whether or not he was an impostor.

Imagine when Jesus marched into a church one Sabbath, read the Scriptures, and then calmly announced to the congregation that He was, in fact, the Messiah that Isaiah had promised would save them from their sins. He had always been a nice kid, but the Messiah? Please. How could they believe such a wild claim?

Let's review the tools for discovering the truth:

Tool 1—Was reasonable evidence given for the claims the contestants made?
Tool 2—Did the person seem believable?
Tool 3—Over the course of the game, did a contestant's answer ever contradict information that they had given before?

Look at the story from the beginning of Jesus' ministry and see for yourself. Think about how you would have felt if it had been your church in which He made such a startling announcement. How would you know if this bold young man was telling the truth? What tools would *you* use?

Life of Christ

Luke 4:14-21

"Jesus returned to Galilee in the power of the Spirit, and news about him spread through the whole countryside. He taught in their synagogues, and everyone praised him. He went to Nazareth, where he had been brought up, and on the Sabbath day he went into the synagogue, as was his custom. And he stood up to read. The scroll of the prophet Isaiah was handed to him. Unrolling it, he found the place where it is written: 'The Spirit of the Lord is on me, because he has anointed me to preach good news to the poor. He has sent me to proclaim freedom for the prisoners and recovery of sight for the blind, to release the oppressed, to proclaim the year of the Lord's favor.' Then he rolled up the scroll, gave it back to the attendant and sat down. The eyes of everyone in the synagogue were fastened on him, and he began by saying to them, 'Today this scripture is fulfilled in your hearing.'"

What is this book called the Bible? Why do we have it? How do we know it's true? Can I really trust this book to be God's word?

Look up the Old Testament passages and the corresponding New Testament passages and write what was prophesied about the Messiah and fulfilled in the life of Christ.

OT Prophecy	What Was Prophesied and Fulfilled	NT Fulfillment
1. Micah 5:2	_____	Luke 2:1-7
2. Isaiah 7:14	_____	Matthew 1:23
3. Genesis 49:8-10	_____	Luke 1:30-32
4. Numbers 24:17	_____	Matthew 2:1, 2
5. Isaiah 61:1-3	_____	Luke 4:16-21
6. Psalm 55:12, 13	_____	Matthew 26:47-50
7. Zechariah 11:12, 13	_____	Matthew 27:3-9
8. Isaiah 53:4-7	_____	John 1:29; Acts 8:32
9. Psalm 22:16	_____	Luke 23:33; 24:39

10. Psalm 22:18 _____ Matthew 27:35

11. Psalm 22:1 _____ Matthew 27:46

12. Psalm 34:20 _____ John 19:36

13. Isaiah 53:9 _____ Matthew 27:57-60

14. Psalm 16:10 _____ Matthew 28:2-7

The **We Believe** section has two parts: The statement of belief, and the verses that support that belief. Have the students read this out loud and ask them if they find any words in the statement that they don't understand. The language of the fundamental beliefs was not intended for 10-year-olds so you may have to paraphrase it for them. Many of the phrases in this belief, however, come directly from the Scripture itself.

We Believe

The Holy Scriptures

"The Holy Scriptures . . . are the written Word of God, given by divine inspiration through holy men of God who spoke and wrote as they were moved by the Holy Spirit."[1] Everything we need for salvation is available in the Bible. The Bible is really about God revealing to us who He is and who we are in relation to Him. It reveals a trustworthy picture of God and becomes the authoritative guide for people as they follow Him.

As the students look up each verse they will be doing two things at once: paraphrasing—writing in their own words what they think it means—and making a chain reference as they mark their Bibles. Have them make a topical reference guide in the front of their Bibles so they can refer to the passages later on.

Make sure they understand how to mark their Bible. If you begin to mark your own Bible with them, it will be easier for them to follow along. Put the name of the study and the first text of the study in the front of their Bible: "1—The Scriptures a. 2 Peter 1:20, 21," then go to 2 Peter 1:20, 21 and read the verse, and write in your study guide a short paraphrase in simple everyday language. Have the students do the same. Highlight the verse in your Bible (you can use colored pencils and have each study color-coded or just employ a pen and a ruler—whatever you choose to do). At the end of the verse or in the margin next to it write the next verse in the study: "1b. 2 Timothy 3:16." Have the students continue the process of looking up the passage, paraphrasing it in their own words, then chain-referencing the verses. After a few times it will go faster and easier.

Juniors are very concrete in their thinking, so be patient through the first few lessons. The clearer it is to them, the more they will appreciate it. At first it will seem slow and tedious, but once they have done a few lessons and have started to mark up their Bibles, they tend to get more excited about it.

If you don't finish the verses in time, have them continue the process by themselves throughout the week.

Read the following verses and rewrite them in your own words, then chain-reference them in your Bible:

a. 2 Peter 1:20, 21
b. 2 Timothy 3:16
c. Hebrews 1:1, 2
d. Hebrews 4:12
e. John 5:39
f. Psalm 119:105
g. Proverbs 30:5
h. 1 Thessalonians 2:13
i. James 1:22-25

Before you end the study with prayer, make sure the students understand that the activities below are personal and practical applications. They can choose to talk about them when you meet again, or leave them as private. Simply challenge them to try these activities during the week.

It is important to remember that juniors are in their prime for memorizing Scripture. As they pick a verse to memorize, choose one yourself or the same one they selected, and commit the passage to memory throughout the week.

Choose the verse that you believe describes the power of God's Word the best and memorize it this week.

Pray with the student before you leave and assure them that you will be praying for them during the week. You might ask them to pray for something specific for you as well. This will make them feel like a partner instead of a student.

Way to Pray

Write a letter to God about a verse or story in the Bible that helps you to know Jesus more. Discuss how the story helps you believe in Him. Thank Him for what the story says about God and how it makes you feel.

Powerful Parable

Read the parable in Matthew 7:24-27. What do you think is the lesson Jesus was trying to teach in it? How is that lesson important to learn in your life today?

> This exercise seeks to get the student to simulate how the Bible might have been written. You might have to assure them that you are not trying to add to the Bible, but are simply allowing them to experience the way the writers chose to communicate the gospel as the Holy Spirit guided them.

More Than Words

Luke 1:1-4 (John 20:19, 20)

Write your own Bible. The purpose of Scripture is to speak to people about what God is like, who He is, and why we should follow Him. Here are the instructions:

> Ask them if they have an idea whom they might interview. You may want to offer some suggestions. The point of this exercise is for them to actively hear another person's story so that it will reinforce their faith. Juniors look to people for their faith, not to abstract ideas. So the most important thing you can do as a leader is to help them interview people who will spiritually strengthen them.

Interview at least three people and ask them:

What story would you tell from the Bible if you could tell only one? Why?

What verse in the Bible would you say has changed your life the most? Why?

Ask the same questions to yourself and compile a list of powerful verses and stories that help you understand God. Arrange them in a way that seems logical to you. Give it a title (other than the Bible).

In the Mirror is for their personal reflection. Their study guide provides room for their thoughts and ideas. Challenge them to write their thoughts down. Once again, the junior-age person will probably not create a collage of ideas, but will say what they think in factual, concrete terms. Affirm them for it.

In the Mirror

Think about your interview and share a few insights you gained.

Think also about what you love most about the Bible. Also write about what is difficult about studying the Bible.

Lesson 2
The Trinity

Objective: Students will encounter the mystery and marvelous relationship of the Trinity and see how an unfathomable God becomes real to people.

Last week we studied what the Bible said about itself. The fact that Scripture proves itself to be true age after age gives us confidence to live our lives by every word written in these pages. This week we will look at God as He reveals Himself through three personalities. The Father, Son, and Holy Spirit are all God. This study will not try to figure everything out. We just want to meet this great God in the pages of Scripture and let Him tell us about Himself.

The opening story is a list of children's statements that reveal who they think God is, followed by a story of a boy who realizes that his father is also a war hero. Like Willie, there is more to God than what we see or know. But what we do know is enough to give our lives fully to God. The disciples struggled with how much they didn't know about Jesus. They had a number of ideas about what they thought He should be, but moment by moment Christ revealed more and more about Himself.

Have the students underline the different members of the Godhead as they read the **Life of Christ** story. As Jesus leaves for heaven, He promises that the Holy Spirit will come. Emphasize Their different roles and functions as you go through the study with the students. For juniors it will be important to focus on what each member of the Godhead "does."

Opening Story

"Dr. Mr. God, I wish you would not make it so easy for people to come apart. I had three stitches and a shot. Janet."

I'm sure that when little Janet penned her letter to God she had no idea it would be published in a book entitled *Children's Letters to God.* Nor did the others. Take a look at some more:

"Dear God, How come you did all those miracles in the old days and don't do any now? Seymour."

"Dear God, I bet it is very hard for you to love all of everybody in the world. There are only four people in our family and I can never do it. Nan."

"Dear God, If you watch in church on Sunday I will show you my new shoes. Mickey D."

"Dear God, I didn't think orange went with purple until I saw the sunset you made on Tuesday. That was cool. Eugene."

"Dear God, Are you really invisible or is that just a trick? Lucy."

"Dear God, My brother is a rat. You should have given him a tail. Ha ha. Danny."

"Dear God, I do not think anyone could be a better God. Well, I just want you to know, but I'm not just saying that because you are God. Charles."

"Dear God, It rained for [our] whole vacation and is my father mad! He said some things about you that people are not supposed to say, but I hope you will not hurt him anyway. Your friend—but I'm not going to tell you who I am."[2]

Little kids are funny, aren't they? So innocent. They have so much to learn and are so limited in their understanding of God. Right? Actually, when you look at the letters above, some sound as if they could have come from someone older, though maybe with different words. What strikes me about these letters is the fact that there is a lot we don't know about God. The question for you and me is Do we know enough about God to love Him and serve Him?

Willie loved his father. He was funny, playful, smart, helpful, and a war hero. War hero? That's right. The last one, however, was kind of a surprise to the boy. One day as Willie sat in the fourth row of his classroom the teacher announced a special guest who would share a few thoughts about the upcoming Veterans Day holiday. Willie's heart jumped as he saw his father come through the door in full uniform. His father smiled at him as the teacher introduced Willie's dad as a decorated war hero. The teacher continued to describe the deeds of bravery Willie's father had shown under fire. For the first time the boy heard about a side of his father that he had never known before. Pride boiled over at recess when everyone mentioned to Willie how cool it must be to have a father like his. One thing is true: We don't always know everything there is to know about our parents.

The same is true with God. After Jesus had risen from the dead in victory the disciples wanted to know what His next move was going to be. When would things really happen for them? Jesus told them something new about Him—He was going to leave and go to heaven. It was something the Father had been planning all along. And Jesus added something new about the Holy Spirit—"He's on His way, and things are going to get a little crazy down here, so pay attention and be ready!"

As you look at this section of Scripture, imagine how the disciples must have felt with the news. How would you feel?

Life of Christ

Acts 1:4-9

"On one occasion, while he was eating with them, he gave them this command: 'Do not leave Jerusalem, but wait for the gift my Father promised, which you have heard me speak about. For John baptized with water, but in a few days you will be baptized with the Holy Spirit.' So when they met together, they asked him, 'Lord, are you at this time going to restore the kingdom to Israel?' He said to them: 'It is not for you to know the times or dates the Father has set by his own authority. But you will receive power when the Holy Spirit comes on you; and you will be my witnesses in Jerusalem, and in all Judea and Samaria, and to the ends of the earth.' After he said this, he was taken up before their very eyes, and a cloud hid him from their sight."

As the students study each member of the Trinity individually, it is possible that they may not have time to finish. Make sure you continue to walk them through the steps of chain-referencing and writing the verses in their own words. For this lesson, it is probably most important to chain-reference the "Trinity" passages first.

We Believe

> Have the students read the statement below and share with each other some of the explanations they may have heard about the Trinity (God being both three and one).

The Trinity

Read the statement below and share with each other some of the explanations you have heard about the Trinity (God being both three and one).

As you look up each verse, be sure to mark and chain-reference your Bible as you go through the study. Also, write what you think the verse says, but try not to use the exact same words the Bible does.

The Trinity

"There is one God: Father, Son, and Holy Spirit, a unity of co-eternal Persons. God is immortal, all-powerful, all-knowing, above all, and ever present. He is infinite and beyond human comprehension, yet known through His self-revelation. He is forever worthy of worship, adoration, and service by the whole creation." [3]

   a. Deuteronomy 6:4
   b. Matthew 28:19, 20
   c. 2 Corinthians 13:14

The Father

"God the Eternal Father is the Creator, Source, Sustainer, and Sovereign of all creation. He is just and holy, merciful and gracious, slow to anger, and abounding in steadfast love and faithfulness. The qualities and powers exhibited in the Son and the Holy Spirit are also revelations of the Father." [4]

As you look up each verse, be sure to mark and chain-reference your Bible as you go through the study. How does God's Word describe the Father?

   a. Genesis 1:1
   b. John 3:16
   c. John 14:8-11

The Son

"God the Eternal Son became incarnate in Jesus Christ. Through Him all things were created, the character of God is revealed, the salvation of humanity is accomplished, and the world is judged. Forever truly God, He became also truly man, Jesus the Christ. He was conceived of the Holy Spirit and born of the virgin Mary. He lived and experienced temptation as a human being, but perfectly exemplified the righteousness and love of God. By His miracles He manifested God's power and was attested as God's promised Messiah. He suffered and died voluntarily on the cross for our sins and in our place, was raised from the dead, and ascended to minister in the heavenly sanctuary in our behalf. He will come again in glory for the final deliverance of His people and the restoration of all things."[5]

a. John 1:1-3, 14

b. Luke 1:35

c. Colossians 1:13-20

d. John 10:30

As you have read these verses and marked them in your Bible, what three characteristics of God the Son are most meaningful to you? Which passages describe those qualities?

The Holy Spirit

"God the eternal Spirit was active with the Father and the Son in Creation, incarnation, and redemption. He inspired the writers of Scripture. He filled Christ's life with power. He draws and convicts human beings; and those who respond He renews and transforms into the image of God. Sent by the Father and the Son to be always with His children, He extends spiritual gifts to the church, empowers it to bear witness to Christ, and in harmony with the Scriptures leads it into all truth."[6]

a. Genesis 1:1, 2

b. John 14:16-18, 26

c. Acts 1:8

d. Ephesians 4:11, 12

As you have read these verses and marked them in your Bible, what three characteristics of God the Holy Spirit are most meaningful to you? Which passages describe those qualities?

> This prayer exercise starts young people on the road to praying to God as a friend. It is often the case that this age group simply parrots the words and phrases they have heard adults use in prayer. Thus this exercise challenges them to say to God what they actually think about Him.

Way to Pray

Make a top 10 list of what you know is true about God. As you pray this week, tell Him what you believe about Him and ask Him to show you something new.

Help the student choose a person for this interview. You might have to assist or prod the student a time or two to do this, but after they conduct a few interviews they will be confident enough to proceed without your help. Remind the student to write or summarize in their notebooks what the subject says in order that they can share it later.

More Than Words

Interview someone who you think would answer these questions for you:
When did you first realize that you knew enough about God to love Him and serve Him?
What do you think the job descriptions are for the Father, the Son, and the Holy Spirit?
What do you love most about each member of the Godhead? Why?

Remind the students to journal about the study and the interview they conducted. Let them know they can write down questions or comments as well throughout the week in this section.

In the Mirror

Think about your interview and share a few insights you gained.
Take a few minutes and journal about the people you know who remind you of a loving God.

Lesson 3
The Great Controversy

Objective: Students will observe the nature of evil and the core issues of how people can better understand such characteristics of God as His freedom, will, and love.

Last week we studied the Trinity. God is much bigger, of course, than the way we have described Him.

This is a good time to review their interview and share some of the insights they gained.

This week we study the conflict that started long ago when Lucifer chose to rebel against God in heaven. The struggle that rages is not a cosmic war with lasers and pyrotechnics, but a battle over God's reputation and the redemption of His fallen creation. Ask the students if they have heard people say things that would hurt another person's reputation. That is Satan's goal—to get us to think wrongly about God.

The **Opening Story** sets the philosophical background through a series of scenes. Have the students venture through them, and as you turn to the **Life of Christ** section, they will be ready for war in the desert.

Opening Story

"It's my word against yours!" he sneers as he looks at the detective with that confident untouchable glare. "I say I'm innocent. You say I'm not. You know you can't hold me, much less convict me, on your word alone. I'm out of here."

When have you had to make a judgment between one person's word over another? It's not always easy. People lie. So how do you know if they're telling the truth? Think of a time you might have heard someone say, "I give you my word on it." What was it worth?

Integrity basically means that what you say you are—you are. As two men wandered through a cemetery on the property of a historic mansion in Alabama they stumbled on some tombstones. "My brother and I walked among the ruins of the mansion and then crossed the country road into the dense forest on the other side. After a quarter mile we found the Jackson family cemetery. There is no sign marking the spot, only a five-foot-high stone wall surrounding about 50 graves. Inside we found a tall marker over James Jackson's grave, with a long inscription extolling his virtues, which were many. As I walked along, my eyes fastened on the marker for one of his sons, William Moore Jackson. There was his name, the dates 1824-1891, and a simple five-word epitaph: 'A man of unquestioned integrity.'"[7]

Five words—that's it. But I have no doubt that when William Moore Jackson said "I give you my word," it meant something more than just words. That is the point of the great controversy between Christ and Satan. It is about God's word and about Satan's word. One is described as love and the other as a liar. As you witness this clash in the desert, take notice of the One who's word is trustworthy and make your choice.

> After the students read this passage with their partners ask them, "Why do you think Satan keeps saying, 'If you are the Son of God . . . ?' What is Satan really trying to do here?" Satan's only hope at victory is to derail Jesus from the mission. If he can get Jesus to take any other way than God's, Satan wins. Ask the students: "How does Jesus respond to every temptation?" (His defense is a full knowledge of Scripture.)

Life of Christ

Matthew 4:1-11

"Then Jesus was led by the Spirit into the desert to be tempted by the devil. After fasting forty days and forty nights, he was hungry. The tempter came to him and said, 'If you are the Son of God, tell these stones to become bread.' Jesus answered, 'It is written: "Man does not live on bread alone, but on every word that comes from the mouth of God."' Then the devil took him to the holy city and had him stand on the highest point of the temple. 'If you are the Son of God,' he said, 'throw yourself down. For it is written: "He will command his angels concerning you, and they will lift you up in their hands, so that you will not strike your foot against a stone."' Jesus answered him, 'It is also written: "Do not put the Lord your God to the test."' Again, the devil took him to a very high mountain and showed him all the kingdoms of the world and their splendor. 'All this I will give you,' he said, 'if you will bow down and worship me.' Jesus said to him, 'Away from me, Satan! For it is written: "Worship the Lord your God, and serve him only."' Then the devil left him, and angels came and attended him."

> The great controversy doctrine is mostly one long story. The verses you study will wander through the fall of Lucifer, what caused it, and how the world is the arena of the conflict between him and Christ.
>
> Make sure you have a modern translation handy for any passages in Romans. They can be tricky, even for older students. If you focus on anything in this study, make it the world's desperate need for a Savior as a result of what Satan has done. This will prepare the student for next week's lesson on the experience of salvation.

We Believe

The Great Controversy

"All humanity is now involved in a great controversy between Christ and Satan regarding the character of God, His law, and His sovereignty over the universe. This conflict originated in heaven when a created being, endowed with freedom of choice, in self-exaltation became Satan, God's adversary, and led into rebellion a portion of the angels. He introduced the spirit of rebellion into this world when he led Adam and Eve into sin. This human sin resulted in the distortion of the image of God in humanity, the disordering of the created world, and its eventual devastation at the time of the worldwide flood. Observed by the whole creation, this world became the arena of the universal conflict, out of which the God of love will ultimately be vindicated. To assist His people in this controversy, Christ sends the Holy Spirit and the loyal angels to guide, protect, and sustain them in the way of salvation." [8]

Read the following verses and rewrite them in your owns words and then chain reference them in your Bible:

a. Revelation 12:4-9

b. Isaiah 14:12-14

c. Ezekiel 28:12-18

d. Genesis 3

e. Genesis 6-8

f. 2 Peter 3:6

g. 1 Corinthians 4:9

> As the student partners share the great controversy in a nutshell, they should affirm each other for their perspective. Each student should mention something that specifically spoke to them. Such affirmation will continue to stimulate more thoughtful conversation in the future.

In a few sentences, tell the story of the great controversy in your own words.

Choose from the verses you studied one passage that you want to commit to memory this week and work on it every day.

> This prayer is suggested so they can begin to be ready like Jesus was in the

desert. You might mention that they can read a verse or two while they pray to God.

Way to Pray

As you pray this week, ask for the ability to understand and remember God's Word.

Help the students choose someone to interview if they don't know anyone to ask. They can pick a teacher, a grandparent, a person in their congregation, or a friend of the family.

More Than Words

Interview someone who you think has an idea of what God's Word says, using the following questions:

What story from the Bible gives you the most confidence that God's Word is true? Why did you pick that story?

If you could remember one verse from the Bible when you are tempted, what would that verse be?

What advice would you give someone my age who wants to trust God's Word over the lies of the devil? How does someone like me overcome temptation?

Remind them to write their notes from their interview down in their books and be ready to share their insights at the next meeting.

In the Mirror

Think about your interview and share a few insights you gained.

Take a moment to journal about the evidence you see in the world of good and evil. Be specific.

Lesson 4
The Experience of Salvation

Stress to the students that since we have started this study we have discovered a trustworthy message in the Bible and have looked at the mysterious way God chooses to reveal Himself to us. Last week we watched as Lucifer sought to destroy God's name and His children. Invite your students to share the insights they gained from their interview last week.

Objective: The goal of this study is to communicate clearly the sinner's need for a Savior, the abundant grace that comes from Christ, and ultimately the confidence we can have in a relationship with Him.

The **Opening Story** demonstrates how hard it is to grasp the message of grace and salvation. The story evokes a sense of the value that Christ places on every human He died for. The birth of Christ further demonstrates the message of salvation. The key phrase in the story from the Gospels is "a Savior is born." You can ask the students if when they think of heroes they first think of babies. Many heroes save with might and force, but Jesus came to save by becoming a sacrifice.

The middle of the story section asks the students to make a list of the facts that describe the process of salvation. At this age they need to see things in steps. Try to help them arrange a list of facts that move a person from death to life (see the gift of grace, realize one's sinfulness, accept and receive the promise of salvation, and live with assurance).

Opening Story

"The story has been told of a missionary who became a good friend of an Indian pearl diver. The two had spent many hours together discussing salvation, but the Indian could not understand anything so precious being free. Instead, in making preparation for the life to come, the diver was going to walk nine hundred miles to Delhi on his knees. He thought this would buy entrance into heaven for him. The missionary struggled to communicate to his friend that it is impossible to buy entrance into heaven because the price would be too costly. Instead, he said, Jesus had died to buy it for us.

"Before he left for his pilgrimage, the Indian gave the missionary the largest and most perfect pearl he had ever seen. The missionary offered to buy it, but the diver became upset and said that the pearl was beyond price, that his only son had lost his life in the attempt to get it. The pearl was worth the lifeblood of his son. As he said this, suddenly the diver understood that God was offering him salvation as a priceless gift. It is so precious that no man could buy it. It had cost God the life's blood of His Son. The veil was lifted; he understood at last."[9]

> Compile a list of facts in this story that show how a person comes to experience salvation.

(Make a list of facts in this story that show how a person comes to experience salvation.)

Sometimes it takes extreme action to catch someone's attention. But the work of salvation was more than God just trying to get us to notice Him. In the following story from the life of Christ the angel said to the people, "A Savior is born." Jesus came to earth and became one of us not just for a while, but forever. His hands were not always pierced. Once they were soft like any newborn's. The Savior made a commitment to you and to me when He came to earth as a baby, and He waits for you and me to make the commitment of our lives to Him. Is that what you want to do?

Life of Christ

Luke 2:4-12

"Joseph also went up from the town of Nazareth in Galilee to Judea, to Bethlehem the town of David, because he belonged to the house and line of David. He went there to register with Mary, who was pledged to be married to him and was expecting a child. While they were there, the time came for the baby to be born, and she gave birth to her firstborn, a son. She wrapped him in cloths and placed him in a manger, because there was no room for them in the inn. And there were shepherds living out in the fields nearby, keeping watch over their flocks at night. An angel of the Lord appeared to them, and the glory of the Lord shone around them, and they were terrified. But the angel said to them, 'Do not be afraid. I bring you good news of great joy that will be for all the people. Today in the town of David a Savior has been born to you; he is Christ the Lord. This will be a sign to you: You will find a baby wrapped in cloths and lying in a manger.'"

What other story from the Bible is a good illustration of someone who makes a commitment to God and devotes their life to Him?

> **We Believe** contains words such as "justified," "adopted," "divine power," "grace," "assurance," etc. Don't think you have to explain the terms. The stories will do more to communicate the message than the theological terminology. As the students paraphrase and chain-reference their Bibles, elaborate on the simple facts that the various passages demonstrate. If the students restate the passage in language similar to the text itself, say, "So, Susan, what does that really mean to you?" As they finish, have them choose the verse that really speaks to them about salvation so they can memorize it this week.

We Believe

The Experience of Salvation

"In infinite love and mercy God made Christ, who knew no sin, to be sin for us, so that in Him we might be made the righteousness of God. Led by the Holy Spirit we sense our need, acknowledge our sinfulness, repent of our transgressions, and exercise faith in Jesus as Lord and Christ, as Substitute and Example. This faith which receives salvation comes through the divine power of the Word and is the gift of God's grace. Through Christ we are justified, adopted as God's sons and daughters, and delivered from the lordship of sin. Through the Spirit we are born again and sanctified; the Spirit renews our minds, writes God's law of love in our hearts, and we are given the power to live a holy life. Abiding in Him we become partakers of the divine nature and have the assurance of salvation now and in the judgment."[10]

Read the following verses and rewrite them in your owns words while you chain-reference them in your Bible:

    a. John 3:16

    b. Romans 3:21

    c. 2 Corinthians 5:17-21

    d. Galatians 4:4-7

    e. Titus 3:3-7

    f. Romans 8:14-17

    g. Romans 10:17

    h. Galatians 3:2

    i. Romans 8:1-4

    j. Romans 12:2

Choose from the verses you studied one passage that you want to commit to memory this week and work on it every day.

Before you end the lesson, have a prayer of commitment with the students affirming their decision to receive the gift of salvation.

Way to Pray

As you pray this week, make a point to thank God for His gift of salvation to you.

Ask the students how the interviews are going. Invite them to share what they appreciate about the interviews the most. Then for the next interview choose someone both you and they believe has experienced the surety of God's salvation.

More Than Words

Interview someone who you think has a close walk with God, using the following questions:

Tell me about a moment in your life when you invited Jesus into your heart and received the gift of salvation. What happened? What were the circumstances? What did you do?

How do you live each day and have assurance and certainty that God will take you to heaven with Him when He comes?

Which verse speaks to you the most about salvation?

In the Mirror

Think about your interview and share a few insights you gained. Also think about the times you remember asking God to come into your heart. Make a short list of those times as best as you can.

Lesson 5
Baptism

Objective: Students understand the nature, purpose, and awesome privilege of baptism.

As you begin the lesson on baptism, start by having the students review the insights and stories they gained from their interviews. Continue to affirm the juniors for working hard, because it fosters more involvement. Invite them to share what they have heard people say about the meaning of baptism.

The **Opening Story** and the section from the **Life of Christ** target the heart of what should motivate people to the waters of baptism—repentance. It is not a word we use often, but it actually means to change your mind—so much so that your life changes as well.

The stories center around two facts. The first involves what baptism means from our viewpoint—a change of mind about God and us. The second fact concerns our changed identity at baptism—God claims us as His own child.

You might ask the students, "What biblical characters do you recall who changed their minds and eventually their lives?" For this age group, attaching stories and facts to truths builds their confidence in them.

Ask the students if there is a vegetable they just can't stand. Five years ago I could have bet my life on the fact that no one could get me to swallow one slimy stem of asparagus. I don't know where or when the change of mind came, but all I can say now is "Bring on the asparagus!" Have them share a food, a type of music, or a certain game that they don't particularly care for and talk about how hard it is for them to imagine changing their mind about something like that. The change of mind for the believer in baptism involves deciding whether to go their way or God's way.

Opening Story

When the Jews came to the Jordan to be baptized by John, it was the first time a Jew was ever baptized. Baptism was for outsiders, a ritual non-Jewish people had to go through to become a member of the Jewish faith. Jews would never be baptized, because they were already the children of God. So when the Jewish people came to be baptized, they must have had some change of mind. But that is exactly what repentance means—to change your mind in such a way that your life changes too. Here's an example:

"The American Red Cross was gathering supplies, medicine, clothing, food and the like for the suffering people of Biafra. Inside one of the boxes that showed up at the collecting depot one day was a letter. It said, 'We have recently been converted, and because of our conversion we want to try to help. We won't ever need these again. Can you use them for something?' Inside the box were several Ku Klux Klan sheets. The sheets were cut down to strips and eventually used to bandage the wounds of black persons in Africa."[11]

A change of mind. Repentance. If you want to be baptized, it is because you have already changed your mind—or you want to. "Changed my mind about what?" you ask. About who you are going to belong to. Are you going to belong to the living Lord? Or are you going to join many others and say, "My life belongs to me"? Repentance is a change of mind that transforms your life.

When you are baptized you announce to the world, the heavens, and to all the angels, good and bad, that you belong to God. At the baptism of Jesus the words came back from the Father, "This is My Son, whom I love, with Him I am well pleased." And as you are baptized that is what God says to you and to the entire listening universe.

What baptism have you witnessed that sticks in your memory the most? Why?

> **Passage to focus on:** "This is my Son, whom I love; with him I am well pleased." Expect to have a discussion as to why Christ was baptized. Though you could give many thoughtful responses, it might be more effective to focus on what God says at the baptism of Christ. Was there any question in Jesus' mind about His relationship to the Father? Why were these words necessary? Does God say this about us at baptism?

Life of Christ

Matthew 3:13-17

"Then Jesus came from Galilee to the Jordan to be baptized by John. But John tried to deter him, saying, 'I need to be baptized by you, and do you come to me?' Jesus replied, 'Let it be so now; it is proper for us to do this to fulfill all righteousness.' Then John consented. As soon as Jesus was baptized, he went up out of the water. At that moment heaven was opened, and he saw the Spirit of God descending like a dove and lighting on him. And a voice from heaven said, 'This is my Son, whom I love; with him I am well pleased.'"

> What you believe about baptism and what you experience at it can be two different things. As they paraphrase and mark their Bibles, take a moment to personalize each aspect of baptism with the students.

We Believe

Baptism

"By baptism we confess our faith in the death and resurrection of Jesus Christ, and testify of our death to sin and of our purpose to walk in newness of life. Thus we acknowledge Christ as Lord and Saviour, become His people, and are received as members by His church. Baptism is a symbol of our union with Christ, the forgiveness of our sins, and our reception of the Holy Spirit. It is by immersion in water and is contingent on an affirmation of faith in Jesus and evidence of repentance of sin. It follows instruction in the Holy Scriptures and acceptance of their teachings." [12]

Read the following verses and rewrite them in your owns words while you chain-reference them in your Bible:

    a. Romans 6:1-6

    b. Acts 2:38

    c. Acts 16:30-33

    d. Acts 22:16

    e. Colossians 2:12, 13

    f. Matthew 28:19, 20

    g. 1 Corinthians 12:13

Choose from the verses you studied one passage that you want to commit to memory this week and work on it every day.

> The opportunity to thoroughly write out what they want to say to God in baptism can be very meaningful for the student. It might be a prayer that they read. What we want to avoid is children who, once they have dried off, cannot remember why they were baptized in the first place. A letter can be one way to make their experience more memorable.

Way to Pray

As you pray this week, start by writing a prayer to God that contains everything you want to say to Him by your baptism. "Dear God, when I'm baptized on Sabbath I want it to say to You . . . "

More Than Words

Begin planning your baptism with your partner or group and especially your family. Make everything about it say what you want to tell God.

Using the following questions, interview someone who has been a positive influence in your life:

Describe the most memorable baptism you have ever experienced. Why do you think it sticks out in your mind so well?

In a nutshell, what does it mean when a person goes into the water to be baptized?

What passage of Scripture most speaks to you about the significance of baptism?

Find an example of a before and after set of photos that have the subject in the before picture unsmiling or that uses other intentionally deceptive tricks. Invite the student to discuss with you the before and after expectations of baptism. Instead of constantly telling children that "they will stumble and fall," I ask permission—and give them mine as well—to hold them accountable to their choice to follow God. That means, if they start to stumble, fall away, or just get disinterested, you have the right to gracefully remind them of their good choice.

In the Mirror

Think about your interview and share a few insights you gained.

What are some things you want to do before your baptism? Are there people you need to have a conversation with, people to thank, etc.? What do you want to do after your baptism? What do you expect will be different about you, if anything?

Lesson 6
Creation

Objective: Students will discuss the significance of Christ as the Creator and embrace His re-creative work in their lives.

One of the attributes of junior-age students is that they can understand and accept the reality that a Grand Designer made the world. Millions of lessons from nature demonstrate this. Ask the students to share with you a fact or truth from nature that they believe offers evidence that God created the world. See what they come up with.

The story of the front-yard showdown introduces a confrontation in the life of Christ. In both scenarios the situation reached the place where neither person could back away. "The line was drawn. From the perspective of the Jewish leaders Jesus must have been insane. He was either exactly who He said He was, or completely possessed by a demon. But their minds were already made up. As you have the students look at both of these stories, have them consider how unbelievable it must have been for people to hear Christ's words. Imagine, also, what it would mean if His words were true.

The phrase to focus on is "Before Abraham was born, I AM." No one but a crazy blasphemer or God would made such a claim. Ask the students why they think it was so hard for the leaders back then to see what seems easy for us to believe.

Opening Story

"Go ahead. Step across that line. I dare you." Joey's eyes were wild. He was protecting our turf on the block. We may have been only third graders, but we still had turf.

I knew it was going to get ugly when Tina took the confrontation to the next level. "Oh yeah. What are you going to do if I step over your stupid line?" We looked at Joey, and for a moment he appeared shaken and confused. I don't think he had thought that far ahead. Most people who throw threats around don't get called on them, so they just learn to get really good at making threats—until someone challenges their bluff.

"Well, you just step across that line and you'll see what happens to you," Joey replied with newfound resolve. He turned and smiled at us boys.

Tina never said another word. She not only crossed the line, but walked right up into Joey's face with her lips curled back in a snarl that I will never forget. "OK, Joey," she sneered. "What are you going to do about it?"

It would not have been a good fight if it had come to that. Joey didn't have a chance against Tina, so it was best that he just walked away muttering something about not being allowed to hit girls.

Their showdown reminded me of the encounter between Jesus and the Pharisees. As He taught that day the Pharisees pushed Him and moved the conversation up to the next level.

"You're demon-possessed, because no one talks like that about death! You young up-start. So you think you have been around, huh? Have you been around so long that you know Abraham?" the Pharisees chided.

Uh-oh. They had drawn the line on the ground right in front of Jesus. Walk away? Not a chance. He stepped over it. No, not only did He step over, but He stepped right onto the church leaders' toes—so to speak.

"Before Abraham was even thinking about a Promised Land I was around!"

They picked up stones because Jesus had uttered something that only God could say. In His case, He was. Which brings us to the point: You can't believe in Christ and not be-lieve He created the world. As John said:

"In the beginning was the Word, and the Word was with God, and the Word was God. He was with God in the beginning. Through him all things were made; without him noth-ing was made that has been made. In him was life, and that life was the light of men" (John 1:1-4).

Check out the story.

Life of Christ

John 8:51-59

" 'I tell you the truth, if anyone keeps my word, he will never see death.' At this the Jews exclaimed, 'Now we know that you are demon-possessed! Abraham died and so did the prophets, yet you say that if anyone keeps your word, he will never taste death. Are you greater than our father Abraham? He died, and so did the prophets. Who do you think you are?' Jesus replied, 'If I glorify myself, my glory means nothing. My Father, whom you claim as your God, is the one who glorifies me. Though you do not know him, I know him. If I said I did not, I would be a liar like you, but I do know him and keep his word. Your father Abraham rejoiced at the thought of seeing my day; he saw it and was glad.' 'You are not yet fifty years old,' the Jews said to him, 'and you have seen Abraham!' 'I tell you the truth,' Jesus answered, 'before Abraham was born, I am!' At this, they picked up stones to stone him, but Jesus hid himself, slipping away from the temple grounds."

How would you have responded to this Carpenter who declared, "I am the eternal God"? Would you have stared at the man who looked a lot like the guy next door and thought, *I wonder if he is God?* It is hard to imagine. But Jesus did the unimaginable. He created the world. He created us. And He became one of us to save us.

Sometimes we don't think beyond the notion that Jesus loves us to the truth that He made us, but that's why He loves us. As a Christian, celebrating God's creation and His creative power is a big part of your journey.

Ask the students if they can think of something that is precious to them or their family only because it was made by hand. What is it?

As the students study the verses that describe God's creative work and they mark their Bibles, they may want to highlight the essential parts of the Creation week in Genesis 1 and 2, such as "Let there be light" or "Let the land produce living creatures." Finding and marking just the salient parts makes the passage easier to refer to later if they see the divisions of days instead of two chapters of solid color.

We Believe

Creation

"God is Creator of all things, and has revealed in Scripture the authentic account of His creative activity. In six days the Lord made 'the heaven and the earth' and all living things upon the earth, and rested on the seventh day of that first week. Thus He established the Sabbath as a perpetual memorial of His completed creative work. The first man and woman were made in the image of God as the crowning work of Creation, given dominion over the world, and charged with responsibility to care for it. When the world was finished it was 'very good,' declaring the glory of God."[13]

Read the following verses and rewrite them in your own words while you chain-reference them in your Bible:

a. Genesis 1
b. Genesis 2
c. Exodus 20:8-11
d. Psalm 19:1-6
e. Psalm 33:6, 9
f. Psalm 104
g. Hebrews 11:3

Suggest a verse to memorize that specifically mentions Christ as the Creator or one on creation from the Psalms. "In the beginning" is a little too easy and familiar. Challenge them to memorize passages they don't already know.

Choose from the verses you studied one passage that you want to commit to memory this week and work on it every day.

Sometimes the active events and practical application of this series of lessons can get lost if the students don't plan well. I find that reminders increase the effectiveness of the activities. You may want to call during the week and send a note to remind them to do this exercise. Sometimes they let the simple exercises get pushed to the back burner unless we intentionally challenge them. Invite them to share, either during the week or at the next meeting, what happened when they did the exercises.

Way to Pray

As you pray this week, do it outside. Find a way to talk to God about His creation, especially His plan for you. After all, the crowning work of Creation is people.

The goal is to have the students interview someone who has thought about the topic enough to have something meaningful to say. You may make some suggestions as to whom they might choose, or decide to do this interview together with them on the phone or at church.

More Than Words

Interview a member of the church who loves biology, astronomy, or science as a whole with the following questions:

What are some real evidences in the natural world that demonstrate to you that a great designer created this world? Share a few.

Have you ever talked with people who don't believe in God as our Creator? What were those conversations like? How do you relate to them?

In the Mirror

Think about your interview and share a few insights that you gained with your partner.

Lesson 7
The Law of God

Objective: Students will discover the primary principle of God's government (love) and determine how the rules of God's kingdom apply to life.

Tell the students that as their relationship with their partners begins to get stronger they should invite them to share with each other what part of the lessons has been most helpful for them. It is OK to admit that not everyone has the same taste or learning style.

The lesson on the law opens with a popular and powerful business leader undermining the need for the Ten Commandments. Discuss what the world would be like without them. Ted Turner's statements contain contradictions and inconsistencies, but let the students discover this for themselves. Invite them to respond to the statements.

The passage to focus on is clearly "Love the Lord your God with all your heart and with all your soul and with . . . all your strength. . . . Love your neighbor as yourself." Both young and old assume that the Old Testament is all about rules. Discuss the reference in Deuteronomy 6:4-6, in which God wanted His people to love Him from their hearts. Invite the students to share their thoughts about the Old Testament. Ask them: "When you think of the Old Testament, what comes to mind?"

Jesus here and other places (for example, the Sermon on the Mount, Matthew 5-7) shows clearly how He tried to deepen our love for the law of God and not to distract us from it by false concepts of grace.

Opening Story

Make a list of the top 10 biggest problems that our world faces today.

As you think of the problems challenging our world, consider what Ted Turner had to say about God's law and world problems.

Several years ago the cable TV mogul declared the Ten Commandments obsolete. Turner, creator of the Cable News Network, told members of the Newspaper Association of America in Atlanta that the biblical Ten Commandments do not relate to current global issues, such as overpopulation and the arms race. "We're living with outmoded rules," he claimed. "The rules we're living under are the Ten Commandments, and I bet nobody even pays much attention to them, because they are too old. When Moses went up on the mountain there were no nuclear weapons, there was no poverty. Today, the commandments wouldn't go over. Nobody around likes to be commanded. Commandments are out."

Was Ted Turner right? Discuss with your partner the relationship between world problems and the Ten Commandments.

> Have the students discuss with each other the relationship between the problems of the world and the Ten Commandments.

Without question, God's law is not only still relevant, but obedience to them would solve the majority of the problems we encounter in the world. But I can understand why people want to throw the stone tablets out, and there are usually a couple of reasons:

1. They want to live their own life by their own rules. Fair enough.

2. They don't know or love the One who made the rules.

I have been told, "If you love the King, you live joyfully by the laws of the kingdom."

Jesus used the phrase "love the Lord with all your heart" when asked about the commandments, because "love" does what "obey" cannot do—inspire a heartfelt response that goes beyond the minimum. The minimum isn't hard to do:

I can go a lifetime without bending to the temptation to murder someone. I get mad, but not that mad.

I'm going to honor my parents with my life—it's not that hard to do.

I can keep the Sabbath holy. While I may not do it perfectly, I want to and try to.

I have no graven images in my room that I choose to bow down to and worship.

I adore my wife and will be faithful to her until I die. Lots of people do this.

I know people who would rather die than be dishonest—and they are not even Christians.

The Ten Commandments—are they really that hard to keep? I'm going to leap out and take a risk and say no, not on the surface. At least not at a minimum level. But God never wanted us to keep His law without keeping Him in mind. He never wanted us to scratch the surface of the list of rules, but to have them engraved deep within our heart of hearts. The law of God is not for the surface but the center of the heart.

"'This is the covenant I will make with the house of Israel after that time,' declares the Lord. 'I will put my law in their minds and write it on their hearts. I will be their God, and they will be my people'" (Jeremiah 31:33).

Notice that when you start thinking like this, you're getting closer to what God really wants for you.

Life of Christ

Mark 12:28-34

"One of the teachers of the law came and heard them debating. Noticing that Jesus had given them a good answer, he asked him, 'Of all the commandments, which is the most important?' 'The most important one,' answered Jesus, 'is this: "Hear, O Israel, the Lord our God, the Lord is one. Love the Lord your God with all your heart and with all your soul and with all your mind and with all your strength." The second is this: "Love your neighbor as yourself." There is no commandment greater than these.' 'Well said, teacher,' the man replied. 'You are right in saying that God is one and there is no other but him. To love him with all your heart, with all your understanding and with all your strength, and to love your neighbor as yourself is more important than all burnt offerings and sacrifices.' When Jesus saw that he had answered wisely, he said to him, 'You are not far from the kingdom of God.'"

> Ask the students if there is anything about the way the doctrinal statement is stated that they have a question about. As they mark and paraphrase the verses, they should remind each other that God meant the law for the heart.

We Believe

The Law of God

"The great principles of God's law are embodied in the Ten Commandments and exemplified in the life of Christ. They express God's love, will, and purposes concerning human conduct and relationships and are binding upon all people in every age. These precepts are the basis of God's covenant with His people and the standard in God's judgment. Through the agency of the Holy Spirit they point out sin and awaken a sense of need for a Saviour. Salvation is all of grace and not of works, but its fruitage is obedience to the Commandments. This obedience develops Christian character and results in a sense of well-being. It is an evidence of our love for the Lord and our concern for our fellow men. The obedience of faith demonstrates the power of Christ to transform lives, and therefore strengthens Christian witness." [14]

Read the following verses and rewrite them in your owns words while you chain-reference them in your Bible:

a. Exodus 20:1-17

b. Psalm 40:7, 8

c. Matthew 22:36-40

d. Deuteronomy 28:1-14

e. Matthew 5:17-20

f. John 15:7-10

g. 1 John 5:3

h. Psalm 19:7-14

Choose from the verses you studied one passage that you want to commit to memory this week and work on it every day.

> Have the students see if they can summarize each command in one word: Purity. Justice. Respect. Content. Faithfulness. (9- to 12-year-olds don't usually worry about committing adultery—but they should be considering the virtues of faithfulness and purity.)

Way to Pray

One by one, pray about the commandments this week, asking God to show you ways you can change His law from being a list of rules to a living love deep within your heart. Talk with your partner about how you can experiment with having God write them on your heart.

> **Reminder:** Make sure the students keep good notes of their interviews in their books. Such notes provide for later reflection and help when they debrief with you. The students may choose to debrief with each other right after the interview is done. To debrief with you may require a phone call, a visit, or doing the interview together

with the student. Either way, make sure you talk about the interview they had before you move on to the next lesson.

More Than Words

Interview someone who you believe loves God from their heart and use the following questions:

What are some characteristics about God that inspire you to love and serve Him?

What do you think it means to have God's law written on your heart?

What commandment seems to be the hardest to keep in today's world?

In the Mirror

Think about your interview and share a few insights you gained.

Lesson 8
The Sabbath

Objective: Students will explore the beauty and promise that exist in keeping the Sabbath as a permanent reminder of God's claim on humanity.

The Sabbath stands as the moment of celebration that joyfully reminds people of their relationship to God. Ask the students: "Can you think of ways that people use to jog their memories about their relationships?"

The parable is ridiculous in a way, but ask the students in what way it is true about keeping Sabbath. Jesus faced constant reprimands from religious leaders for His Sabbathbreaking. Ask the students what point the leaders were missing. What do they think people are missing today?

The passage to focus on in the **Life of Christ** section is "The Sabbath was made for man, not man for the Sabbath." If we get the order right, the rest follows. The Sabbath is a gift for people.

Opening Story

Imagine it's your birthday. Your friends have arrived dressed up and bearing gifts in brightly colored packages of every shape and size. The cake is amazing! It is such a work of art that you almost don't want to cut it. Almost. Everyone gathers in a large room to sing "Happy Birthday" and watch you open your presents and devour cake and ice cream.

Just as the singing begins, someone interrupts, "I want the corner piece of the cake with all the icing!"

The next-door neighbor shouts, "I don't think so. I called it when I first saw the cake."

"It's mine!" a soft-spoken boy comments loud enough for everyone to hear.

"The cake is wonderful. Maybe none of us should eat it," someone else suggests. "Maybe we should take a picture of it and have copies made so we'll all remember what a beautiful cake this was."

Everyone looks in shock at the timid boy who made the suggestion. The silence breaks when an overgrown neighbor boy from down the street erupts, "Are you crazy? I didn't come here for a picture of cake! We're going to cut this baby!"

A frenzied argument builds until Sally screeches, "Quiet!" Everyone stares at her as she gathers herself for one of her famous speeches. "All of you are acting like animals. We are here to celebrate—uh, what was your name again? I, uh, forgot."

Once again everyone goes silent. "Yeah, what's your name again?" "Check the name on the gifts," another kid volunteers.

"The gifts! That's right! We brought gifts for you! Let's open them up!"

The crowd cheers. They begin ripping open the packages on the table. By now you can't believe what just happened. You want to shout, "Hey, everyone! What's going on here? It's *my* birthday party!" They continue to play with toys and games with greater and greater intensity. Finally you go to your room until they leave. When it's all quiet, you walk downstairs to the mess. *They didn't even know my name,* you think to yourself.

Now, I can't imagine this ever taking place. Birthdays are a celebration of a person—an individual's life. The gifts, the cake, the party are all about the person. This little parable I call "A party for the party." But where is the person? Over time the Sabbath became a party for the celebration of the party. People missed the point. A party is for a person. The Sabbath is for you. A gift. A celebration of Creation—especially the crowning work of Creation, people! Notice how this happened in the days of Jesus.

Life of Christ

Mark 2:23-28

"One Sabbath Jesus was going through the grainfields, and as his disciples walked along, they began to pick some heads of grain. The Pharisees said to him, 'Look, why are they doing what is unlawful on the Sabbath?' He answered, 'Have you never read what David did when he and his companions were hungry and in need? In the days of Abiathar the high priest, he entered the house of God and ate the consecrated bread, which is lawful only for priests to eat. And he also gave some to his companions.' Then he said to them, 'The Sabbath was made for man, not man for the Sabbath. So the Son of Man is Lord even of the Sabbath.'"

The Adventist message has among its pillars the law and the Sabbath. The aspect that we need to emphasize to young people is the tremendous relational importance the Sabbath has. In the past, many have suggested the Sabbath is a time for family. While it can be and should be, family time is not the primary focus of the Sabbath— the most important point of observing the seventh-day Sabbath is to be "mindful" of our Creator. Mind. Full. Full of God's grace, beauty, and powerful work in our lives and in the world we live in.

You can illustrate this with a pitcher of water and a cup of water. Fill the cup halfway with water. Add to the water other substances such as juice, dirt, milk, etc. None of these are bad in themselves. However, it is hard to tell what they are when they are all mixed together. Put the cup in a sink—so you don't make a mess—and begin to pour the pitcher of water into the cup. Continue pouring, although it overflows, until the cup of water is again clear. The pure water is the undivided attention God wants from us one day a week.

As the students mark and share the essential meaning of the scriptures together, they should begin to think of ways to keep Sabbath with an undivided heart. It will keep them from forgetting what the day is really about.

We Believe

The Sabbath

"The beneficent Creator, after the six days of Creation, rested on the seventh day and instituted the Sabbath for all people as a memorial of Creation. The fourth commandment of God's unchangeable law requires the observance of this seventh-day Sabbath as the day of rest, worship, and ministry in harmony with the teaching and practice of

Jesus, the Lord of the Sabbath. The Sabbath is a day of delightful communion with God and one another. It is a symbol of our redemption in Christ, a sign of our sanctification, a token of our allegiance, and a foretaste of our eternal future in God's kingdom. The Sabbath is God's perpetual sign of His eternal covenant between Him and His people. Joyful observance of this holy time from evening to evening, sunset to sunset, is a celebration of God's creative and redemptive acts." [15]

Read the following verses and rewrite them in your owns words while you chain-reference them in your Bible:

a. Genesis 2:1-3
b. Exodus 20:8-11
c. Deuteronomy 5:12-15
d. Exodus 31:13-17
e. Luke 4:16
f. Ezekiel 20:12, 20
g. Matthew 12:1-12
h. Isaiah 58:13, 14
i. Isaiah 56:5, 6

Choose from the verses you studied one passage that you want to commit to memory this week and work on it every day.

Way to Pray

As you pray this week, ask God to show you ways to remember Him and be mindful that Sabbath is a celebration of *you* as well. It sounds kind of funny, but you are the center of God's creative and redemptive activity. Enjoy it.

> When the students make their lists, have them share with each other and then choose at least one suggestion to work on for the coming Sabbath. Encourage them to commit to this before they leave, and make sure they debrief about it later.

More Than Words

Make a list of the things you can do to celebrate and commune with your Creator and share them with your partner.

Interview someone who you believe has a joyful walk with God on the Sabbath. Ask the person:

In your own words, share what you think the Sabbath day is all about.

Describe the Sabbath day that is the most memorable for you. What happened? What did you do? Why is this a good memory for you?

What passage or story from the Bible demonstrates the importance of the Sabbath the most to you?

In the Mirror

Think about your interview and share a few insights you gained.

Lesson 9
The Life, Death, and Resurrection of Christ

Objective: Students will immerse themselves in stories that depict the significance of Christ's life, death, and resurrection and then determine how they will respond to the claims of Christ.

The **Opening Story** challenges the students to find the passages that describe Christ's mission—the "I came to . . ." statements. This lesson presents the Crucifixion scene for the students to respond to. Ask them to underline or circle the words, phrases, or sentences that really speak to them about the meaning of Christ's life.

The passage to focus on is "Come down from the cross, if you are the Son of God!" The mob obviously misunderstood what His life was about.

Have the students make a list of some of the most popular people in the world today. Then ask them what they think their life goals are. What would be their mottos? Compare them with the motto Christ lived by—to serve, to give His life as a ransom, to seek the lost, to save the dying, to live out the law. Have them discuss why Christ's life is so significant.

Opening Story

Napoléon Bonaparte once said:

"I know men; and I tell you that Jesus Christ is no mere man. Between him and every other person in the world there is no possible term of comparison. Alexander, Caesar, Charlemagne, and I myself have founded empires; but upon what do these creations of our genius depend? Upon force. Jesus alone founded His empire on love; and to this very day millions would die for Him." [16]

Let there be no misunderstanding of the purpose and plan of Jesus. He came to: (underline the phrase that describes Christ's mission):

"The Son of Man did not come to destroy men's lives, but to save them" (Luke 9:56, NKJV).

"Do not think that I have come to abolish the Law or the Prophets; I have not come to abolish them but to fulfill them" (Matthew 5:17).

"For the Son of Man came to seek and to save what was lost" (Luke 19:10).

"Not so with you. Instead, whoever wants to become great among you must be your servant, and whoever wants to be first must be your slave—just as the Son of Man did not come to be served, but to serve, and to give his life as a ransom for many" (Matthew 20:26-28).

"When the Pharisees saw this, they asked his disciples, 'Why does your teacher eat with tax collectors and "sinners"?' On hearing this, Jesus said, 'It is not the healthy who need a doctor, but the sick. But go and learn what this means: "I desire mercy, not sacrifice." For I have not come to call the righteous, but sinners'" (Matthew 9:11-13).

What a job description. Apparently we were worth it.

Life of Christ

Matthew 27:38-54

"Two robbers were crucified with him, one on his right and one on his left. Those who passed by hurled insults at him, shaking their heads and saying, 'You who are going to destroy the temple and build it in three days, save yourself! Come down from the cross, if you are the Son of God!' In the same way the chief priests, the teachers of the law and the elders mocked him. 'He saved others,' they said, 'but he can't save himself! He's the King of Israel! Let him come down now from the cross, and we will believe in him. He trusts in God. Let God rescue him now if he wants him, for he said, "I am the Son of God."' In the same way the robbers who were crucified with him also heaped insults on him. From the sixth hour until the ninth hour darkness came over all the land. About the ninth hour Jesus cried out in a loud voice, 'Eloi, Eloi, lama sabachthani?'—which means, 'My God, my God, why have you forsaken me?'

"When some of those standing there heard this, they said, 'He's calling Elijah.' Immediately one of them ran and got a sponge. He filled it with wine vinegar, put it on a stick, and offered it to Jesus to drink. The rest said, 'Now leave him alone. Let's see if Elijah comes to save him.' And when Jesus had cried out again in a loud voice, he gave up his spirit. At that moment the curtain of the temple was torn in two from top to bottom. The earth shook and the rocks split. The tombs broke open and the bodies of many holy people who had died were raised to life. They came out of the tombs, and after Jesus' resurrection they went into the holy city and appeared to many people. When the centurion and those with him who were guarding Jesus saw the earthquake and all that had happened, they were terrified, and exclaimed, 'Surely he was the Son of God!'"

We Believe

Life, Death, and Resurrection of Christ

"In Christ's life of perfect obedience to God's will, His suffering, death, and resurrection, God provided the only means of atonement for human sin, so that those who by faith accept this atonement may have eternal life, and the whole creation may better understand the infinite and holy love of the Creator. This perfect atonement vindicates the righteousness of God's law and the graciousness of His character; for it both condemns our sin and provides for our forgiveness. The death of Christ is substitutionary and expiatory, reconciling and transforming. The resurrection of Christ proclaims God's triumph over the forces of evil, and for those who accept the atonement assures their final victory over sin and death. It declares the Lordship of Jesus Christ, before whom every knee in heaven and on earth will bow." [17]

Read the following verses and rewrite them in your owns words while you chain-reference them in your Bible:
   a. John 3:16
   b. Isaiah 53
   c. 1 Peter 2:21, 22
   d. 1 John 2:2; 4:10
   e. Colossians 2:15
   f. Philippians 2:6-11

Choose from the verses you studied one passage that you want to commit to memory this week and work on it every day.

Introduce to your student the idea of meditating on the **Life of Christ**. Clearly, we are talking about focusing our minds on the details of His life, as though we were watching a movie or standing right there with the disciples. Have the students make a list of the types of things they would need to envision to be true to the biblical world (landscape, the way the people appeared, the weather, the sounds and smells of life in the Middle East). The purpose is to teach young people to visualize the biblical stories so they become more real to them.

Way to Pray

As you pray this week, simply think about the things that Christ did while He was on earth—His ministry, His teaching, the miracles and moments of healing, and especially Calvary.

More Than Words

Ask someone you know to be a serious student of the life of Christ to respond to the following interview questions:

If you had three stories or events to share from the life of Christ, which ones would you share and why?

What do you think is the most important saying from the four Gospels?

Share an experience, a story, or an event from your own life in which the life of Christ was especially meaningful to you. (Give them time for this question.)

In the Mirror

Think about your interview and share a few insights you gained from listening to other people.

Lesson 10
The Lord's Supper

Objective: Students will understand the importance of symbols that bring remembrance and renewal of their faith as well as discover the sacred joy that believers experience as they celebrate grace with others.

Have the students suggest some symbols or signs in everyday life that need very little explanation. (For example, a swastika, a Christmas tree, or a peace symbol.) Ask them to explain the meaning of each symbol. The bread and the grape juice in the Communion service symbolize the Lord's death. Foot washing represents His service to people and humility. While understanding what the elements represent is not hard for most young people, experiencing such moments as times of renewal is harder to achieve.

Have the students think of some Old Testament Bible stories, then create a symbol for each story and write or draw only the symbol on a sheet of paper. Their partners can then guess the story by looking at the symbol. The key is to not make it hard, but easy, to identify.

The phrases to focus on are "This is my body" and "This is my blood." When reading the **Opening Story** and the **Life of Christ** section, have the students think of some ways to help people see the meaning of Communion more fully.

Opening Story

To me the meaning of Communion centers on two events that happened when I was about 11.

I grew up in the Roman Catholic faith. I remember the order of events in the Mass well. At a certain time in the service I came forward. The priest went to the back where the emblems sat. He took the bread and dipped it into the bowl of wine. I reverently lifted my head and opened my mouth as the priest placed the wine-soaked bread in it. Done. Grace received. But one thing bothered me about that process. It was the table—it was so far away. The table of grace was at the back of the church, and the priest was the one who had to go get the bread and wine. The thought occurred to me a couple times simply to bypass the priest and get it myself—but that would not have been a good idea.

When I participated in the Communion service in a small Adventist church as a young person, however, I noticed the table was right in front of me. I could reach out and grab it from where I sat.

Lesson 1—The death of Christ on Calvary gives me direct access to God and His grace. It means that no one stands in between me and God's amazing grace.

"Therefore, since we have been justified through faith, we have peace with God through our Lord Jesus Christ, through whom we have gained access by faith into this grace in which we now stand. And we rejoice in the hope of the glory of God" (Romans 5:1, 2).

Lesson 2—The death of Christ abundantly makes up for every failure and more.

I sat at the back of the church as the deacons passed the emblems around for people. They passed me up. I was old enough to know how to make a big deal out of their ignoring me, so I planned to pout and work the situation for all it was worth afterward. But I never got a chance. As I left the church and shook Pastor White's hand he grabbed me and led me down the hall, apologizing about the deacons passing me over at Communion. I hardly had time to pout or object. In a matter of seconds I was in his study sitting before his desk. He left for a moment and returned with a silver plate full of bread and two large 16-ounce glasses full of deep-red grape juice. The bread was not the small finger-sized crackers that get lost between the third and fourth molars. The pieces were hefty. He didn't miss a beat. Again he apologized for my being left out of Communion, then prayed over the bread and the juice. I sat there stunned. When he said "Amen" he noticed I was in shock.

"What's wrong, Troy?" he asked with genuine concern.

"I—uh—well—the—um . . . bread . . . I mean—shouldn't we break it? And the juice?" I fumbled.

He recovered. "Troy," he said in a warm but serious voice, "God's grace and forgiveness are abundant, overflowing, more than we can possibly contain. Big grace calls for big bread. Big forgiveness calls for big glasses." He leaned closer to me and said, "I don't want you ever to remember this service with an empty feeling in your stomach. I want you full—now eat." Pastor White was bold, and sometimes a little brash. But I guarantee you this much—I got the message of God's grace at Communion. Let's start a revolution in which we use bigger cups. What do you say?

Life of Christ

Matthew 26:20-30

"When evening came, Jesus was reclining at the table with the Twelve. And while they were eating, he said, 'I tell you the truth, one of you will betray me.' They were very sad and began to say to him one after the other, 'Surely not I, Lord?' Jesus replied, 'The one who has dipped his hand into the bowl with me will betray me. The Son of Man will go just as it is written about him. But woe to that man who betrays the Son of Man! It would be better for him if he had not been born.' Then Judas, the one who would betray him, said, 'Surely not I, Rabbi?' Jesus answered, 'Yes, it is you.' While they were eating, Jesus took bread, gave thanks and broke it, and gave it to his disciples, saying, 'Take and eat; this is my body.' Then he took the cup, gave thanks and offered it to them, saying, 'Drink from it, all of you. This is my blood of the covenant, which is poured out for many for the forgiveness of sins. I tell you, I will not drink of this fruit of the vine from now on until that day when I drink it anew with you in my Father's kingdom.' When they had sung a hymn, they went out to the Mount of Olives."

> As the students read and study the following passages, they should consider some of the things Christians do to prepare for the service (self-examination, repentance, confession, service, worshiping joyfully in the hope of the Second Coming).

We Believe

The Lord's Supper

"The Lord's Supper is a participation in the emblems of the body and blood of Jesus as an expression of faith in Him, our Lord and Saviour. In this experience of Communion Christ is present to meet and strengthen His people. As we partake, we joyfully proclaim the Lord's death until He comes again. Preparation for the Supper includes self-examination, repentance, and confession. The Master ordained the service of foot washing to signify renewed cleansing, to express a willingness to serve one another in Christlike humility, and to unite our hearts in love. The Communion service is open to all believing Christians."[18]

Read the following verses and rewrite them in your owns words while you chain-reference them in your Bible:

    a. 1 Corinthians 10:16, 17; 11:23-30
    b. Matthew 26:17-30
    c. Revelation 3:20
    d. John 6:48-63
    e. John 13:1-17

Choose from the verses you studied one passage that you want to commit to memory this week and work on it every day.

John 17 records, in a way, the real Lord's Prayer. It is a great way to pray in preparation for the Lord's Supper. Have the students find out the date of the next Communion service and make an appointment to pray together and model this prayer. As they practice praying this way during the week, they should find a way to send a note to their partners to let them know that they have prayed for them this way.

Way to Pray

Read John 17 and notice how Jesus prays first for Himself, then for His disciples, and finally for those who will believe because of them. Pray in the same way: first for yourself, that you will be one with God. Then pray for your friends and fellow believers in the church. And finally, pray for those who might come to know Jesus because of them.

More Than Words

Interview someone in your church family, preferably someone a little older than you. Ask the following questions:

What is your most memorable moment in a Communion service? Why does it stick out in your mind?

What passage or story from Scripture helps you remember God's grace the most?

What are some rituals or reminders you do or know others do that remind you of God's love and presence?

In the Mirror

Think about your interview and share a few insights you gained.

Lesson 11
Spiritual Gifts

Objective: Students will seek to interact with God about their spiritual gifts and their identity and purpose as Christians as they learn to serve God by His Spirit.

This study contains a 70-question survey. Plan for time to complete it together, or make time to do the survey at another time when both you and the students can discuss the results. The survey should take about 20 to 30 minutes to complete and tabulate. You may want to look at the "What's in the Box?" and arrange the lesson appropriately.

The next two lessons address the practical aspects of church life. Young people who prepare for baptism rarely have a thorough discussion and follow-through about their spiritual gifts. God bestows spiritual gifts to each member to build up the kingdom of God through the church. Most of those baptized in North America consist of children, yet rarely do their conversion experience and baptism deal with their giftedness. In this study we begin a process to discover their gifts and deploy them into active ministry. Our church cannot sustain another decade of young people who remain bystanders or spectators. As you work with a young person, involving them in meaningful work is more important than any other activity.

The **Opening Story** builds the groundwork for the concept that the church needs everyone, and that they have a role to fulfill. The key word is "needed." As the students study this section, invite them to share a time when they felt most needed, most useful to God's work.

The passage to focus on in this study is "You have been faithful with a few things; I will put you in charge of many."

Opening Story

One of the activities I had my summer campers try to do was build a fort—but each member of the group had either their hands tied, their feet tied, or their eyes blindfolded. At first they grumbled, stumbled, and accidentally stuck each other with sticks. Usually it took a little while for them to catch on to how to do it. Think about it: If you had to build a fort out in the woods with only three people, including yourself, how would you proceed if your feet, hands, and eyes were limited? (Share with your partner your plan of action.)

One cabin of boys finally "got it" after almost killing each other. One young man learned that you can't throw sticks to a blindfolded person—you can imagine how he discovered this fact. Johnny could see and use his hands but couldn't move his feet, so they built the fort where he was standing. Reuben, who could not see (blindfolded), carried wood, rocks, and other items from the forest. Frank, who could walk and see but couldn't use his hands, guided him. Soon the fort came together, and we sat inside and talked about the exercise. We all had strengths and all had weaknesses. The group needed all the strengths. If one were missing, we'd be in trouble. The same is true for believers. God gives us all gifts. The gifts are different, but He expects us to use them for His work. Consider the parable of the tools of the carpenter's shop.

Imagine the tools of a carpenter's workshop holding a conference:

"Brother Hammer presided. Several suggested he leave the meeting because he was too noisy. Replied the Hammer, 'If I have to leave this shop, Brother Screw must go also. You have to turn him around again and again to get him to accomplish anything.' Brother Screw then spoke up. 'If you wish, I'll leave. But Brother Plane must leave too. All his work is on the surface. His efforts have no depth.' To this Brother Plane responded, 'Brother Rule will also have to withdraw, for he is always measuring folks as though he were the only one who is right.' Brother Rule then complained against Brother Sandpaper, 'You ought to leave too because you're so rough and always rubbing people the wrong way.' In the midst of all the discussion, in walked the Carpenter of Nazareth. He had arrived to start His day's work. Putting on His apron, He went to the bench to make a pulpit from which to proclaim the Gospel. He employed the hammer, screw, plane, rule, sandpaper, and all the other tools. After the day's work when the pulpit was finished, Brother Saw arose and remarked, 'Brethren, I observe that all of us are workers together with the Lord.'"[19]

Life of Christ

Matthew 25:14-30

"Again, it will be like a man going on a journey, who called his servants and entrusted his property to them. To one he gave five talents of money, to another two talents, and to another one talent, each according to his ability. Then he went on his journey. The man who had received the five talents went at once and put his money to work and gained five more. So also, the one with the two talents gained two more. But the man who had received the one talent went off, dug a hole in the ground and hid his master's money. After a long time the master of those servants returned and settled accounts with them. The man who had received the five talents brought the other five. 'Master,' he said, 'you entrusted me with five talents. See, I have gained five more.' His master replied, 'Well-done, good and faithful servant! You have been faithful with a few things; I will put you in charge of many things. Come and share your master's happiness!' The man with the two talents also came. 'Master,' he said, 'you entrusted me with two talents; see, I have gained two more.' His master replied, 'Well-done, good and faithful servant! You have been faithful with a few things; I will put you in charge of many things. Come and share your master's happiness!' Then the man who had received the one talent came. 'Master,' he said, 'I knew that you are a hard man, harvesting where you have not sown and gathering where you have not scattered seed. So I was afraid and went out and hid your talent in the ground. See, here is what belongs to you.' His master replied, 'You wicked, lazy servant! So you knew that I harvest where I have not sown and gather where I have not scattered seed? Well then, you should have put my money on deposit with the bankers, so that when I returned I would have received it back with interest. Take the talent from him and give it to the one who has the ten talents. For everyone who has will be given more, and he will have abundance. Whoever does not have, even what he has will be taken from him. And throw that worthless servant outside, into the darkness, where there will be weeping and gnashing of teeth.'"

What are the hard, real facts that this story teaches about God giving people spiritual gifts?

> As they mark their Bibles and paraphrase each passage, the students should think of people in the church who demonstrate the various gifts. Have them personalize each verse with the names of familiar people. For instance: "I can see that Pastor Karl has the gift of teaching." Or "Mrs. Johnson is a builder. She always finds a way to say the right thing to make others feel better." "Frank is always the first person to show up and help. I can see his spiritual gift is serving or helping." "I have noticed that when Beverly says something in church, people listen, because I think they sense that what she says is what God would say if He were here." This exercise will prepare the students to think about their place in the church.

We Believe

Spiritual Gifts

"God bestows upon all members of His church in every age spiritual gifts which each member is to employ in loving ministry for the common good of the church and of humanity. Given by the agency of the Holy Spirit, who apportions to each member as He wills, the gifts provide all abilities and ministries needed by the church to fulfill its divinely ordained functions. According to the Scriptures, these gifts include such ministries as faith, healing, prophecy, proclamation, teaching, administration, reconciliation, compassion, and self-sacrificing service and charity for the help and encouragement of people. Some members are called of God and endowed by the Spirit for functions recognized by the church in pastoral, evangelistic, apostolic, and teaching ministries particularly needed to equip the members for service, to build up the church to spiritual maturity, and to foster unity of the faith and knowledge of God. When members employ these spiritual gifts as faithful stewards of God's varied grace, the church is protected from the destructive influence of false doctrine, grows with a growth that is from God, and is built up in faith and love." [20]

Read the following verses and rewrite them in your owns words while you chain-reference them in your Bible:

a. Romans 12:4-8

b. 1 Corinthians 12:9-11, 27, 28

c. Ephesians 4:8, 11-16

d. Acts 6:1-7

e. 1 Timothy 3:1-13

f. 1 Peter 4:10, 11

Choose from the verses you studied one passage that you want to commit to memory this week and work on it every day.

Way to Pray

As you pray this week, ask God to teach you what He wants you to do in His church. Then, as you take the "What's in the Box?" survey, invite God to show you ways you can practice your gifts.

Make sure the students fill the survey out together so they can discuss the results as a group. As with any survey, it is a human construction. But it does seek to get in touch with the students' self-description, providing a basis for further consideration and experimentation. If a student scores high in the area of leadership, it doesn't mean they are scientifically proven leaders. Rather, it simply means that leadership is something they should pray about and practice, because God may have gifted them to function as a leader in the church. The only way to know the end result is actually to become involved. The same principle applies to every other gift.

Have the students go through the instructions given at the beginning of the survey so they can assist their partners. They may want to let their parents and their pastor or other church leaders know where they are in the study and should briefly describe what this lesson is about so the adults can be helpful in this process. The goal is to enable the students to sense their calling for ministry in the life of the church. When they have finished the survey and have the results, they should debrief with their partners about the findings. Ask them: "Were you surprised by the scores you have? How do you feel about the area(s) that you scored the highest in? Out of the seven gifts this survey focuses on, do you feel that the gift you scored highest in is something that interests you? Why/why not? Are you willing to experiment with some of the different activities in the church to see if this might really be a gift you have?"

Another way to affirm the gifts God gave the students is to have them ask godly people to give insight and advice. It can be a teacher, a relative, a Sabbath school or Pathfinder leader—anyone who might know the student well enough to share how they feel God has gifted this particular young person. Questions you might ask such adults include: "What examples can you share that demonstrate this particular gift (higher scores) in Susie's life? What other gifts (lower scores) would you recommend that Susie give some prayer and attention to? Why? What specific activities would you recommend she participate in to help her discover her spiritual gifts?"

There is no magical formula other than allowing the Spirit to guide us and engage us in activities that build the ministry and mission of the church. The greatest indicator of giftedness is success in a particular area.

More Than Words

Take the "What's in the Box?" survey with your partner or group. Share with each other the results and make plans as to how you are going to find ways to use your gift for God's service.

Write a letter to your pastor or the church board sharing with them what gifts you think you have and invite them to put you to work. See what happens.

Interview someone you know who has made an impact on the church or in the community. Use the following questions:

Tell me a story or experience from your life in which you felt God was able to use your gifts in a special way.

How would you explain the idea that the different gifts are equal? Is the gift of preaching the sermon more valuable than the gift of quietly serving in the background? Explain how this works.

What advice do you have for someone like me who wants to serve God through this church?

In the Mirror

Think about your interview and share a few insights you gained.

Look up 1 Timothy 4:12 and journal some ideas you have about how you can apply this verse to your life. Be specific.

Lesson 12
The Church

Especially as we seek to discover our spiritual gifts, the study of the church and its life is an important part of life as a Seventh-day Adventist.

Objective: Students will deepen their sense of understanding what church members are in light of the biblical descriptions of church and church life.

The before and after pictures in the New Testament clearly describe two different groups of believers. While their names are the same, their attitudes and actions greatly change during the course of a couple weeks. Ask the students what made the difference. (Just before Christ left for heaven He promised the Holy Spirit. When the Holy Spirit came, people began to live differently.)

Tell the students to think of a time when they may have seen similar things happen in their own church and share a few of those experiences.

The phrase to focus on is "You are witnesses of these things." The church is a body of believers who differ in their gifts and are unique in their individual personalities, but are united in mission.

Opening Story

Before and after photos can sometimes seem really convincing. One time I looked at a tabloid in the grocery store line after first checking to see if anybody I knew was watching. I would not want my educational curiosity misunderstood. As I studied the before and after pictures littering the pages of the tabloid, I noticed a common characteristic—people in the before pictures were not smiling, while those in the after pictures were. Whether it be for weight loss or hairstyles, tanned skin or makeovers, the before people were never smiling. Those in the after picture always were.

Take a look at this before and after picture in the Bible and see what you think.

Before

"They began to question among themselves which of them it might be who would do this. Also a dispute arose among them as to which of them was considered to be greatest" (Luke 22:23, 24).

After

"All the believers were together and had everything in common. Selling their possessions and goods, they gave to anyone as he had need. Every day they continued to meet together in the temple courts. They broke bread in their homes and ate together with glad and sincere hearts, praising God and enjoying the favor of all the people. And the Lord added to their number daily those who were being saved" (Acts 2:44-47).

Now, that's a change. And the purpose of every good before and after picture is to sell you a product, an idea, or a service. So what makes the selfish, self-centered disciples into selfless servants? It is what happened in between the fighting and the feasting together. Jesus gave them a mission, a message, and the might to do it.

In the story below, what was the mission Jesus gave? What was the message for the world? And what was the "might" that would empower them to be successful?

Life of Christ

Luke 24:36-53

"While they were still talking about this, Jesus himself stood among them and said to them, 'Peace be with you.' They were startled and frightened, thinking they saw a ghost. He said to them, 'Why are you troubled, and why do doubts rise in your minds? Look at my hands and my feet. It is I myself! Touch me and see; a ghost does not have flesh and bones, as you see I have.' When he had said this, he showed them his hands and feet. And while they still did not believe it because of joy and amazement, he asked them, 'Do you have anything here to eat?' They gave him a piece of broiled fish, and he took it and ate it in their presence. He said to them, 'This is what I told you while I was still with you: Everything must be fulfilled that is written about me in the Law of Moses, the Prophets and the Psalms.' Then he opened their minds so they could understand the Scriptures. He told them, 'This is what is written: The Christ will suffer and rise from the dead on the third day, and repentance and forgiveness of sins will be preached in his name to all nations, beginning at Jerusalem. You are witnesses of these things. I am going to send you what my Father has promised; but stay in the city until you have been clothed with power from on high.' When he had led them out to the vicinity of Bethany, he lifted up his hands and blessed them. While he was blessing them, he left them and was taken up into heaven. Then they worshiped him and returned to Jerusalem with great joy. And they stayed continually at the temple, praising God."

We Believe

The Church

"The church is the community of believers who confess Jesus Christ as Lord and Saviour. In continuity with the people of God in Old Testament times, we are called out from the world; and we join together for worship, for fellowship, for instruction in the Word, for the celebration of the Lord's Supper, for service to all mankind, and for the worldwide proclamation of the gospel. The church derives its authority from Christ, who is the incarnate Word, and from the Scriptures, which are the written Word. The church is God's family; adopted by Him as children, its members live on the basis of the new covenant. The church is the body of Christ, a community of faith of which Christ Himself is the Head. The church is the bride for whom Christ died that He might sanctify and cleanse her. At His return in triumph, He will present her to Himself a glorious church, the faithful of all the ages, the purchase of His blood, not having spot or wrinkle, but holy and without blemish." [21]

Read the following verses and rewrite them in your owns words while you chain-reference them in your Bible:

    a. Genesis 12:3
    b. Acts 7:38
    c. Ephesians 4:11-15; 3:8-11
    d. Matthew 28:19, 20
    e. Matthew 16:13-20; 18:17, 18
    f. Ephesians 2:19-22; 1:22, 23; 5:23-27
    g. Colossians 1:17, 18

Choose from the verses you studied one passage that you want to commit to memory this week and work on it every day.

Way to Pray

If you could pray for a before and an after picture of your church, what changes would you hope to see? What would be the source of those changes?

More Than Words

Interview someone who has a deep love for their local church. Use the following questions:

What do you love most about your local church congregation? What would you like to change?

Share a story or experience that you have had that inspires you to remain dedicated to the service of the church.

What passage or story from Scripture especially speaks to you about how we should live as a body of believers?

In the Mirror

Think about your interview and share a few insights you gained.

Lesson 13
Death and
Resurrection

Objective: Students will integrate the biblical view of death and resurrection into a hopeful and confident trust in Christ.

The **Opening Story** and the incident from the life of Christ both describe two processions, one filled with joy and life and the other with sorrow and despair. While Jesus raises someone from the dead in only a few stories, this particular episode rings true with its clear picture of death and its temporary grip on the lives of God's people. The story of the widow of Nain is especially dramatic. Jesus disrupts the funeral by doing four things: 1. He saw the woman in her misery and pain. A widow, she had been to this graveyard before. Since it was her only son who had died, she now was left alone. As Jesus saw her, the scene stirred Him deep within. 2. He gave her words of encouragement and hope. Actually, He told her not to cry, perhaps not the most polite thing to say at a funeral, but He was already heading for the coffin. 3. He put His hand against the coffin and stopped the funeral. In Jewish thought, to touch the dead defiled a person. But He put His hand up to say, "Death stops here. I'm keeping this one for now." 4. He woke the boy from death by the words of His mouth and returned the child to his mother.

Ask the students if they have ever attended a funeral. What do they remember about the service? the people? the words and actions of others?

Bring a local newspaper to the study and have a look at the obituaries together. Ask the students what they think Peter, Paul, or even Christ Himself would say in a card of sympathy to the family members.

Choose one of the four statements you think is the most powerful statement about death and resurrection 1. Jesus saw her. 2. He said, "Don't cry." 3. He stopped the funeral with His hand. 4. He spoke life to the boy and returned him to his mother.

Opening Story

With birdseed still in my hair and the windshield covered with shaving cream, lipstick, and colored ribbons, I pressed the button that locked the doors of my car. That sound signified safety. Safety from my brothers and friends. I looked over at my brand-new bride and let out a sigh of relief. I didn't really feel married, with all the festivities, practical jokes and jabs, and goodbye hugs and kisses. But now we were off to our honeymoon and a couple of weeks of vacation.

The farther from the church we drove, the more excited we became. As I was talking, my wife, Julie, glanced over my shoulder and pointed to my left. There he was—a policeman on a motorcycle five feet from our car and staring directly at me. His face had a blank stare that I recognized from previous experiences. *What did I do now?* I thought to myself. I must have thought it louder than normal because at that moment his face broke into a smile and he gave me the old thumbs-up. Turning red, I waved as he drove by. Whew.

As Julie and I talked about our plans—the beach, snorkeling, fruity tropical nonalcoholic drinks, and lots of sun—suddenly I slammed on the brakes. The car screeched slightly. "What's going on? The light is green, and everyone is . . ." As the cars crossing the intersection in front of us drove slowly by, I noticed the little orange flags. They stopped my complaining in midsentence. I didn't say a word.

The thought popped into my head how strange this seemed. Two processions. One filled with joy, life, and hopeful expectation, and the other involving death, pain, and unbelievable sadness. Just the sight of those cars driving by could steal away the joy from the biggest party. The last car passed and it was our turn to go, so we moved forward, but not without thinking. Just the thought of death stops people in their tracks—stops the joking, the joy, the hope, the happiness. It halts right in our throats. I couldn't say a word.

I have known since childhood that at funerals you don't say much. Instantly you just show that you care and that you are hurting with the family and friends. So you don't say a word. That is, unless You are Jesus and the whole point of Your life is to put an end to funerals. You have to see this story! While I keep quiet at funerals, Jesus speaks up with the most unexpected words you'd ever hear, and then—well, see for yourself what Jesus thinks about funerals.

Life of Christ

Luke 7:11-17

"Soon afterward, Jesus went to a town called Nain, and his disciples and a large crowd went along with him. As he approached the town gate, a dead person was being carried out—the only son of his mother, and she was a widow. And a large crowd from the town was with her. When the Lord saw her, his heart went out to her and he said, 'Don't cry.' Then he went up and touched the coffin, and those carrying it stood still. He said, 'Young man, I say to you, get up!' The dead man sat up and began to talk, and Jesus gave him back to his mother. They were all filled with awe and praised God. 'A great prophet has appeared among us,' they said. 'God has come to help his people.' This news about Jesus spread throughout Judea and the surrounding country."

> As you study the condition of humanity in death and the resurrection, be mindful that juniors respond well to clearly stated facts. Deepen their confidence in God's Word by amplifying the key attributes of death and resurrection. For example: "John 11 shows Jesus referring to death as a sleep." "The dead know nothing." "When Jesus comes, the dead in Christ will rise first."

We Believe

Death and Resurrection

"The wages of sin is death. But God, who alone is immortal, will grant eternal life to

His redeemed. Until that day death is an unconscious state for all people. When Christ, who is our life, appears, the resurrected righteous and the living righteous will be glorified and caught up to meet their Lord. The second resurrection, the resurrection of the unrighteous, will take place a thousand years later." [22]

Read the following verses and rewrite them in your owns words while you chain-reference them in your Bible:

a. Romans 6:23
b. 1 Timothy 6:15, 16
c. Ecclesiastes 9:5, 6
d. Psalm 146:3, 4
e. John 11:11-14
f. Colossians 3:4
g. 1 Corinthians 15:51-54
h. 1 Thessalonians 4:13-17
i. John 5:28, 29
j. Revelation 20:1-10

Choose from the verses you studied one passage that you want to commit to memory this week and work on it every day.

Way to Pray

As you pray this week, remember those who need comfort and the hope of the resurrection. Maybe you could write a note to someone who has lost a loved one and share with the individual the promises of the resurrection.

More Than Words

Interview someone you think has attended a few funerals in their lifetime. Use the following questions:

What is the most inspiring, encouraging thing you have ever heard or seen at a funeral?

What passage or story from Scripture gives you the most comfort about death and the resurrection?

What can we do for people who experience the loss of loved ones that nonbelievers would have a difficult time doing?

In the Mirror

Think about your interview and share a few insights you gained.

Lesson 14
The Second Coming

As you meet together this week, remember to have the students debrief and share the insights they gained from their interviews.

Objective: Students will understand the second coming of Christ and experience the personal assurance that believers enjoy as they watch and work for the approaching day.

The **Opening Story** is short because the lesson has three parables to take a look at. In them Jesus describes either what God's people are like at His coming or what they are doing then. 1. Five maidens are prepared for the Advent, not because they were watching (everyone was sleeping up until the time he arrived), but because they had extra oil. 2. The master gave money to each of his workers. Most of them did well and used their gift wisely. The master rewarded them when he returned—that is, all but the one who chose not to use his gift for the master's work. When Jesus returns, He will find us faithfully using the gifts He gave us to His glory. 3. The parable of the sheep and the goats focuses on what people will be doing when He returns. God's people will be active agents in bringing hope, comfort, and care to hurting people.

The phrases to focus on are the parts that describe the people, not the time of Christ's coming.

Opening Story

Some signs crack me up. "Slow men at work" or "Slow children at play." The one I love the most is on the fast-food window at the Taco Bell near my house. The sign reads, "Drive through window." I'm not sure that's the message they want to send. Signs are everywhere.

"Look out for signs," the preacher said. We could interpret that one two different ways. It could mean, "Keep your eyes peeled, because the signs you need to see are ahead." It could also be a warning against even looking for signs at all. Sound strange? Matthew 24 and 25 are all about "Looking out for the sign." Look at this:

"As Jesus was sitting on the Mount of Olives, the disciples came to him privately. 'Tell us,' they said, 'when will this happen, and what will be the sign of your coming and of the end of the age?'" (Matthew 24:3).

OK, English scholars. The word "sign"—is it singular or plural? Please say "singular."

Thanks. So if the sign is singular, how many signs should we look for? Come on, now; it's not a trick question. The answer is "one." But what about the wars and rumors of wars, the earthquakes and antichrists, floods, hurricanes, and fake messiahs? Read Matthew 24:3-29 and list as many "signs" as you can see. Now read the next verse:

"At that time the sign of the Son of Man will appear in the sky, and all the nations of the earth will mourn. They will see the Son of Man coming on the clouds of the sky, with power and great glory" (verse 30).

Did you see it? The "sign" of the second coming of Jesus is—the second coming of Jesus. But what about the other things? It seems as if God is more interested in what His people are doing at the time of the Second Coming than the events that signify the time of His return. Call me crazy, but the three parables that follow in Matthew 25 are all about what "being ready" actually consists of.

Life of Christ

Matthew 25:1-13

"At that time the kingdom of heaven will be like ten virgins who took their lamps and went out to meet the bridegroom. Five of them were foolish and five were wise. The foolish ones took their lamps but did not take any oil with them. The wise, however, took oil in jars along with their lamps. The bridegroom was a long time in coming, and they all became drowsy and fell asleep. At midnight the cry rang out: 'Here's the bridegroom! Come out to meet him!' Then all the virgins woke up and trimmed their lamps. The foolish ones said to the wise, 'Give us some of your oil; our lamps are going out.' 'No,' they replied, 'there may not be enough for both us and you. Instead, go to those who sell oil and buy some for yourselves.' But while they were on their way to buy the oil, the bridegroom arrived. The virgins who were ready went in with him to the wedding banquet. And the door was shut. Later the others also came. 'Sir! Sir!' they said. 'Open the door for us!' But he replied, 'I tell you the truth, I don't know you.' Therefore keep watch, because you do not know the day or the hour."

Matthew 25:14-29

"Again, it will be like a man going on a journey, who called his servants and entrusted his property to them. To one he gave five talents of money, to another two talents, and to another one talent, each according to his ability. Then he went on his journey. The man who had received the five talents went at once and put his money to work and gained five more. So also, the one with the two talents gained two more. But the man who had received the one talent went off, dug a hole in the ground and hid his master's money. After a long time the master of those servants returned and settled accounts with them. The man who had received the five talents brought the other five. 'Master,' he said, 'you entrusted me with five talents. See, I have gained five more.' His master replied, 'Well done, good and faithful servant! You have been faithful with a few things; I will put you in charge of many things. Come and share your master's happiness!' The man with the two talents also came. 'Master,' he said, 'you entrusted me with two talents; see, I have gained two more.' His master replied, 'Well done, good and faithful servant! You have been faithful with a few things; I will put you in charge of many things. Come and share your master's happiness!' Then the man who had received the one talent came. 'Master,' he said, 'I knew that you are a hard man, harvesting where you have not sown and gathering where you have not scattered seed. So I was afraid and went out and hid your talent in the ground. See, here is what belongs to you.' His master replied, 'You wicked, lazy servant! So you knew that I harvest where I have not sown and gather where I have not scattered seed? Well then, you should have put my money on deposit with the bankers, so that when I returned I would have received it back with interest. Take the talent from him and give it to the one who has the ten talents. For everyone who has will be given more, and he will have an abundance. Whoever does not have, even what he has will be taken from him.'"

Matthew 25:31-46

"When the Son of Man comes in his glory, and all the angels with him, he will sit on his throne in heavenly glory. All the nations will be gathered before him, and he will separate the people one from another as a shepherd separates the sheep from the goats. He will put the sheep on his right and the goats on his left. Then the King will say to those on his right, 'Come, you who are blessed by my Father; take your inheritance, the kingdom prepared for you since the creation of the world. For I was hungry and you gave me something to eat, I was thirsty and you gave me something to drink, I was a stranger and you invited me in, I needed clothes and you clothed me, I was sick and you looked after me, I was in prison and you came to visit me.' Then the righteous will answer him, 'Lord, when did we see you hungry and feed you, or thirsty and give you something to drink? When did we see you a stranger and invite you in, or needing clothes and clothe you? When did we see you sick or in prison and go to visit you?' The King will reply, 'I tell you the truth, whatever you did for one of the least of these brothers of mine, you did for me.' Then he will say to those on his left, 'Depart from me, you who are cursed, into the eternal fire prepared for the devil and his angels. For I was hungry and you gave me nothing to eat, I was thirsty and you gave me nothing to drink, I was a stranger and you did not invite me in, I needed clothes and you did not clothe me, I was sick and in prison and you did not look after me.' They also will answer, 'Lord, when did we see you hungry or thirsty or a stranger or needing clothes or sick or in prison, and did not help you?' He will reply, 'I tell you the truth, whatever you did not do for one of the least of these, you did not do for me.' Then they will go away to eternal punishment, but the righteous to eternal life."

> As the students paraphrase each verse and mark their Bibles, affirm the clear teaching that the Second Coming will be a literal, personal, visual, audible, death-smashing, earth-quaking event that marks the end of the era of sin and the beginning of the era of glory.

According to the above stories, what do the people who are ready for Christ's return look like? What are they busy with?

We Believe

The Second Coming

"The second coming of Christ is the blessed hope of the church, the grand climax of the gospel. The Saviour's coming will be literal, personal, visible, and worldwide. When He returns, the righteous dead will be resurrected, and together with the righteous living will be glorified and taken to heaven, but the unrighteous will die. The almost complete fulfillment of most lines of prophecy, together with the present condition of the world, indicates that Christ's coming is imminent. The time of that event has not been revealed, and we are therefore exhorted to be ready at all times." [23]

Read the following verses and rewrite them in your owns words as you chain-reference them in your Bible:

a. Revelation 1:7
b. Matthew 24:43, 44
c. 1 Thessalonians 4:13-18
d. 1 Corinthians 15:51-54
e. 2 Thessalonians 1:7-10; 2:8
f. Revelation 14:14-20
g. Revelation 19:11-21
h. Matthew 24
i. 2 Timothy 3:1-5
j. 1 Thessalonians 5:1-6

Choose from the verses you studied one passage that you want to commit to memory this week and work on it every day.

Way to Pray

Pray this week for a spirit of readiness. Pray throughout the day for your friends, relatives, and others in your community. Make this week a time to pray for others.

More Than Words

Interview someone in your congregation who is at least 50 years old. Use the following questions:

What events made you think, *Surely Christ is coming this year?*

What aspect of the Second Coming are you really looking forward to the most?

What do you want to be doing, or caught doing, when Jesus returns in the clouds of glory?

In the Mirror

Think about your interview and share a few insights you gained.

Lesson 15
The Millennium and
the End of Sin

As you begin this study, review the salient parts of the Second Coming with your students and finish by talking about their interviews.

Topics of last week's lesson:

The dead in Christ are raised to life (the wicked dead remain in their graves).

Those who are in Christ and alive at His coming will be caught up to meet Him.

Those who are lost and alive at His coming will die from the brightness.

Topics of this week's lesson:
The righteous will live with Christ in heaven.
The dead will remain in their graves until the end of the millennium, when Christ will resurrect them to face judgment and will then cleanse the earth entirely of sin by fire.

Objective: Students will see the compassion and justice of God as He finally removes sin from the universe.

The **Opening Story** describes how surprising the end will be, especially in light of those we thought would successfully finish the spiritual race. The point of the story is not to focus on who we think will be there or not there, but to concentrate on running the race. The millennium will provide time for questions and a thorough searching of God's ways. When it is done we will know without a doubt that God not only has been just, but merciful. The final punishment of the wicked is just and right, and everyone who is lost will agree that it was their own choice. It is vital to remind ourselves that God lets us choose our eternal home. Satan's deceitful slander accuses God of being unjust, overbearing, and forceful. But one day it will be clear to all that sin is the result of a lie that Lucifer told. Sin, God promises us, will never rise again.

In the **Life of Christ** the passage to focus on is "I tell you the truth, at the renewal of all things, when the Son of Man sits on his glorious throne, you who have followed me will also sit on twelve thrones, judging the twelve tribes of Israel. And everyone who has left houses or brothers or sisters or father or mother or children or fields for my sake will receive a hundred times as much and will inherit eternal life. But many who are first will be last, and many who are last will be first."

Opening Story

Racing around the block became a popular pastime for our neighborhood. Anyone could join in. The girls usually won, since they were slightly older than we were. I loved to watch them race off and about five minutes later hurtle around the opposite corner, huffing, puffing, snarling, and scratching their way to the finish line. Gregg was our best chance at winning, and it seemed he had this race won because the girls stumbled over each other at the start. By the time the girls got up and running the boys were around the corner. Watching the corner, I planned my victory dance. I envisioned Gregg rounding the corner, long stringy hair blowing in the wind, followed by the other determined male athletes.

But instead I stood there in shock as Christina showed up first, her long black hair flowing in the wind. Next came Tonya. Then Shonna. *What is going on here?* I thought. They smirked as they crossed the finish line. "You better go help your buddies out, Troy," they mocked and did their own victory dance.

Hopping on my bike, I soon discovered what had happened. From a distance I could hear one of our neighborhood gardeners screaming, "My new plants . . . I just planted the seeds for grass yesterday and look what you've done . . . irresponsible . . . rebellious . . . trespassers . . . jail . . ." Quickly I turned my bike around. Apparently the boys tried a short-cut through the neighbor's yard and got caught red-handed.

As I think about that day I wonder how the end of the world might be similar. The millennium is much like the finish line at which everyone watches and wonders at the way things turned out. What kinds of questions do you think people will need to have answered? What do you think Jesus will need to explain to us? Before the wicked receive their punishment, what is it that we will want to be sure of?

The great controversy has to do with God's reputation. Satan has spread a subtle, but highly deceptive rumor: God is harsh, exacting, too demanding, and if you cross Him, you're a goner. I could not serve a God like that out of anything but fear. When God's people who are alive at His coming and those who are resurrected in Christ go with Him to the city in heaven, what will we need to know? I'm sure I don't know a large chunk of what will take place, but one thing I am sure we will do is to see the beginning, the middle, and the end of the cosmic race between good and evil. When some that we expect to cross the finish line don't, we will need to know why. When the fire comes, not only will we understand that God did the right thing, but we will sing from our hearts our deepest praise because He did everything He possibly could to save them all—except save them against their will. It's heavy stuff—but it's very real.

Sometimes we get scared or anxious, or we simply try to predict what we think is going to happen during this time. One thing is for sure: We will agree that God is just and that He is good.

Life of Christ

Matthew 19:16-30

"Now a man came up to Jesus and asked, 'Teacher, what good thing must I do to get eternal life?' 'Why do you ask me about what is good?' Jesus replied. 'There is only One who is good. If you want to enter life, obey the commandments.' 'Which ones?' the man inquired. Jesus replied, '"Do not murder, do not commit adultery, do not steal, do not give false testimony, honor your father and mother," and "love your neighbor as yourself."'

"'All these I have kept,' the young man said. 'What do I still lack?'

"Jesus answered, 'If you want to be perfect, go, sell your possessions and give to the poor, and you will have treasure in heaven. Then come, follow me.

"When the young man heard this, he went away sad, because he had great wealth.

Then Jesus said to his disciples, 'I tell you the truth, it is hard for a rich man to enter the kingdom of heaven. Again I tell you, it is easier for a camel to go through the eye of a needle than for a rich man to enter the kingdom of God.' When the disciples heard this, they were greatly astonished and asked, 'Who then can be saved?' Jesus looked at them and said, 'With man this is impossible, but with God all things are possible.'

"Peter answered him, 'We have left everything to follow you! What then will there be for us?'

"Jesus said to them, 'I tell you the truth, at the renewal of all things, when the Son of Man sits on his glorious throne, you who have followed me will also sit on twelve thrones, judging the twelve tribes of Israel. And everyone who has left houses or brothers or sisters or father or mother or children or fields for my sake will receive a hundred times as much and will inherit eternal life. But many who are first will be last, and many who are last will be first.'"

As the students study the events of the millennium and the destruction of the wicked, have them make a time line.

We Believe

The Millennium and the End of Sin

"The millennium is the thousand-year reign of Christ with His saints in heaven between the first and second resurrections. During this time the wicked dead will be judged; the earth will be utterly desolate, without living human inhabitants, but occupied by Satan and his angels. At its close Christ with His saints and the Holy City will descend from heaven to earth. The unrighteous dead will then be resurrected, and with Satan and his angels will surround the city; but fire from God will consume them and cleanse the earth. The universe will thus be freed of sin and sinners forever." [24]

Read the following verses and rewrite them in your owns words while you chain-reference them in your Bible:

a. Revelation 20
b. 1 Corinthians 6:2, 3
c. Jeremiah 4:23-26
d. Revelation 21:1-5
e. Malachi 4:1
f. Ezekiel 28:18, 19

Choose from the verses you studied one passage that you want to commit to memory this week. Work on it every day.

Way to Pray

Think about the verses you have studied. God has given enough information to you to make you confident about where you stand now and in the days to come. Pray this week in thankfulness for what God has done and what He promises to do in the end.

More Than Words

Interview someone with the following questions:

How could a God of love destroy the world by fire? Doesn't that seem harsh to you? Explain.

What story or passage from the Bible gives you the most confidence and assurance that your life is safe in God's hands?

In the Mirror

Think about your interview and share a few insights you gained.

Lesson 16
The New Earth

One of the beauties of the Adventist message is the big picture it presents to us about God, His character, and His plan for people. The new earth teaching powerfully encourages the believer, because we can rest in confidence that we will eternally live in the unbelievable joy and love of the Savior.

Objective: Students will discover God's marvelous plan for restoring and re-creating the earth. The lesson will seek to create ways in which they can foster the reality of a place called Paradise.

Sometimes we hear people talk about life on the new earth as though it were all up to us. But the thief on the cross is a good example of one who will trust his Savior with the details.

Imagine you have a chance to choose whatever you want for your birthday. Most would be thinking, *How much is too much?* But it all depends on the giver. I don't want to minimize what Christ has planned for me by saying, "I'm going to snowboard throughout eternity and have lime-green hair." We must learn to trust God. One question you can ask the students is: "How will life in the new earth be like life now? How will it be different?"

Have the students take a glance at the last few pages of *The Great Controversy* and read together some of the paragraphs that depict existence on the new earth, especially pages 675, 676, in which Ellen White describes the way we will live in the new earth and the New Jerusalem.

Opening Story

I love rice. But after spending several weeks in Asia I was ready for a potato. Pasta. A burrito. Anything but rice. When my wife asked, "What do you want to eat when you get back from the airport?" I answered, "I don't care—anything but rice." She understood.

How would you describe Paradise? What will the houses look like? How big will the mangoes really be? Will there really be chocolate doughnut trees everywhere?—that's what the evangelist who came to my church said in his sermon. I'll be honest with you. I don't care what the new earth looks like. I could eat whatever is there for the ceaseless ages of eternity—even rice. What I'll be glad to miss is the following headlines:

"Mother and child badly beaten by drunken husband. They both remain in critical condition."

"House fire claims the life of a 12-year-old boy."

"Sweet-natured 4-year-old girl loses battle with cancer."

"Tragic accident claims the life of a 3-year-old boy."

"Hate crimes increase and local minorities live in fear."

"Rape crimes surge on college campuses."

"Bombs, war, innocent victims."

I could go on—but you get the idea. Make no mistake, whatever the new earth is like, I'm OK with it. Why? Look at this!

"Then I saw a new heaven and a new earth, for the first heaven and the first earth had passed away, and there was no longer any sea. I saw the Holy City, the new Jerusalem, coming down out of heaven from God, prepared as a bride beautifully dressed for her husband. And I heard a loud voice from the throne saying, 'Now the dwelling of God is with men, and he will live with them. They will be his people, and God himself will be with them and be their God. He will wipe every tear from their eyes. There will be no more death or mourning or crying or pain, for the old order of things has passed away.' He who was seated on the throne said, 'I am making everything new!' Then he said, 'Write this down, for these words are trustworthy and true'" (Revelation 21:1-5).

(Underline the three facts about the new earth that you look forward to the most. Share them with your partner.)

Imagine the thief on the cross. Do you believe he has his mind on chocolate doughnuts and mango trees? Not a chance. He's probably thinking, *If what He says is true, I'm not leaving that guy's side no matter how long eternity lasts.*

Life of Christ

Luke 23:39-43

"One of the criminals who hung there hurled insults at him: 'Aren't you the Christ? Save yourself and us!' But the other criminal rebuked him. 'Don't you fear God,' he said, 'since you are under the same sentence? We are punished justly, for we are getting what our deeds deserve. But this man has done nothing wrong.' Then he said, 'Jesus, remember me when you come into your kingdom.' Jesus answered him, 'I tell you the truth, . . . you will be with me in paradise.'"

We Believe

The New Earth

"On the new earth, in which righteousness dwells, God will provide an eternal home for the redeemed and a perfect environment for everlasting life, love, joy, and learning in His presence. For here God Himself will dwell with His people, and suffering and death will have passed away. The great controversy will be ended, and sin will be no more. All things, animate and inanimate, will declare that God is love; and He shall reign forever. Amen." [25]

Read the following verses and rewrite them in your owns words while you chain-reference them in your Bible:

a. 2 Peter 3:13
b. Isaiah 35
c. Isaiah 65:17-25

d. Matthew 5:5

e. Revelation 21:1-7; 22:1-5; 11:15

Choose from the verses you studied one passage that you want to commit to memory this week and work on it every day.

Now is the time to practice for life in the new earth. This exercise is the beginning of a way of life. One student sectioned off a 5' x 5' section of his backyard and planted a grapevine. He keeps it absolutely free from weeds as a reminder of the days to come. Have the students think of some everyday things they can do to live as though heaven had already arrived.

Way to Pray

As you pray this week, remember those who desperately need a taste of heaven now.

More Than Words

Interview someone who you think has thought about heaven and the new earth. Use the following questions:

What are you looking forward to the most in the new earth? What will you miss the least?

What promise from Scripture best helps you understand what heaven will be like?

Why do you think sin will never reign again on the new earth?

In the Mirror

Think about your interview and share a few insights you gained.

Lesson 17
Stewardship

Having examined the big picture events (death, resurrection, Second Coming, millennium, new earth), we now focus on how to live lives that glorify the Savior and prepare our world for God's kingdom.

By now you and the students should have established a consistent routine of activities—interviewing, Bible marking, praying and serving, sharing, thinking and journaling.

Objective: Students will deepen their understanding of the way God calls believers to a complete surrender of their lives, resources, and hearts for the work and glory of His kingdom.

It is hard for the believer to fight over money, adornment, or what music is appropriate in light of the events that we have just studied. The task for leaders and teachers is to refer to the big picture when looking at the duties of the Christian life now.

Lessons 1 through 12 build on the foundation of our relationship to God and to each other. Lessons 13 through 16 examine events that frame God's plan of redemption through history. Finally, lessons 17 through 21 will explore practical ways to live as believers.

The key to teaching this section is to model a positive, joyful lifestyle deeply committed to the truths we have already studied.

In this lesson we will study the topic of Christian stewardship. The opening stories depict a lifestyle committed to heaven's ways of giving, sharing, and selflessness.

As they read the stories, have the students notice the thoughtlessness of the givers. Ask the questions: "How are the givers in both stories thoughtless? What are they thoughtless about? What are they thoughtful about?"

The phrase to focus on in the **Life of Christ** section is "She has done a beautiful thing to me." Our giving to Christ of our time, self, energy, and money for His cause is personal. The woman gave to Him. Our giving, although it may be directly to a church, is really "to Him."

Opening Story

"I have more change in the ashtray of my car. May I go get it?" Rebekah asked as she dumped wads of crumpled dollar bills in both my hands. She and other students in my class had begun to respond to a prayer request. Finley needed a plane ticket to attend his birth mother's funeral. His adopted parents could not afford to fly him across the country, so my class took it upon themselves to make it happen. Finley was a giver. No matter who needed help with math, he would stay up at night on the phone or after school until late. Those who had received help from Finley wanted to give back something to him in a tangible way. The theme of the morning was "Whatever it takes—all that we have for Finley." I hadn't expected this kind of response:

"Here's the title to my car. It's wrecked and the junkyard is giving me $50 for it today. It's not much, but it's what I have."

One girl left the class without permission and interrupted basketball practice to do a little fund-raising. She returned with $36, saying, "The basketball team just gave me this," as she dumped the money on my desk.

It just seemed unreal. Here were 26 high school students. One minute they had been whining about the cost of lunch meals. The next they were balancing their checkbooks to see what they had left to give. When they didn't have money, they gave their time. If that was not enough, they found more of both. "Whatever it takes—all that we have for Finley." Why such a response?

I think it had to do with Finley. His constant gifts prompted people to give the way he did. That's all this woman in the following story was trying to do for Jesus—give back the way He gave to her. It is not about the number of dollars spent but the size of the heart that gives. Imagine what a gift like that would look like today? As you read this story, consider how much this act of kindness cost the woman, not just in money.

Life of Christ

Mark 14:1-9

"Now the Passover and the Feast of Unleavened Bread were only two days away, and the chief priests and the teachers of the law were looking for some sly way to arrest Jesus and kill him. 'But not during the Feast,' they said, 'or the people may riot.' While he was in Bethany, reclining at the table in the home of a man known as Simon the Leper, a woman came with an alabaster jar of very expensive perfume, made of pure nard. She broke the jar and poured the perfume on his head. Some of those present were saying indignantly to one another, 'Why this waste of perfume? It could have been sold for more than a year's wages and the money given to the poor.' And they rebuked her harshly. 'Leave her alone,' said Jesus. 'Why are you bothering her? She has done a beautiful thing to me. The poor you will always have with you, and you can help them any time you want. But you will not always have me. She did what she could. She poured perfume on my body beforehand to prepare for my burial. I tell you the truth, wherever the gospel is preached throughout the world, what she has done will also be told, in memory of her.'"

> As the students mark their Bible and paraphrase the verses, encourage them to note the passages that describe how God planned very specific ways for His people to spread the good news of God's love to the world.
>
> Consider the following definition of tithe:
>
> "In the Old Testament the purpose of the giving of a tenth was to meet the material need of the Levite, the stranger, the fatherless (the orphan), and the widow (Deut. 26:12, 13). The tithe was an expression of gratitude to God by His people. Basic to tithing was the acknowledgment of God's ownership of everything in the earth." [26]

We Believe

Stewardship

"We are God's stewards, entrusted by Him with time and opportunities, abilities and possessions, and the blessings of the earth and its resources. We are responsible to Him for their proper use. We acknowledge God's ownership by faithful service to Him and our fellow men, and by returning tithes and giving offerings for the proclamation of His gospel and the support and growth of His church. Stewardship is a privilege given to us by God for nurture in love and the victory over selfishness and covetousness. The steward rejoices in the blessings that come to others as a result of his faithfulness." [27]

Read the following verses and rewrite them in your owns words while you chain-reference them in your Bible:

    a. Genesis 1:26-28; 2:15

    b. 1 Chronicles 29:14

    c. Haggai 1:3-11

    d. Malachi 3:8-12

    e. 1 Corinthians 9:9-14

    f. Matthew 23:23

    g. 2 Corinthians 8:1-15

    h. Romans 15:26, 27

Choose from the verses you studied one passage that you want to commit to memory this week and work on it every day.

Way to Pray

As you pray this week, make a commitment to God to be faithful to Him by giving not just your money but your time and talents—the way He gave to you.

Many youth in the church have an unclear idea what the tithe and offering are for. It is helpful to show them clearly how the various funds relate both to the global church and the local church. The tithe does not remain in the local congregation, but gets spread throughout the world for the work of the church as a whole. The offerings collected each Sabbath remain in the local congregation to pay for the facility, the resources, and the ministries that it operates. As a member of a local church, we should give what God has commanded (10 percent tithe) as well as an offering to help keep the church open and running.

More Than Words

Interview someone who has children in college or older. Use the following questions:

When in your life has God come through miraculously for you as a result of your faithful giving?

Why do you think it is hard for us to consider our things or even time as belonging to God and not to ourselves?

What words of wisdom do you have for someone my age about giving and working in the church?

In the Mirror

Think about your interview and share a few insights you gained. Write about the ways that God has blessed you and given you reasons to be thankful.

Lesson 18
Christian Behavior

As the students meet to start another lesson, have them take a few moments to share the insights from the interview and other stories they might have heard about God's wonderful way of providing for people who spend themselves for His cause.

Objective: Students will understand the importance of living by the principles that God gave His children so that they might experience the abundant life.

The focus of the following passage from the **Life of Christ** section involves the difference between the lifestyle of the thief and that of the Savior: "The thief comes only to steal and kill and destroy; I have come that they may have life . . . to the full."

The students may have questions, but those converted in their heart have no problem wanting to live the good life. I use an illustration to describe the struggle over lifestyle decisions. We are either feeding one of two dogs—the good dog (blue) or the bad dog (red). These two dogs war with each other every moment. If you feed the red dog more than the blue dog, it wins the battle every time. Or if you feed the blue dog and starve the red dog, the blue dog will triumph. But if you feed them equally, it becomes a bloody, tiring dogfight. When it comes to Christian standards, inspire the student, in light of the big picture, to choose the most excellent way.

Opening Story

Questions that scare me to death:

"What movies are 'OK' to watch?"

"What's wrong with the way I dress?"

"Is there anything really bad about my music—isn't it just talking about 'real life'?"

"Jesus ate meat! Are people going to be kept out of heaven for that? The Bible doesn't say . . ."

And so on . . .

Do you know why these kinds of questions scare me? Because many of them are not really questions at all, but personal statements in disguise. Christian living is not about seeing what parts of "the world" legally fit in our life but how our lives can bring a smell of God's love to our world. Smell? Did I say, "Smell?"

No, Paul did. Check it out:

"But thanks be to God, who always leads us in triumphal procession in Christ and through us spreads everywhere the fragrance of the knowledge of him. For we are to God the aroma of Christ among those who are being saved and those who are perishing" (2 Corinthians 2:14, 15).

God's heart beats with joy when our sole passion in life is radiating His goodness and wonder. As our world gets darker we, as God's children, need to burn brighter, work harder, give more, sing louder, smell stronger! It doesn't sound like it fits, but when you approach a bakery, you know what it is. And when you drive by a dead skunk on the road, everyone notices.

Those other questions? I think it depends on who you ask. If your hope is to fit what you want into your world, then you already have your answers. But if your desire is to sell out completely to Jesus, then you ask Him and His Word for answers—they are there!

As my son and I stomped through the backyard full of snow, I turned to look back. The little guy was exhausted. His short legs would plummet into thick snow, and every step was hard work. But he wanted to blaze his own trail. I waited for him to catch up. Then as we continued I glanced back again and, to my surprise, discovered my son trucking along at a fast clip, right on my heels. "Get moving, slowpoke!" he chided. He had found the secret to speeding through the snow—walking in his father's footsteps. There are two ways to go: your own way or following in the footsteps of Christ. Jesus spoke of the two different lives you can choose to live.

Life of Christ

John 10:7-16

"Therefore Jesus said again, 'I tell you the truth, I am the gate for the sheep. All who ever came before me were thieves and robbers, but the sheep did not listen to them. I am the gate; whoever enters through me will be saved. He will come in and go out, and find pasture. The thief comes only to steal and kill and destroy; I have come that they may have life, and have it to the full.

"'I am the good shepherd. The good shepherd lays down his life for the sheep. The hired hand is not the shepherd who owns the sheep. So when he sees the wolf coming, he abandons the sheep and runs away. Then the wolf attacks the flock and scatters it. The man runs away because he is a hired hand and cares nothing for the sheep.

"'I am the good shepherd; I know my sheep and my sheep know me—just as the Father knows me and I know the Father—and I lay down my life for the sheep. I have other sheep that are not of this sheep pen. I must bring them also. They too will listen to my voice, and there shall be one flock and one shepherd.'"

To use the analogy of a fruit tree, what would the students think if they walked into an apple orchard during harvest season and found a tree with no fruit. Something was definitely wrong, but you would not be sure what the problem might be. If the tree was gnarled and leafless, you would know that it was probably dead. Or suppose the tree did have leaves and beautiful red apples—but they were mixed together with deep-green cucumbers. You would know that something was definitely wrong. If these trees represent believers in the church, how would the students explain the different kinds of trees?

Suggest to the students that as they mark their Bibles and paraphrase each verse, they should think about the kind of fruit they want to bear this year.

We Believe

Christian Behavior

"We are called to be a godly people who think, feel, and act in harmony with the principles of heaven. For the Spirit to re-create in us the character of our Lord we involve ourselves only in those things which will produce Christlike purity, health, and joy in our lives. This means that our amusement and entertainment should meet the highest standards of Christian taste and beauty. While recognizing cultural differences, our dress is to be simple, modest, and neat, befitting those whose true beauty does not consist of outward adornment but in the imperishable ornament of a gentle and quiet spirit. It also means that because our bodies are the temple of the Holy Spirit, we are to care for them intelligently. Along with adequate exercise and rest, we are to adopt the most healthful diet possible and abstain from the unclean foods identified in the Scriptures. Since alcoholic beverages, tobacco, and the irresponsible use of drugs and narcotics are harmful to our bodies, we are to abstain from them as well. Instead, we are to engage in whatever brings our thoughts and bodies into the discipline of Christ, who desires our wholesomeness, joy, and goodness." [28]

Read the following verses and rewrite them in your owns words while you chain-reference them in your Bible:

   a. Romans 12:1, 2
   b. 1 John 2:6
   c. Ephesians 5:16-26
   d. Philippians 4:8
   e. 1 Peter 3:1-4
   f. 1 Corinthians 6:19, 20
   g. Leviticus 11

h. 3 John 2

Choose from the verses you studied one passage that you want to commit to memory this week and work on it every day.

Have the students discuss with their partners how their prayer life has changed since they started these lessons. Invite them to share also what is different about the way they pray now than they did before.

Way to Pray

As you pray this week, make a list of a few parts of your life that you are uncomfortable with because of what you studied in this lesson. These are things you do that may or may not be moving you closer to Christ. Ask God to give you courage to do something about them.

More Than Words

Interview someone whose life really shines for God. Use the following questions:

Who has been the greatest influence on you in the choices you have made about living every day for Christ? How did they influence the decisions you made about: dress, entertainment, healthy living, etc.?

What passage or story from Scripture speaks to you about how to live a godly life in a godless world?

Do you think Christians should stand out in our world? In what ways do you think they should be different and in what ways do you think they should blend in?

In the Mirror

Think about and share a few insights you gained from your interview. Write about some of the choices and commitments you want to make today about your lifestyle.

Lesson 19
Marriage and the Family

Before the students start this lesson on marriage and the family, they should share any insights that emerged from their interviews. The transition between the last lesson and this one has to do with the way our personal choices about lifestyle eventually make us who we are later on in life. Ray Pritchard said, "We make decisions and our decisions make us." This is certainly true about the way an individual approaches marriage.

Objective: Students will discuss God's original plan for the family and the reason for the brokenness that plagues families today as the students set goals for their own lives based on Scripture.

The **Opening Story** depicts the ideal family by contrasting geese with gulls. Have the students think of a family (but not out loud) that represents both types of relationships—the cooperative and selfless geese, or the independent and competitive gulls.

Ask them what everyday activities a family can do to foster the geese-like V formation. Have them be specific. What are some attitudes and actions to avoid the gull-like lifestyle?

The passages to focus on in the **Life of Christ** section are the salt and light ones. Salt is an interesting metaphor because the substance has so many uses. Have the students make a list of the things salt is good for.

Take two clear glass saltshakers and put sugar in one and salt in the other. As you hold both shakers at a distance, it is very difficult to tell which is salt and which is sugar. Ask the student to guess which is which. When I have done this with entire classrooms, usually 50 percent get it wrong. Ask the students what this illustration can teach about families and how to tell whether they are healthy or not.

The truth is that when a family starts falling apart, it usually surprises most people, and by the time others discover and see the problems, it is often too late. The chances are good that you are studying with one or more young people who come from broken or divided homes.

Opening Story

Independence. Countries fight for it. Teenagers demand it. Most people today consider independence a positive virtue. Parents of college students eagerly wait for their grown-up kids to become independent. I want my son to be independent so he can tie his own shoes. But never, never ever did God want us to be alone.

"The Lord God said, 'It is not good for the man to be alone. I will make a helper suitable for him'" (Genesis 2:18).

So begins a family, the need for a partner, a community, a team to help us grow toward God and His chosen plan. The illustration that captures this plan for me is the difference between the seagulls and Canada geese:

"A seagull exults in freedom. When flying alone, he thrusts his wings back with powerful strokes, climbs higher and higher, and then swoops down in majestic loops and circles. In a flock, though, the seagull is a different bird. His majesty dissolves into in-fights and cruelty. Concepts of sharing and manners do not seem to exist among gulls. They are so fiercely competitive and jealous that if you tie a ribbon around the leg of a gull, making him stand out from the rest, you sentence him to death. The others in his flock will furiously attack him with claws and beaks, hammering through feathers and flesh to draw blood. They'll continue until he is a bloody heap.

"Consider the wild goose. The V formation they use in flying enables them to fly with more ease and speed. The point position is the most difficult because of wind resistance, so the geese rotate this position every few minutes. The easiest flight is experienced in the two rear sections of the formation, and the stronger geese permit the young, weak, and older birds to occupy these positions." [29]

Several facts stand out. 1. God created us as individuals, each one of us precious and unique to the Father in heaven. 2. God created individuals to live in harmony together for His purpose. 3. The result of unity in a family is joy and success. 4. The power of a harmonious family is more than a little flashlight in the forest—it is a spotlight that shines bright in the darkness.

Life of Christ

Matthew 5:13-16

"You are the salt of the earth. But if the salt loses its saltiness, how can it be made salty again? It is no longer good for anything, except to be thrown out and trampled by men.

"You are the light of the world. A city on a hill cannot be hidden. Neither do people light a lamp and put it under a bowl. Instead they put it on its stand, and it gives light to everyone in the house. In the same way, let your light shine before men, that they may see your good deeds and praise your Father in heaven."

In what ways can a family, of any size or shape, be a witness to others? If you know a family that is a light, write an anonymous note to them thanking them for their example. (Do this with your partner.)

> Encourage the students to write the letters with their partners.
> As they mark their Bibles and paraphrase the following passages, have them share what they think are the important parts to building an eternal marriage.

We Believe

Marriage and Family

"Marriage was divinely established in Eden and affirmed by Jesus to be a lifelong union between a man and a woman in loving companionship. For the Christian, a marriage commitment is to God as well as to the spouse, and should be entered into only between partners who share a common faith. Mutual love, honor, respect, and responsibility are the fabric of this relationship, which is to reflect the love, sanctity, closeness, and permanence of the relationship between Christ and His church. Regarding divorce, Jesus taught that the person who divorces a spouse, except for fornication, and marries another, commits adultery. Although some family relationships may fall short of the ideal, marriage partners who fully commit themselves to each other in Christ may achieve loving unity through the guidance of the Spirit and the nurture of the church. God blesses the family and intends that its members shall assist each other toward complete maturity. Parents are to bring up their children to love and obey the Lord. By their example and their words they are to teach them that Christ is a loving disciplinarian, ever tender and caring, who wants them to become members of His body, the family of God. Increasing family closeness is one of the earmarks of the final gospel message." [30]

Read the following verses and rewrite them in your owns words while you chain-reference them in your Bible:

a. Genesis 2:18-25
b. Matthew 19:3-9
c. 2 Corinthians 6:14
d. Ephesians 5:21-33
e. Matthew 5:31, 32
f. Exodus 20:12
g. Ephesians 6:1-4
h. Proverbs 22:6

Choose from the verses you studied one passage that you want to commit to memory this week and work on it every day.

> This week have the students encourage each other to do what they can to help build peace and joy in their homes. An analogy that may help involves the difference between a thermostat and thermometer. The thermometer simply reflects and registers the current temperature, but the thermostat regulates the temperature. If it should be 75 degrees, the thermostat does whatever is needed—kicking on the heat or the air-conditioning—to make the room the required temperature. How could they be a thermostat this week? But be careful that you don't make it seem as if happiness and unity depend completely on them. Young people can carry guilt that a broken family is their fault.

Way to Pray

Pray for the members of your family individually throughout the week. Ask God to help you to be a blessing to your family, instead of a pain. Share with your partner how you will work toward this goal this week. Be specific. (Call each other during the week as a reminder.)

> Encourage the student partners to do all they can to help their families. Have them call each other during the week to remind themselves about their goals.

More Than Words

Interview a parent who you think would have a lot to share about the importance of a family to the mission of God's church. Ask:

What do you think are the most important tools to help families grow closer together?

Who has been your example for family life and what are some of the things they do that made such an impression on you?

What passage or story from Scripture is your greatest source of help as a parent? as a spouse?

What advice would you give a young person who is considering whom they might marry?

In the Mirror

Think about your interview and share a few insights you gained.

Lesson 20
Christ's Ministry in the Heavenly Sanctuary

Have the students share some of their experiences in being "geese" or "thermostats" during the past week. Also let them take a minute or two to share a few insights they gained from their interviews.

As you move into the doctrine of the sanctuary, it is important to remember that the teaching is what we would call a pillar in Adventist faith. If you look at the whole of Scripture, you cannot avoid the message of the sanctuary.

Objective: Students will survey the meaning and purpose of the sanctuary (on earth and in heaven) and discover the incredible significance of the events that mark the beginning of the Adventist movement.

The **Opening Story** introduces the Lamb. The people of Israel, even though they lived and breathed the very air of the sanctuary, still were not ready for a Messiah that came as a lamb. But John saw Jesus and knew without question who He was. He was not a general, a politician, or a warrior, but a Lamb. The sanctuary service centers on the lamb, and therefore centers on Christ.

The phrase to focus on is "Look, the Lamb of God, who takes away the sin of the world!" The statement makes no sense without a sanctuary. As you study the sanctuary on earth, you will see that it is patterned after the sanctuary in heaven.

Opening Story

Jesus was not the first man to be considered the Messiah by people. As a matter of fact, He came some 60 years after several so-called messiahs. After His death a group of wild-eyed rebels with political and religious ideas made a lot of noise. Called Zealots, they sought to take down Rome one official, one soldier at a time. Good with a knife, they had no problem finding a place for it as they slipped through the crowded streets full of soldiers. Another name for them was the Sicarii, or the daggermen.

"Fortified with apocalyptic notions of the imminent arrival of a Davidic messiah, they were eager to fight the Romans. They seized control of Jerusalem early in the war, defending it with a fanaticism which made any solution except destruction of the city impossible."[31]

Many of the leaders considered themselves to be the Messiah, and their idea of a revolution was to bring glory back to Israel by bloodshed and force. During this century of wanna-be messiahs Jesus walked up the banks of the Jordan River not banging a drum and waving a sword or shouting the war cry of frenzied rebels. Jesus came to the water to be baptized. The One who stood before John in the water would be no flash-in-the-pan leader. His work, like that of the other leaders before Him, would involve knife and blood, but not the knife of a murderer and the blood of trained soldiers, but His own. His fight would be different from that of all the others in that He would be the only one to die. That's why John could say, "Behold the Lamb of God who takes away the sins of the world." Now, that's a revolution. But why lambs and why blood?

Take a look at the story first, and then, as you study the purpose and meaning of the sanctuary, you'll notice three important players in the sanctuary service that are hard to miss: the sinner, the lamb, and the high priest.

Believe me, when it comes to sin and God's plan to redeem and restore the earth, the sanctuary is the centerpiece you can't overlook. You'll notice no military leaders, no loudmouths waving a knife and banging a drum—just a sinner, a lamb, and the high priest. This is what John saw when he saw Jesus approaching. What will you see?

Life of Christ

John 1:29-37

"The next day John saw Jesus coming toward him and said, 'Look, the Lamb of God, who takes away the sin of the world! This is the one I meant when I said, "A man who comes after me has surpassed me because he was before me." I myself did not know him, but the reason I came baptizing with water was that he might be revealed to Israel.' Then John gave this testimony: 'I saw the Spirit come down from heaven as a dove and remain on him. I would not have known him, except that the one who sent me to baptize with water told me, "The man on whom you see the Spirit come down and remain is he who will baptize with the Holy Spirit." I have seen and I testify that this is the Son of God.' The next day John was there again with two of his disciples. When he saw Jesus passing by, he said, 'Look, the Lamb of God!' When the two disciples heard him say this, they followed Jesus."

A Look at the Sanctuary

The elements of the sanctuary show Christ's ministry to us, not only at Calvary but also today in heaven. Ultimately, the sanctuary was then, and still is, about Jesus.

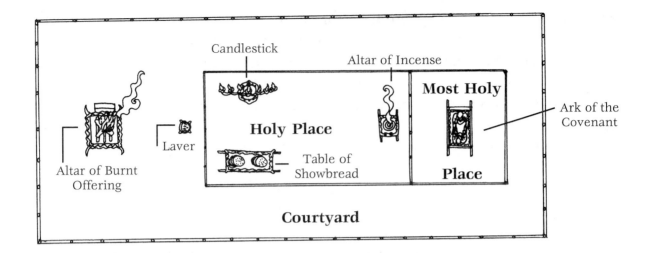

What is the sanctuary?

The courtyard contained the altar of burnt offering and the laver.

The tent of the sanctuary had two parts: the holy place and the Most Holy Place. The holy place housed the seven-branched candlestick (lampstand), the table of showbread, and the altar of incense. The Most Holy Place held the ark of the covenant, which contained the Ten Commandments, written by God on two tables of stone. Two golden cherubim stood facing each other, and in the middle of the covering was the mercy seat.

What happened at the sanctuary?

As a sinner, you would bring a sacrifice (usually a lamb) and place your hands on the innocent animal. The animal was killed as you confessed your sins, thus in a way placing them on the victim. The high priest sprinkled the blood of the animal on the alter of burnt offering or in the holy place. Every day sinners transferred their sins to the sanctuary through what we call the daily sacrifice. Those who confessed their sins walked away forgiven.

The sanctuary would be cleansed once a year, an event Scripture calls the Day of Atonement. Essentially, it was a day of judgment for everyone who had confessed their sins throughout the year. It was a time of awe and solemn reverence. The Levites brought two goats to the sanctuary on the Day of Atonement. One goat, "the Lord's goat," would be sacrificed. The other was the scapegoat. The high priest would sacrifice the Lord's goat and take its blood into the Most Holy Place. The high priest entered this room once a year and only on this special day. He sprinkled the blood on the mercy seat. Then the high priest returned to the holy place and spattered blood on the altar of incense. He finally returned to the courtyard, where he put the blood on the altar of burnt offering.

After this was done, the high priest placed his hands on the head of the other goat (the scapegoat) and confessed the sins of all the people of Israel for a whole year and symbolically placed them on the scapegoat. A Levite sent the scapegoat into the wilderness to wander around until it died with the sins of Israel.

What does it mean?

God showed Moses the sanctuary in heaven, and Moses then built a model of the heavenly one. The parts of the sanctuary have tremendous meaning and purpose. The sanctuary service demonstrated the two parts of the ministry of Christ (the work of intercession and the work of judgment).

The First Part (the Courtyard and the Holy Place)

When people confessed their sin over the lamb and the high priest killed and placed it on the altar, it symbolized the sacrifice of Christ as He died on Calvary. (Remember, John the Baptist said, "Behold the Lamb of God who takes away the sins of the world.")

The laver, filled with water, illustrates baptism and the forgiveness of sins as the water washes away the old person of sin.

In the holy place the table of showbread stands for Christ, the Bread of Life (John 6:35). The candlestick portrays Jesus as the light of the world (John 8:12). The altar of incense illustrates the way Christ intercedes for sinners (John 17).

The Second Part (the Most Holy Place)

The ministry of the second compartment is one of judgment. The truth of sin is that even though there is forgiveness for sin, someone has to pay. The ark of the covenant is a timeless symbol of God's unchanging law of righteousness. It is important to remember that God's law makes the sacrifice and the blood and death necessary. Sin (transgression of the law) brings death. The ark represents God's throne, at which His justice calls for an answer to the sin problem.

The scapegoat depicts Satan, who is banished from the sanctuary with the sins of the people. Thus justice is served. Sin, death, and shame die with the one responsible for them.

The sanctuary is not a sick ritual demanded by an angry God who wants blood. No, quite the opposite; it is a moment to participate with and to witness a loving God who deals with the sin problem by becoming the payment for sin Himself. Scripture has many warm and fuzzy stories of God's love. But the sanctuary service is not warm and fuzzy—it is God's love conquering the cold, cruel effects of sin. Although not pretty, it does save us.

As you read the passages below that describe the heavenly sanctuary and God's plan of salvation, also read chapters 23 and 24 in *The Great Controversy* for a more thorough explanation on the work of the sanctuary and of Christ's ministry in the sanctuary.

We Believe

Christ's Ministry in the Heavenly Sanctuary

"There is a sanctuary in heaven, the true tabernacle which the Lord set up and not man. In it Christ ministers on our behalf, making available to believers the benefits of His atoning sacrifice offered once for all on the cross. He was inaugurated as our great High Priest and began His intercessory ministry at the time of His ascension. In 1844, at the end of the prophetic period of 2300 days, He entered the second and last phase of His atoning ministry. It is a work of investigative judgment, which is part of the ultimate disposition of all sin, typified by the cleansing of the ancient Hebrew sanctuary on the Day of Atonement. In that typical service the sanctuary was cleansed with the blood of animal sacrifices, but the heavenly things are purified with the perfect sacrifice of the blood of Jesus. The investigative judgment reveals to heavenly intelligences who among the dead are asleep in Christ and therefore, in Him, are deemed worthy to have part in the first resurrection. It also makes manifest who among the living are abiding in Christ, keeping the commandments of God and the faith of Jesus, and in Him, therefore, are ready for translation into His everlasting kingdom. This judgment vindicates the justice of God in saving those who believe in Jesus. It declares that those who have remained loyal to God shall receive the kingdom. The completion of this ministry of Christ will mark the close of human probation before the Second Advent." [32]

Read the following verses and rewrite them in your own words while you chain-reference them in your Bible:

a. Hebrews 8:1-5; 4:14-16

b. Daniel 7:9-27; 8:13, 14; 9:24-27

c. Numbers 14:34

d. Ezekiel 4:6

e. Leviticus 16

f. Revelation 14:6, 7; 20:12; 14:12; 22:12

Choose from the verses you studied one passage that you want to commit to memory this week and work on it every day.

What part of the sanctuary service do you think is the most important feature? Why? What parts of this do you still have questions about? Share them with your partner.

> This prayer is designed to enable the students to experience the beauty of the sanctuary as they pray. Juniors have great imaginations, but since this is not the type of exercise they would feel comfortable doing in a public or group setting, have them do it alone at home.

Way to Pray

As you pray this week, imagine yourself at the sanctuary and think about what it must have been like in the desert or at Jerusalem during a sacrifice. Here are some of the steps to praying your way through the sanctuary:

1. Enter with praise (Psalm 100). "Dear God, I want to praise You today for the way You love people . . ."

2. Confess your sins (1 John 1:8, 9). "Lord, You know how I have let You down this week. . . . I want to confess to You how much I need your forgiveness . . ."

3. Ask for spiritual washing through the Word (Titus 3:5, 6). "Father, You have spoken to me in Your Word about the way You want me to live . . ."

4. Ask for the baptism of the Spirit (Galatians 5:22-25). "God, please bring Your Spirit to me so I can have Your presence with me throughout the day . . ."

5. Receive strength for the day ahead (John 6:32, 33 and Romans 13:12-14). "Jesus, give me the strength and courage I need to be what you want me to be . . ."

6. Intercede wuth God (Philippians 1:3, 4). "Father, because You ask us to bring our needs and wants to You, I ask You to provide a way for . . ."

7. Experience intimate communion with God (Psalm 16:8, 11). "Father, thank You for making this possible. . . . I sense You are with me now, and I want to live each day like this . . ."

More Than Words

Interview a pastor, teacher, elder, or someone who you think has a pretty good knowledge of the meaning and purpose of the sanctuary. Ask the following questions:

What do you think is the most significant feature of the sanctuary service?

What story or passage from Scripture reminds you most of God's great work of salvation?

What do you think the sanctuary in heaven is all about?

In the Mirror

Think about your interview and share a few insights you gained.

Lesson 21
The Remnant and the Mission of the Church

Have the students take a few minutes to share the results from their interviews during the past week.

Objective: Students will discover the wonderful and sacred responsibility of inviting people to know the Savior and unite together to communicate the truth of the gospel to the world.

The stories that open this lesson involve young people who have chosen to remain faithful to Jesus in spite of the odds against them or the pressure around them. The remnant is not an exclusive group of know-it-alls, but a group of people who just happen to be in the right place at the right time with their eyes open and their minds attentive. The core concept of the remnant is not their purity, but their mission.

The aspect to focus the students' attention on in the **Life of Christ** section is not a phrase, but a word. Ask the students if they can guess what it is. You don't have to read far into the verse to find the word "Go." Get a copy of the *Seventh-day Adventist Yearbook* and have the students scan through it. Have them study the names and the places. As they look at India, for example, have them imagine the thousands who will come to know Christ this week. Get a copy of *Adventist Frontier Missions* magazine and read about people serving around the world. All who become Seventh-day Adventist Christians must let the mission of the remnant sink deep into their souls.

Opening Story

Six bystanders stood silently as the vehicle sped from the scene of the crime. Two women leaving a department store, arms full of shopping bags, witnessed the truck skid and crash into a parked car. An elderly couple sitting by the window of an Italian restaurant looked in horror as the driver of the truck backed up and raced away. While talking on a pay phone, a teenage girl surveyed the accident, eyes wide with surprise, as she reported the event to whoever was on the other line. Looking for an opening in traffic, a businessman waited to pull out when—*crash*—the pickup truck smashed into the parked car in front of his. Writing the license plate number on an envelope, he then reached for his cell phone to call the police. Six people witnessed the event. Six witnesses? Maybe, maybe not.

Some see events like this and pretend to have noticed nothing. Many refuse to get involved by testifying, thinking someone else will do it. Others wonder, *Why should I get involved?* while making the excuse "It's not my problem." Still, there are some who witness a crime and willingly cooperate and participate in the process of justice. What would you do?

Witnesses not only see but are willing to testify to what they have seen. Can you imagine how frustrating it would be for Jesus to have all these people who walked with Him, talked to Him, and witnessed the wonders of His life refuse to spread the word? But lepers who were healed, blind men who were made to see—they testified! When Jesus called His disciples to be witnesses to the world, there were only a few, at least 11, maybe 100. But throughout history God has had people who will be faithful witnesses no matter what the cost.

Kevin would faithfully read his Bible every night. When his friends and I were on a campout I noticed that the others didn't even bring a Bible, much less read it. The first night Kevin read as the others joked around, hooting and hollering with the excitement of the first night in the woods. The boys noticed him with his Bible. In the morning, as they ate breakfast around the campfire, someone asked, "Where's Kevin?" He had gathered some wood and returned just in time to hear one of the others say, "He's probably out reading his Bible." Several boys laughed uncomfortably. They all knew the remark was a thoughtless jab at Kevin, but no one said a word as he dropped the wood by the fire. "Just kidding, Kevin!" the boy whose mouth moved faster than his thoughts chuckled. The rest glanced at each other sheepishly, and soon they were off doing boy stuff.

During the afternoon I asked Kevin if the remark bothered him. His face became red and he hesitated a bit, but then he said, "Yeah, I feel kind of funny bringing my Bible with me, but it's just something I've always done."

"What do you think your friends think about you?" I probed.

"Well," he started slowly, a grin forming around the corners of his mouth, "they are coming around. Tonight they want me to read out loud." And I thought I had a delicate boy whom I would have to shelter on the whole camping trip. Instead, he turned out to be a solid oak-tree witness with a clear mission. He was winning his friends right under my nose!

Andrew pops out of the water as the church applauds in joy at his decision for baptism. Christ captured his heart as he learned about the Adventist message from an evangelist on TV. He attends a public high school in a fair-sized city in the Northwest, so I asked him, "Andrew, why don't you come to school at the academy? You would love it!"

His face betrayed his surprise. "Pastor Troy, I'm the only Adventist at my school." He just looked at me as if that explained it. Then I saw it. Right in front of me stood a full-blown missionary in the skin of a teenager. As you read the mission Jesus commits

His disciples to, know this: The first missionaries of the church were not much older than you.

Life of Christ

Matthew 28:19, 20

"Therefore go and make disciples of all nations, baptizing them in the name of the Father and of the Son and of the Holy Spirit, and teaching them to obey everything I have commanded you. And surely I am with you always, to the very end of the age."

We Believe

The Remnant and the Mission of the Church

"The universal church is composed of all who truly believe in Christ, but in the last days, a time of widespread apostasy, a remnant has been called out to keep the commandments of God and the faith of Jesus. This remnant announces the arrival of the judgment hour, proclaims salvation through Christ, and heralds the approach of His second advent. This proclamation is symbolized by the three angels of Revelation 14; it coincides with the work of judgment in heaven and results in a work of repentance and reform on earth. Every believer is called to have a personal part in this worldwide witness."[33]

Read the following verses and rewrite them in your own words while you chain-reference them in your Bible.

a. Revelation 12:17; 14:6-12; 18:1-4
b. 2 Corinthians 5:10
c. Jude 3, 14
d. 1 Peter 1:16-19
e. 2 Peter 3:10-14
f. Revelation 21:1-14

Choose from the verses you studied one passage that you want to commit to memory this week and work on it every day.

Way to Pray

As you pray this week, ask God to remind you of opportunities to be a witness. Think of times in your normal routine that you could share a word of encouragement.

Another option would be for the students to interview either a regular missionary or a student missionary who has returned from service. Have them ask about the people, the church, and the mission overseas. One of the challenges I always make to young people is to begin to save and sacrifice in order to go on a short-term mission trip before they leave high school.

More Than Words

Interview someone this week who you think is a witness to other people. Use the following questions:

Who is the remnant, and how does the Adventist Church relate to that group of people?

What do you think are key marks of God's people in the last days? What do they look like, what are they doing, and how would you characterize them?

Share a story or experience from your life when you were most proud to be a Seventh-day Adventist Christian.

Before they end this study, the students should do three things with their partners.

1. Take five minutes to go through their study guides and just reflect on all the things they wrote about in the journaling section called In the Mirror. Both should look at what they have done together.

2. Pray with them to be faithful witnesses as part of the remnant church.

3. Continue to remind each other throughout the coming months of the commitments both have made to Christ and to His church.

In the Mirror

Think about your interview and share a few insights you gained. Consider how you want to be faithful to the mission Jesus gave years ago.

[1] *Seventh-day Adventists Believe,* p. 4.
[2] Stuart Hample and Eric Marshall, *Children's Letters to God,* pp. 12, 15, 31, 35, 37, 47, 79.
[3] *Seventh-day Adventists Believe,* p.16.
[4] *Ibid.,* p. 28.
[5] *Ibid.,* p. 36.
[6] Ibid., p. 58.
[7] Ray Pritchard, *The ABCs of Wisdom,* pp. 158, 159.
[8] *Seventh-day Adventists Believe,* p. 98.
[9] Michael Green, *1500 Illustrations for Biblical Preaching,* p. 315.
[10] *Seventh-day Adventist Believe,* p. 118.
[11] James S. Hewett, *Illustrations Unlimited,* p. 51.
[12] *Seventh-day Adventists Believe,* p. 180.

[13] *Ibid.,* p. 68.

[14] *Ibid.,* p. 232.

[15] *Ibid.,* p. 249.

[16] Green, p. 47.

[17] *Seventh-day Adventists Believe,* p. 106.

[18] *Ibid.,* p. 194.

[19] *Nelson's Complete Book of Stories, Illustrations, and Quotes,* p. 128.

[20] *Seventh-day Adventists Believe,* p. 206.

[21] *Ibid.,* p. 134.

[22] *Ibid.,* p. 348.

[23] *Ibid.,* p. 332.

[24] *Ibid.,* p. 362.

[25] *Ibid.,* p. 374.

[26] *Nelson's Illustrated Bible Dictionary.*

[27] *Seventh-day Adventists Believe,* p. 268.

[28] *Ibid.,* p. 278.

[29] Green, p. 146.

[30] *Seventh-day Adventists Believe,* p. 294.

[31] Albert Bell, *Exploring the New Testament World,* p. 39.

[32] *Seventh-day Adventists Believe,* p. 312.

[33] *Ibid.,* p. 152.

ChristWise: Teens
Lesson 1
The Scriptures

Objective: Students will discover the purpose, person, and power of God's Word in the life of the believer.

The **Opening Story** demonstrates the dilemma between believing what people say to you and what you see. It is true in life, and especially in the spiritual life, that we believe what we see instead of what God says. The purpose of this story is to cause us to think about how we relate to God's Word.

Opening Story

I stood at the back of the crowd, watching the magic show in the mall. Even more intriguing than the magician, however, was the girl beside me. She bawled like a burst pipe as the magician sliced a woman in half.

"It's OK, honey," her father said. "That woman didn't really get cut in half. It's just a trick. Let's go meet the magician, and he'll show you the woman is OK."

After the show the father escorted his girl to the stage. "Excuse me, sir, but your sawing trick greatly disturbed my daughter, Chelsea. Surely you will tell her that cutting a person in two is a trick, won't you?"

"Well—uh—of course the woman is OK and now in one piece . . ."

"But please show Chelsea that the woman is safe."

After 15 minutes of haggling, the magician surrendered his secret like a monkey giving up his last banana. "Of course she's OK. She is right there."

Because his assistant had changed out of her costume, however, the girl didn't recognize the woman. Ironically, even after the magician walked the girl through a step-by-step drill of the trick, the kid wouldn't buy it. Seeing the real thing did not equate to believing it.

Isn't it amazing how we can refuse to believe what is so clearly real? For example, science keeps documenting the deadly effects of tobacco, yet people still smoke. In a world swarming with sexually transmitted diseases young people remain as promiscuous as ever. The Bible has been around for centuries and has proved itself to be the most trustworthy guideline for living. Nevertheless, many people ignore its counsel.

Why? Because we tend to believe the magic trick rather than the evidence. Consider the story Jesus told about the rich man and Lazarus.

The aspect to focus on in the story of the rich man and Lazarus is not the flames, torture, despair, or supernatural phenomenon. The reason the lessons use this story is that the final issue is about trusting the Scriptures instead of what we see. "'They have Moses and the Prophets; let them listen to them.' 'No, father Abraham,' he said, 'but if someone from the dead goes to them, they will repent.' He said to him, 'If they do not listen to Moses and the Prophets, they will not be convinced even if someone rises from the dead.'"

Think of some scenarios that are like this one; such as consulting a grocery store clerk on how to land a plane, asking a knitting instructor to teach you how to do brain surgery, or questioning a creative storywriter on how to do your taxes. Think of a few of your own.

Life of Christ

Luke 16:19-31

"There was a rich man who was dressed in purple and fine linen and lived in luxury every day. At his gate was laid a beggar named Lazarus, covered with sores and longing to eat what fell from the rich man's table. Even the dogs came and licked his sores. The time came when the beggar died and the angels carried him to Abraham's side. The rich man also died and was buried. In hell, where he was in torment, he looked up and saw Abraham far away, with Lazarus by his side. So he called to him, 'Father Abraham, have pity on me and send Lazarus to dip the tip of his finger in water and cool my tongue, because I am in agony in this fire.' But Abraham replied, 'Son, remember that in your lifetime you received your good things, while Lazarus received bad things, but now he is comforted here and you are in agony. And besides all this, between us and you a great chasm has been fixed, so that those who want to go from here to you cannot, nor can anyone cross over from there to us.' He answered, 'Then I beg you, father, send Lazarus to my father's house, for I have five brothers. Let him warn them, so that they will not also come to this place of torment.' Abraham replied, 'They have Moses and the Prophets; let them listen to them.' 'No, father Abraham,' he said, 'but if someone from the dead goes to them, they will repent.' He said to him, 'If they do not listen to Moses and the Prophets, they will not be convinced even if someone rises from the dead.'"

Open Questions

Do you think it is easier to believe your eyes or what was written years ago in the Bible? Why?

> Before they dive into the Scriptures, have the students ask themselves, "If you had to share what you believe about this book (Bible) to someone else, how would you say it in one sentence?"

We Believe

The Holy Scriptures

Jesus spoke to the religious leaders so pointedly because they knew the Scriptures but didn't "live them." Read the statement below and mark or chain-reference the verses in your Bible.

"The Holy Scriptures . . . are the written Word of God, given by divine inspiration through holy men of God who spoke and wrote as they were moved by the Holy Spirit."[1] Everything we need for salvation is available in the Bible. The Bible is really about God revealing to us who He is and who we are in relation to Him. It reveals a trustworthy picture of God and becomes the authoritative guide for people as they follow Him.

   a. 2 Peter 1:20, 21
   b. 2 Timothy 3:16
   c. Hebrews 1:1, 2
   d. Hebrews 4:12
   e. John 5:39
   f. Psalm 119:105
   g. Proverbs 30:5
   h. 1 Thessalonians 2:13
   i. James 1:22-25

Which verses help you understand the purpose of the Bible the most?
Write a brief statement of your belief about the Bible.

Way to Pray

Scan through Psalm 119 and notice what David says in prayer to God about Scripture. Write a short prayer to God about what you want to say to Him about His Word.

More Than Words

Interview someone you know about their faith in the Bible. Here are a few questions to ask them:

1. When in your life did you come to trust the Bible as God's word for you?
2. When has the Bible been a real source of strength to you? Have you had times when you had doubts about God's Word?
3. If you could tell only one story from Scripture, which one would you choose to help a friend know God? Why?

In the Mirror

Think about how important the Bible is to your life now. Does it point out some things in your life that you would you like to change?

Remind the students to work on the practical applications at the end of the lesson **(Way to Pray, More Than Words, In the Mirror)** and be ready to share their thoughts and insights the next week.

Lesson 2
The Trinity

Before they move into the lesson, have the students share their experiences with the interviews. As the leader, you need to model this activity, because it is a little awkward for many to engage an adult in an interview, but it is ultimately well worth it for them to hear what they think.

Objective: Students will encounter the mystery and marvelous relationship of the Trinity and see how an unfathomable God becomes real to people.

The **Opening Story** is really not a story, but quotes and statements from the world's most renown skateboarders. The magazine asked the skaters, "Do you believe in God?" Their responses reflect whether they believe in God, but mostly what they believe and think *about* Him. As they read through their "beliefs," have the students evaluate each statement. Ask the teens, "Where do they obtain their information about God?" This question is key for the believer because we get our data only because God chose to reveal it to us in His Word. It is clear that many have ideas, beliefs, and opinions, but most are based on nonbiblical sources.

Opening Story

Transworld Skateboarding asked some famous skateboarders the question "Do you believe in God?" Here are some of the responses:

"Not in the traditional sense of a supreme being. I believe in a more unified force in the world."—Tony Hawk.

"I believe in my brain: God's in there, and it's really small. . . . We're just here, man. We don't know what's going on. All we know is that we don't know."—Tim O'Connor.

"I don't know if there is one physical man, but I do [believe in God] in one form or another."—Rick Howard.

"Yes, I do. I believe in God, and I think everyone has their own interpretation of what God is and who they know to be their God. I'm not really close with my god right now, but I do believe in God, for sure."—Reese Forbes.

"I believe there is something. I don't know if it's a someone, a female, or a male. I couldn't tell you what it is. But there's definitely something that is greater than ourselves. I do feel we were created somehow, but do I believe in God? I don't think I believe in God because God is just a word that was given to it. Like I could call my skateboard my god, you know?"—Ricky Oyola.

"No, I don't. I just can't see it. It's not real to me. It just feels like something so that people won't be so scared of dying—something to look forward to. I'm just meat and bones, and then it's done."—Rick McCrank.

"I do believe in something, you know? I don't know enough about God, you know? I know that I want to believe . . . I feel some spirit. Maybe if you just feel good about yourself and what you're doing . . . maybe that's what exists."—Brad Staba.

"Absolutely. I'm sure because something has to come from something. It can't just come from nothing. And we all know that there's a force that separates good from evil."—Rob Dyrdek.

"No. I don't believe in God. I think that when I die I'm gonna rot in the ground just like every other animal."—Moses Itkonen.

"Of course I believe in God. If you don't believe in God, then you think you're God."—Jamie Thomas.[2]

What do you think of their impression of God? A couple of thoughts popped into my mind as I thought about their answers:

The God I know not only wants us to know Him personally, but also goes out of His way to make it happen.

The God I know is a person, or has personlike qualities, for He created us "in His image."

The only way to really know God is through the ways He reveals Himself to us—primarily through Scripture.

As you study the Trinity, notice this supernatural encounter with Christ and think about what it really means both to believe in God and to know Him.

> This lesson is on the Trinity. Only a small number of passages contain all three members of the Godhead in the same section. This is one of those passages. Have the student underline the words or phrases that refer to either the Father, Son, or Holy Spirit.

Life of Christ

Luke 24:36-49

"While they were still talking about this, Jesus himself stood among them and said to them, 'Peace be with you.' They were startled and frightened, thinking they saw a ghost. He said to them, 'Why are you troubled, and why do doubts rise in your minds? Look at my hands and my feet. It is I myself! Touch me and see; a ghost does not have flesh and bones, as you see I have.' When he had said this, he showed them his hands and feet. And while they still did not believe it because of joy and amazement, he asked them, 'Do you have anything here to eat?' They gave him a piece of broiled fish, and he took it and ate it in their presence. He said to them, 'This is what I told you while I was still with you: Everything must be fulfilled that is written about me in the Law of Moses, the Prophets and the Psalms.' Then he opened their minds so they could understand the Scriptures. He told them, 'This is what is written: The Christ will suffer and rise from the dead on the third day, and repentance and forgiveness of sins will be preached in his name to all nations, beginning at Jerusalem. You are witnesses of these things. I am going to send you what my Father has promised; but stay in the city until you have been clothed with power from on high.'"

Here is one of the many sections of Scripture that mention the Son, the Father, and the Holy Spirit in the same place.

What can you tell about the different roles that the members of the Trinity have by looking at this story?

The doctrine of the Trinity challenges the mind. Scholars and theologians have been trying to describe God for centuries now. The point of this lesson is not to define God or describe the way His nature works—but to know Him. How do you know someone you can't figure out? The answer to that question is that nobody knows anyone completely. We know only what the other person has revealed.

As the students look up each verse they will be doing two things at once: paraphrasing (write in your own words what you think it means) and making a chain reference as they mark their Bibles (have them make a topical reference guide in the front of their Bible so they can refer to the passages later on).

Make sure they understand how to mark their Bible. If you begin to mark your Bible with them, it will be easier for them to follow you. Put the name of the study and the first text of the study in the front of their Bible (for example, "1—The Scriptures a. 2 Peter 1:20, 21") then go to 2 Peter 1:20, 21, read the verse, and write in your study guide a short paraphrase of that verse in simple everyday language. Have the students do the same. Have them highlight the verse in their Bibles (they can use colored pencils and have each study color-coded or just employ a pen and a ruler—whatever they choose to do), and at the end of the verse or in the margin next to it write the next verse in the study (1 b. 2 Timothy 3:16). Continue the process of looking up the passages, paraphrasing them in their own words, then chain-referencing the verses. After a few times it will go faster and easier.

We Believe

The Trinity

"There is one God: Father, Son, and Holy Spirit, a unity of co-eternal Persons. God is immortal, all-powerful, all-knowing, above all, and ever present. He is infinite and beyond human comprehension, yet known through His self-revelation. He is forever worthy of worship, adoration, and service by the whole creation."[3]

Trinity

a. Deuteronomy 6:4
b. Matthew 28:19, 20
c. 2 Corinthians 13:14

The Father

"God the Eternal Father is the Creator, Source, Sustainer, and Sovereign of all creation. He is just and holy, merciful and gracious, slow to anger, and abounding in steadfast love and faithfulness. The qualities and powers exhibited in the Son and the Holy Spirit are also revelations of the Father."[4]

    a. Genesis 1:1

    b. John 3:16

    c. John 14:8-11

The Son

"God the Eternal Son became incarnate in Jesus Christ. Through Him all things were created, the character of God is revealed, the salvation of humanity is accomplished, and the world will is judged. Forever truly God, He became also truly man, Jesus the Christ. He was conceived of the Holy Spirit and born of the virgin Mary. He lived and experienced temptation as a human being, but perfectly exemplified the righteousness and love of God. By His miracles He manifested God's power and was attested as God's promised Messiah. He suffered and died voluntarily on the cross for our sins and in our place, was raised from the dead, and ascended to minister in the heavenly sanctuary in our behalf. He will come again in glory for the final deliverance of His people and the restoration of all things."[5]

    a. John 1:1-3, 14

    b. Luke 1:35

    c. Colossians 1:13-20

    d. John 10:30

The Holy Spirit

"God the eternal Spirit was active with the Father and the Son in Creation, incarnation, and redemption. He inspired the writers of Scripture. He filled Christ's life with power. He draws and convicts human beings; and those who respond He renews and transforms into the image of God. Sent by the Father and the Son to be always with His children, He extends spiritual gifts to the church, empowers it to bear witness to Christ, and in harmony with the Scriptures leads it into all truth."[6]

    a. Genesis 1:1, 2

    b. John 14:16-18, 26

    c. Acts 1:8

    d. Ephesians 4:11, 12

What do you believe about the Trinity—who God is—and what do you think is the best way to describe His many sides?

Way to Pray

As you pray this week, talk openly and honestly about what you think is true about God. Ask Him to reveal Himself to you in as many ways as possible. Prayerfully read through the Bible and discover what He might be trying to say about Himself.

More Than Words

Interview a teacher this week with the following questions:

When did you come to an understanding of the Trinity (God's threefold existence)?

How would you teach this to a fourth grader?

What do you know for sure about the Trinity, and what do you still have questions about?

In the Mirror

Write your thoughts on this mystery of God's existence. Share your own thoughts and questions as well with your partner.

Continue to remind the students throughout the week with a note, e-mail, or phone call to get them into the habit of responding to the application activities, especially the interviews. You might want to say, "I know life gets pretty busy, and I'm easily distracted. What do you think about setting a few minutes aside on Thursday night to e-mail or call and remind each other about following through? Do you think that would work?" The goal is to move the discipleship part of their life up on the list of priorities. That is a daily fight and often a slow-going process, but how else will it happen? There is no magic formula—only to keep plugging away.

Lesson 3
The Great Controversy

Before you begin discussing the next lesson, ask, "What was most helpful about your interview? What insights had you already thought of before? Did you come up with anything new? How did it help you understand the topic better?" Such questions should get them talking. Affirm them for sharing: "I really appreciate what you said. I'm glad you chose that person to interview." When teens respond, also affirm them. It doesn't always happen easily, but will occur more often in the future if you can get them to share, and then affirm what they said. At this stage they are extremely sensitive about what people think of them, and they need to know that we admire and appreciate their input.

Objective: Students will observe the nature of evil and the core issues of how people can better understand the character of God, such as the traits of freedom, will, love, and war.

The **Open Question** seeks to get at the heart of human behavior and perceptions. After they share what they think and why, have the students come up with examples of both of the positions. Here is an example: Racists who commit hate crimes have a belief that determines their behavior. Racists don't randomly do violence and look around at who they hurt and say, "I really hate those people." The violence comes from their beliefs. An example of someone whose actions determine their beliefs might be a person who thinks that drinking and driving is not wrong because they do it all the time and nobody gets hurt—at least not yet.

This study is about how Satan seeks to change our perception of God. The great controversy swirls around God's reputation and whether we can and will trust Him and His Word.

Open Questions

Either/Or

"My beliefs determine my actions" or "My actions determine my beliefs." (Explain) Can you think of examples of both mind-sets in the people you see today?

The **Opening Story** demonstrates how people perceive God by using as an illustration the story of a neighbor man whose character and personality revealed itself at a dinner table. The point of the story is that our perceptions are powerful. What we think of others will affect how we relate to them.

Opening Story

"Art Linkletter saw a small boy scrawling wildly on a sheet of paper. 'What are you drawing?' Linkletter asked.

"'I'm drawing a picture of God.'

"'You can't do that, because nobody knows what God looks like.'

"'They will when I'm finished,' the boy confidently replied."[7]

A. W. Tozer once said that the most important thing about us is what we believe about God. Perceptions—the way we see things—are powerful. The perception I had of my next-door neighbor scared me to death. Mr. Rob was tall and bony with a bushy gray mustache and an Adam's apple the size of—well, an apple. Because he just looked weird, he made me nervous.

One night as we were eating at the dinner table Mr. Rob did something to alter my view of him entirely. I watched him nervously because I never knew when he would attack. During the middle of the meal his expression changed from scary to downright silly. I giggled at the sight. His face returned to its normal scary pose for a moment, then he repeated his silly look when no one else was watching. By now my eyes were riveted on him as I took another bite.

Like the final explosion of fireworks on the Fourth of July Mr. Rob rapidly contorted his face, repeating in a sensational show of tremendous talent all the expressions he had made during dinner. The food in my mouth spewed out like a volcano as I laughed uncontrollably. I laughed so hard that my dinner made its way through my nose, ears, and I think through my eyelids. My mother and father stared in horror at me as Mr. Rob's face effortlessly resumed its gaze back at his plate of food. While I was scolded for my bad manners, I changed my mind about my skinny neighbor. He wasn't a freak—he was a riot. Mr. Rob became an endearing part of my family, and during the years following I saw what the rest of my family had already observed—a brilliant, witty, caring human whose passion in life was to create a moment of artistic surprise.

Perceptions. The fight between Christ and Satan is about perceptions and beliefs. Lucifer—tainted by pride and self-exaltation—saw God as a tyrant. As a result, he deceived the angels and now seeks to convince the world to believe a lie about God's character. The bottom line? The target of Satan's fiery darts is our mind—what we think of

God and what we believe God thinks of us. If Satan can reshape our perspective—our viewpoint—only a little, it is enough to taint, even destroy, our relationship with our Father in heaven. Notice the battle in the life of Jesus.

> This story is a little strange because Jesus does a good thing, yet the leaders (who have their minds made up about Jesus already) attribute His act of grace to the devil. Ask the students, "How is this like what happened in Eden with Adam, Eve, and the snake?"

Life of Christ

Luke 11:14-20

"Jesus was driving out a demon that was mute. When the demon left, the man who had been mute spoke, and the crowd was amazed. But some of them said, 'By Beelzebub, the prince of demons, he is driving out demons.' Others tested him by asking for a sign from heaven. Jesus knew their thoughts and said to them: 'Any kingdom divided against itself will be ruined, and a house divided against itself will fall. If Satan is divided against himself, how can his kingdom stand? I say this because you claim that I drive out demons by Beelzebub. Now if I drive out demons by Beelzebub, by whom do your followers drive them out? So then, they will be your judges. But if I drive out demons by the finger of God, then the kingdom of God has come to you.' "

> Have the students read the belief statement and share any questions or comment they have with their partners. Also, as they paraphrase the passages below and chain-reference them in their Bibles, have them share with their partners what they think the Bible is trying to say.
>
> This doctrine covers the whole time span from the beginning—even before the beginning—to the end. The reason many people do not surrender their lives to God is that they can't imagine how they would love and serve a God who allows innocent people to suffer. Satan has been most effective in his deception. Ask the students if they can think of anyone they know who believes that God is responsible for allowing the wickedness of the world to continue. How would they respond to that?

We Believe

The Great Controversy

"All humanity is now involved in a great controversy between Christ and Satan regarding the character of God, His law, and His sovereignty over the universe. This conflict originated in heaven when a created being, endowed with the freedom of choice, in self-exaltation became Satan, God's adversary, and led into rebellion a portion of the angels. He introduced the spirit of rebellion into this world when he led Adam and Eve into sin. This human sin resulted in the distortion of the image of God in humanity, the disordering of the created world, and its eventual devastation at the time of the worldwide flood. Observed by the whole creation, this world became the arena of the universal conflict, out of which the God of love will ultimately be vindicated. To assist His people in this controversy, Christ sends the Holy Spirit and the loyal angels to guide, protect, and sustain them in the way of salvation."[8]

a. Revelation 12:4-9
b. Isaiah 14:12-14
c. Ezekiel 28:12-18
d. Genesis 3
e. Genesis 6-8
f. 2 Peter 3:6
g. 1 Corinthians 4:9

Which verse speaks to you the most about this topic? Why?

What do you believe about the war between Christ and Satan? In a few sentences, describe how you would teach this to a third grader.

Way to Pray

Take a few moments and write down all the characteristics you can think of about God. In your prayer life this week talk to Him about the character traits you love and are grateful for, and also those qualities you don't quite understand.

More Than Words

Interview a college student this week and ask them the following questions:

How has your view of God changed in the past 10 years?

When in your life have you been most aware that the battle between good and evil involves you personally? Describe that time or the events surrounding it.

What advice would you give a teenager who is seeking to know who God "really" is in a world that misunderstands or misrepresents Him?

In the Mirror

Think about the war between Christ and Satan. What do you believe it was like back when it started? How do you think it will end?

Lesson 4
The Experience
of Salvation

Remember to have the students share the insights they gained from their interviews.

The fall of humanity leaves us all in need of a Savior. This lesson is about the experience of trusting in the grace of Christ and receiving His forgiveness and then embracing a new relationship with Him.

Objective: Students will enter the lives of those who were lost, found, and restored in order to experience the power of God's saving grace in their own lives.

The **Open Question** has no right or wrong answer. Let the student share why they put the stories in their particular order. Through it you see what they value about the salvation experience.

Open Questions

Rank the stories in order of their powerful message of salvation to the lost— 1 being the most powerful and 5 being the least powerful to you:

___ The story of the woman caught in adultery and saved from stoning

___ The story of Zacchaeus and his conversion and renewed lifestyle

___ The leper who came to Christ for healing

___ The story of the thief on the cross who received eternal life through faith

___ The woman who touched the hem of Jesus' garment and was healed of her sickness

Why did you rank them in this order?

> The **Opening Story** is about the experience of being lost and found. Many young people grow up in the Adventist Church and know the right things to say and believe, but they have a difficult time with the experience of being lost. Do you really know what it is like to be lost? In this lesson they will become deeply aware of our lostness and be overwhelmed by God's amazing grace, which finds us.

Opening Story

As I looked out the window of the bus everything was a blur. No, my eyes were not filled with tears and I was not taking hallucinogens. Nor was I suffering from depression and confusion. It was a time when the "wet look" was in, and I always managed to sit in a seat on the bus that had the view of the window distorted by gooey, slimy hair gel (I hope it was hair gel). My two-hour bus ride every day always made me sleepy, but I fought the sleep for fear my head would lean against the window smeared with the yuck. On this particular day, though, I fell fast asleep. Fortunately, my head rolled backward, protecting my hair.

I awoke to the voice of the bus driver announcing, "Last stop!" As I leaped from my seat I felt a cold chill creep over my heart when I saw that the bus was empty, save for the driver and me. "You gotta get off here, pal," the man said. I tried to find a clear piece of window to get my bearings, but couldn't recognize a thing.

"Where are we?"

The bus driver looked at me in disbelief. "You missed your stop, didn't you?" I got off the bus into unknown territory and wanted to cry. It was 5:00 p.m., and my parents would be stuck in traffic and wouldn't be home for a while. I was stranded. Lost. Alone.

Then the sound of a honking car jerked me from my misery as a friend from school pulled up to the bus stop. Christina leaned out the window, shouting, louder than she needed to, "Did you forget to get off at your stop?" It was more of a statement than a question (she always seemed to enjoy humiliating me in public). Glad to see Christina and her mom, however, I didn't care how loud she shouted. She and I took the same bus route, so when she got off and I didn't, she suspected I had been asleep or not paying attention. "When I didn't see you get off the bus," she explained, "we decided to come after you. Finally we caught up with you."

"Actually I thought I'd do a little shopping down here," I felt tempted to tell her. Instead I jumped into her car and confessed, "I fell asleep and woke up way too late." They both looked at my hair, knowing how dangerous sleeping on buses could be. "I can't tell you how glad I am to see you." I rode the rest of the way home with my heart in my throat and a hint of a smile on my face—it was good to be "not lost."

Being lost and being found are two tremendously different experiences, and what happens in between is an incredible journey. The parable of the prodigal son is, I believe, *the* story of the experience of salvation. As you read it, underline or highlight the parts that you think are key words or phrases because they say something about how we are saved and from what are we saved.

> You can focus on many phrases in this passage. Have the students do the activities (underline or highlight the key phrases), and then have them share why those aspects are important to them.

Life of Christ

Luke 15:10-24

"'In the same way, I tell you, there is rejoicing in the presence of the angels of God over one sinner who repents.' Jesus continued: 'There was a man who had two sons. The younger one said to his father, "Father, give me my share of the estate." So he divided his property between them. Not long after that, the younger son got together all he had, set off for a distant country and there squandered his wealth in wild living. After he had spent everything, there was a severe famine in that whole country, and he began to be in need. So he went and hired himself out to a citizen of that country, who sent him to his fields to feed pigs. He longed to fill his stomach with the pods that the pigs were eating, but no one gave him anything. When he came to his senses, he said, "How many of my father's hired men have food to spare, and here I am starving to death! I will set out and go back to my father and say to him: Father, I have sinned against heaven and against you. I am no longer worthy to be called your son; make me like one of your hired men." So he got up and went to his father. But while he was still a long way off, his father saw him and was filled with compassion for him; he ran to his son, threw his arms around him and kissed him. The son said to him, "Father, I have sinned against heaven and against you. I am no longer worthy to be called your son." But the father said to his servants, "Quick! Bring the best robe and put it on him. Put a ring on his finger and sandals on his feet. Bring the fattened calf and kill it. Let's have a feast and celebrate. For this son of mine was dead and is alive again; he was lost and is found." So they began to celebrate.'"

> Have the students read the belief statement and share any questions or comments they have with their partners.
>
> As they paraphrase the passages below and chain-reference them in their Bibles, have them share with their partners what you think God is trying to say to them.
>
> Many denominations believe in God's grace and saving power. One of the reasons the Protestant movement started was a belief that we are saved by God's grace and that we receive it by faith. A topic this big can't be summarized completely, but like a good portrait or a well-made movie, you can focus on something different each time you look at it. As you study this teaching, the most important thing you can do as a leader is kneel down with the students and pray a prayer of belief, acceptance, and thankfulness for the free gift of grace and God's forgiveness.

We Believe

The Experience of Salvation

"In infinite love and mercy God made Christ, who knew no sin, to be sin for us, so that in Him we might be made the righteousness of God. Led by the Holy Spirit we sense our need, acknowledge our sinfulness, repent of our transgressions, and exercise faith in Jesus as Lord and Christ, as Substitute and Example. This faith, which receives salvation, comes through the divine power of the Word and is the gift of God's grace. Through Christ we are justified, adopted as God's sons and daughters, and delivered from the lordship of sin. Through the Spirit we are born again and sanctified; the Spirit renews our minds, writes God's law of love in our hearts, and we are given the power to live a holy life. Abiding in Him we become partakers of the divine nature and have the assurance of salvation now and in the judgment." [9]

a. John 3:16

b. Romans 3:21

c. 2 Corinthians 5:17-21

d. Galatians 4:4-7

e. Titus 3:3-7

f. Romans 8:14-17

g. Romans 10:17

h. Galatians 3:2

i. Romans 8:1-4

j. Romans 12:2

Which three verses especially speak to you about the experience of salvation? Why?

How would you respond to someone asking you, "So, how can I know that I am going to go to heaven?"

Way to Pray

As you have looked at what it means to experience salvation, offer with your partner a prayer that recognizes that you are lost, that you believe in the free gift of grace, and that you accept the assurance of salvation with joy and confidence. Continue to pray throughout the week a prayer of thanksgiving for the work God has done for you on Calvary.

More Than Words

After Jesus had healed the man possessed by demons He told him, "Go home to your family and tell them how much the Lord has done for you, and how he has had mercy on you" (Mark 5:19).

Write a letter to someone who has had a big influence on your life. Tell them about your decision to receive Christ into your life and thank them for their support, then mail it to them or even deliver it personally. (Share in a few words how writing the letter affected you.)

Interview someone who you believe has made a heartfelt decision to follow Christ, using the following questions:

When did you first admit your need of a Savior and invite Christ into your heart? What were the circumstances and how did it happen?

Have you ever doubted the fact that you were saved? If so, how do you respond to such doubts?

What Bible passage best describes the salvation experience to you?

In the Mirror

As you think about your decision to follow Christ, what excites you and what makes you a little nervous? How do you think you should respond to such feelings?

Lesson 5
Baptism

Ask the students: "How did it feel to write that letter to the person who had been influential to you?" Have them share what they said and why they thought the experience was meaningful.

Objective: Students understand the nature, purpose, and awesome privilege of baptism.

Open Questions

When do you think a person is ready for baptism? Why?

What is the most memorable baptism you have ever witnessed? Why?

The **Opening Story** emphasizes our choice to claim God as Father. The great controversy reveals to us that God's way is not to force His will upon us, but to compel us to receive Him as our adopted Father because of His love. While God cheers at our baptism, He is cheering because He finally gets to claim us as His fully adopted children.

Opening Story

A parable: A teenage girl (we'll call her Susan) once became so filled with anger against her parents she decided to run away from home. She scribbled her hatred toward them on a note she left on the breakfast table. "This is my certificate of divorce," she said. "You are no longer my parents. I am no longer your daughter. I'm gone. This divorce is final." And she left just before dawn.

Now, normally when young people run away they go around the block, get hungry, forget their anger, and return home. Not Susan. She was long gone by the time her parents awoke and found the note. The girl hitchhiked her way across the state and into another part of the country. Finally she felt free. Meanwhile, her parents searched frantically for her. The police, the sheriff's office, and the FBI all were looking for Susan, but could not find her anywhere. For three and a half years the parents continued the search, hoping they would find their daughter.

One morning the phone rang and a deep voice on the line said, "We think we have found your daughter. She is alive but part of a prostitution and drug ring, and since she is 17 now, we can't force her to return home to you. We can ask her, and if she responds positively, we will get her out of there and bring her to you. Would you like to send her a message?"

"Yes, tell her we love her and for her to please come home," the mother replied.

The authorities approached the young woman, who was too young to be living on the streets and in seedy hotel rooms. When the message from her parents reached her ears, the empty life she now lived could not match her memories of the safety and comfort she had once known. She returned with the agents to her home.

Needless to say, her mother and father welcomed her with joy. Her room was unchanged. The pictures remained on the walls. For several weeks she tried to settle into the home of her childhood, but something was wrong. The relationship was awkward. Although her mom and dad never once mentioned the way she had left, she remembered clearly the words she wrote and the agony she had put her parents through.

One morning she came downstairs and placed a piece of paper on the table before her parents. On the top of the page were the words "Certificate of Adoption." She drew up an agreement for adoption with a place for her and her parents to sign. Her signature was already on the bottom of the page. Confused, her father looked at her. "Susan," he said cautiously, "I can't sign this. You are my daughter. We have always been your parents. We didn't sign your divorce papers, and we won't sign this. You belong to us, as you have always."

As Susan put her arms around her mom, tears welled up in her eyes. "I know how you feel about me. This is not for your benefit, but for mine. I chose to leave, and this is my way of choosing you back. I need to say this. Please, please do this for me and let me choose you formally." Her parents understood, and both signed the agreement. A smile crept across Susan's face as she signed under the line entitled "Daughter."

From God's point of view you have always been His child. Because of our fallen condition, we must die to our old self and be "born again." The word for it is baptism, a public and formal statement of your decision to be in His family—to be His child. Baptism is like Susan's declaration of adoption. But believe me, when it happens, all heaven erupts with shouts of praise as we formally call God "Father."

Notice how the people came in the days of Christ to signify their surrender to God and claim Him as their Father. As you have made this choice, consider the words spoken at the baptism of Jesus, and recognize that the Father declares them at yours.

Up until this time baptism had been for Gentiles, or nonbelievers, if they chose to become a part of Israel. When they did, they were considered fully Jewish, but they had to be baptized—and sometimes circumcised. The Jews became convinced that if they were born Jewish, they were automatically part of the family of God. But the truth is that none of us are children of God fully until we choose to be. Surely God looks at everyone as His child, but it is legal when we make it so. That is baptism. The fact that the Jews came to the river indicated that something big had taken place in their hearts and that the John the Baptist's message was getting through.

Notice the words that come from heaven at the baptism of Jesus. Ask the student: "Does God say that at every baptism?"

Life of Christ

Mark 1:2-11

"It is written in Isaiah the prophet: 'I will send my messenger ahead of you, who will prepare your way'—'a voice of one calling in the desert, "Prepare the way for the Lord, make straight paths for him."'" And so John came, baptizing in the desert region and preaching a baptism of repentance for the forgiveness of sins. The whole Judean countryside and all the people of Jerusalem went out to him. Confessing their sins, they were baptized by him in the Jordan River. John wore clothing made of camel's hair, with a leather belt around his waist, and he ate locusts and wild honey. And this was his message: 'After me will come one more powerful than I, the thongs of whose sandals I am not worthy to stoop down and untie. I baptize you with water, but he will baptize you with the Holy Spirit.' At that time Jesus came from Nazareth in Galilee and was baptized by John in the Jordan. As Jesus was coming up out of the water, he saw heaven being torn open and the Spirit descending on him like a dove. And a voice came from heaven: 'You are my Son, whom I love; with you I am well pleased.'"

Have the students read the belief statement and share any questions or comments they have with their partners. As they paraphrase the passages below and chain-reference them in their Bibles, they should share with their partners what they think God is trying to say to them.

After they study this section, have the students write out what they are trying to say to God by their baptism. This, in a personal way, can be a baptismal vow. Have them share their vows with each other.

We Believe

Baptism

"By baptism we confess our faith in the death and resurrection of Jesus Christ, and testify of our death to sin and of our purpose to walk in newness of life. Thus we acknowledge Christ as Lord and Saviour, become His people, and are received as members by His church. Baptism is a symbol of our union with Christ, the forgiveness of our sins, and our reception of the Holy Spirit. It is by immersion in water and is contingent on an affirmation of faith in Jesus and evidence of repentance of sin. It follows instruction in the Holy Scriptures and acceptance of their teachings." [10]

    a. Romans 6:1-6

    b. Acts 2:38

    c. Acts 16:30-33

    d. Acts 22:16

    e. Colossians 2:12, 13

    f. Matthew 28:19, 20

    g. 1 Corinthians 12:13

As you study the passages that deal with baptism, which one speaks to you the most about your decision to be baptized? Why?

Way to Pray

As you pray this week, think about the words of Paul, who said, "I have been crucified with Christ and I no longer live, but Christ lives in me. The life I live in the body, I live by faith in the Son of God, who loved me and gave himself for me" (Galatians 2:20).

More Than Words

Make the plans for your baptism, selecting the date, place, pastor, songs, text, testimonies, etc. Then, as you prepare for it, interview an older friend in the church about baptism and ask them the following questions:

What was the most memorable part of your baptism?

What is the significance of baptism as you see it?

If you could again prepare for baptism and plan for the event, what would you do differently?

In the Mirror

Think about your own decision to follow Christ in baptism. What events, people, and experiences have brought you to this decision?

Lesson 6
Creation

As you meet together for this lesson, have the students share some of the insights that came to them from their interviews.

The study of Creation can go in a variety of different directions: thoughtful reflection on nature and the beauty in it; the relationship we have with God as His crowning work of Creation; or the issues the world of philosophy and science struggle with about creation and evolution. Whatever road the students' discussion leads them to, find a way for them to pray together a prayer of praise and thanksgiving for what God has created.

Objective: Students will discuss the significance of Christ as the Creator and embrace His re-creative work in their lives.

The **Open Question** sets up the possibility that we can be certain while being wrong. It happens all the time in the everyday experiences of life, especially in marriage.

Open Questions

Share a time in your life when you thought you were absolutely right and turned out to be dead wrong. What was it like?

The **Opening Story** demonstrates how people can have poor logic and mindless convictions and yet think they are absolutely correct.

Opening Story

"An 8-year-old waving around a $100 bill? He says he earned it? Yeah. Right! He stole the $100 bill, because 8-year-olds don't earn money."

"A corn farmer running for mayor? Only educated people are smart enough for politics. There's no way I'd vote for him, because farmers don't have to make big decisions."

"If you should happen to contract a disease, fever, or inflammation, the best remedy is to either apply leeches or simply poke a hole in the infected area or the region of the pain and let the blood out. Since the ailment travels through the bloodstream, just get rid of the bad blood."

What do you see in these statements? They are ridiculous, full of prejudice, ignorance, and illogic. Although wrongheaded, they are real and stubbornly defended.

Once I asked my 4-year-old son, "Do you want to golf with me and Uncle Mike this weekend?"

He responded without missing a beat, "Dad, I can't because I don't even have a fishing pole."

At first I scratched my head, then it dawned on me that while on vacation we had stayed at a hotel in which the artwork in the lobby had golf pictures next to fishing pictures. Somehow he just connected the two together. You can't really have one without the other, can you? The point is this: Many popular ideas get born out of bad logic or some wild notion that popped into someone's thoughts.

In 1990 the 8-year-old mentioned above won a poetry contest entitled "My Shoes Are Too Tight," in which the grand prize was a $100 bill. The Midwest farmer became mayor, winning by a landslide. Why? He was brilliant, and almost everyone in the town was familiar with his innovative spirit and decision-making skills. He had a degree in biology, but even if he didn't, the fact remains that I have never met a farmer who wasn't sharp as a razor. At one time bloodletting seemed to be a logical remedy for disease. If someone is sick now, would we drain off their blood? .

How could people think in such ways? As in the story of the blind man healed by Christ, the critics miss the truth because they already believe something else. See if you can see in the following story some patterns of thinking that people today still have. At the end of the story notice the last two sentences and discuss them with your partner.

The aspect to focus on in the **Life of Christ** section is the mindless, unbelievably illogical response to Christ's healing: "Some of the Pharisees said, 'This man is not from God, for he does not keep the Sabbath.' But others asked, 'How can a sinner do such miraculous signs?' So they were divided." Divided? Deluded is more like it. How is it that people can be so blind? Talk about this question. What makes people so wrongheaded and stubborn about their ideas? What are they afraid of?

Life of Christ

John 9:1-16

"As he went along, he saw a man blind from birth. His disciples asked him, 'Rabbi, who sinned, this man or his parents, that he was born blind?' 'Neither this man nor his parents sinned,' said Jesus, 'but this happened so that the work of God might be displayed in his life. As long as it is day, we must do the work of him who sent me. Night is coming, when no one can work. While I am in the world, I am the light of the world.' Having said this, he spit on the ground, made some mud with the saliva, and put it on the man's eyes. 'Go,' he told him, 'wash in the Pool of Siloam' (this word means Sent). So the man went and washed, and came home seeing. His neighbors and those who had formerly seen him begging asked, 'Isn't this the same man who used to sit and beg?' Some claimed that he was. Others said, 'No, he only looks like him.' But he himself insisted, 'I am the man.' 'How then were your eyes opened?' they demanded. He replied, 'The man they call Jesus made some mud and put it on my eyes. He told me to go to Siloam and wash. So I went and washed, and then I could see.' 'Where is this man?' they asked him. 'I don't know,' he said. They brought to the Pharisees the man who had been blind. Now the day on which Jesus had made the mud and opened the man's eyes was a Sabbath. Therefore the Pharisees also asked him how he had received his sight. 'He put mud on my eyes,' the man replied, 'and I washed, and now I see.' Some of the Pharisees said, 'This man is not from God, for he does not keep the Sabbath.' But others asked, 'How can a sinner do such miraculous signs?' So they were divided."

Have the students read the belief statement and share any questions or comments they have with their partners.

As they paraphrase the passages below and chain-reference them in their Bibles, have the students share with their partners what they think God is trying to say to them.

Remind the students that as they chain-reference the Creation stories in Genesis 1 and 2, they might want to highlight or underline the key phrases instead of the entire first two chapters of Genesis. It is much easier to see the outline of the Creation week if they just highlight the parts that describe either what was created or the day it was created on.

Until 100 years ago the Western world had only one theory of how the earth began. As the students study this lesson, have them notice the adoration and wonder that grows out of the possibility of being friends with the Creator of the universe.

We Believe

Creation

"God is Creator of all things, and has revealed in Scripture the authentic account of His creative activity. In six days the Lord made 'the heaven and the earth' and all living things upon the earth, and rested on the seventh day of that first week. Thus He established the Sabbath as a perpetual memorial of His completed creative work. The first man and woman were made in the image of God as the crowning work of Creation, given dominion over the world, and charged with responsibility to care for it. When the world was finished it was 'very good,' declaring the glory of God."[11]

- **a.** Genesis 1
- **b.** Genesis 2
- **c.** Exodus 20:8-11
- **d.** Psalm 19:1-6
- **e.** Psalm 33:6, 9
- **f.** Psalm 104
- **g.** Hebrews 11:3

Which verse speaks to you the most about this topic?

Write a statement that describes what you believe to be true about God's work of creation.

Way to Pray

In Job 38 to 40:6 God reminds Job and us who He is. God asks a series of questions about the created world, questions that only a Creator could answer. Breeze through them and look at Job's response in Job 40:4, 5. As you pray this week, pray to God as a close Friend and a mighty Creator.

More Than Words

Interview: Invite someone to share their thoughts on the following questions:

When have you been most awed by God's creative work? Describe what you experienced and why you think it was so powerful.

What story or passage from Scripture stands out as a compelling piece of evidence for God's creative power?

Why do you think people so widely accept evolution in today's world?

In the Mirror

What do you think are the most effective ways for you personally to stay in touch with God as a Creator?

Lesson 7
The Law of God

As the students begin this study, have them share some of the ideas and thoughts they gained from their interviews. Tell them to be sure to remember to write down the things people say as they interview them so that they can recall and share them with their partners.

Objective: Students will discover the primary principle of God's government (love) and determine how the rules of God's kingdom work.

The **Opening Story** targets the essence of God's dream for His children—that His law of love will be deeply embedded in our hearts.

Opening Story

During my first year in college, before I learned to cook, I learned to heat. The culinary skill of heating is by far the most important tool of the bachelor who gets hungry. Today people look down upon the archaic methods of boiling, baking, and "slowly simmering" anything. Heating by microwave is the only way to go. The food that presents the greatest challenge, though, is the frozen burrito.

I returned from my classes starving for something cheap, filling, and easy to prepare. My heart sank into my vacant stomach as I opened the door to my refrigerator. Seeing nothing that resembled a meal, I ventured into the freezer. There they were—frozen burritos. *Oh, great, frozen burritos!* I thought. *Now I have to slave over a hot microwave (at least I think it is hot in there) for at least two minutes before I can eat.* It seemed like a year before the three beeps announced the end of the wait. I grabbed the burritos, carefully left in their plastic package with the ends partially open (a technique popular among young bachelors during the eighties).

Unfortunately, the burrito was so hot that I had to drop it on a small, uncluttered landing space on the counter reserved for just such emergencies. Using a few utensils, a paper plate, and a ravenous appetite, I lunged into the burrito with my fork. The fork cut smoothly into the tortilla, then stopped cold about halfway through the burrito. "No!" It was still frozen. The heat had never penetrated deep enough to heat the inside. The choice? Heat it or eat it. But what does this have to do with God's law?

One time Jesus declared, "Unless your righteousness [rightdoing] surpasses that of the Pharisees and the teachers of the Law, you will not enter the kingdom of heaven." Such news would sap His listeners of their hope for eternal life. Why? All knew the unparalleled obedience of the Pharisees. To imagine anyone being even better was unimaginable. But Jesus makes it clear that the way the Pharisees obeyed the law was a lot like heating the frozen burrito: The heat has to go into the heart of the burrito for it to be good. John referred to it this way: "This is love for God: to obey his commands. And his commands are not burdensome, for everyone born of God overcomes the world. This is the victory that has overcome the world, even our faith" (1 John 5:3, 4). The love and power of God's revealed will in His law must be a matter of the heart—and not just the skin—for it to be meaningful.

> The phrases to focus on in this passage come from the statement "I have not come to abolish them but to fulfill them" and then later as Christ describes what that looks like in everyday life: "For I tell you that unless your righteousness surpasses that of the Pharisees and the teachers of the law . . ." Ask the students: "How are the Pharisees like microwaveable burritos? Can you think of another illustration?"

Life of Christ

Matthew 5:17-20

"Do not think that I have come to abolish the Law or the Prophets; I have not come to abolish them but to fulfill them. I tell you the truth, until heaven and earth disappear, not the smallest letter, not the least stroke of a pen, will by any means disappear from the Law until everything is accomplished. Anyone who breaks one of the least of these commandments and teaches others to do the same will be called least in the kingdom of heaven, but whoever practices and teaches these commands will be called great in the kingdom of heaven. For I tell you that unless your righteousness surpasses that of the Pharisees and the teachers of the law, you will certainly not enter the kingdom of heaven."

> Have the students read the belief statement and share any questions or comments they have with their partner. As they paraphrase the passages below and chain-reference them in their Bibles, they should share with their partners what they think God is trying to say to them.
>
> If you want to flip over to the juniors' lesson on the law and read what Ted Turner says about the Ten Commandments, it might help as you introduce this doctrine. Ask the students: "What is the purpose of the Law? How do we live by it and not be legalists?" In these lessons, every doctrine has a direct basis in one idea: God's Word communicates His will for us. The Sabbath, Creation, and salvation all hang on the written Word of God. People might say, "Those Adventists are all about the law and not about grace." Ask the students: "Do you really want to live in a world, community, or church that does not seek to keep God's law of love? Can you imagine what that would be like?"

We Believe

The Law of God

"The great principles of God's law are embodied in the Ten Commandments and exemplified in the life of Christ. They express God's love, will, and purposes concerning human conduct and relationships and are binding upon all people in every age. These precepts are the basis of God's covenant with His people and the standard in God's judgment. Through the agency of the Holy Spirit they point out sin and awaken a sense of need for a Saviour. Salvation is all of grace and not of works, but its fruitage is obedience to the Commandments. This obedience develops Christian character and results in a sense of well-being. It is an evidence of our love for the Lord and our concern for our fellow men. The obedience of faith demonstrates the power of Christ to transform lives, and therefore strengthens Christian witness." [12]

  a. Exodus 20:1-17
  b. Psalm 40:7, 8
  c. Matthew 22:36-40
  d. Deuteronomy 28:1-14
  e. Matthew 5:17-20
  f. John 15:7-10
  g. 1 John 5:3
  h. Psalm 19:7-14

What verse speaks to you the most about this topic?

As a Christian, how do you explain the importance of the law and also the reality that we are saved by grace, not by our efforts?

Way to Pray

As you pray this week, consider areas of God's law that you struggle with obeying consistently. Talk specifically to God about those problems and invite Him to remind you about them and to strengthen you to be faithful.

More Than Words

Ask the following questions of a young adult you admire and respect:

How did you relate to rules as a teenager?

When did you personally come to understand the value of God's law in your own life?

How does a person get God's law written on their heart? What does that look like to you in everyday life?

In the Mirror

Think and write about the commandments you want written on your heart the most at this stage of your life.

Lesson 8
The Sabbath

Have the students share for a few moments some of the things they learned from the young adults they interviewed.

The Sabbath is a precious teaching and way of life for Adventists. We have concerns and questions about how to maintain and more fully understand how to be Sabbathkeepers, but the Sabbath is a treasure we hold dearly to as a church.

Objective: Students will explore the beauty and promise that exists in keeping Sabbath as a permanent reminder of God's claim on humanity.

The **Open Question** simply sets up the attitudes and feelings that Jesus went through when human beings obscured the goal of the Sabbath.

Open Questions

When have you been so frustrated that you were a little out of control? What happened?

This lesson takes a passionate approach to Sabbath, not to incite anger, but to inspire believers about what Christ will do to make it clear to us that our relationship to the Creator is the very essence of Sabbath.

Opening Story

The graffiti on the side of the church left me more than frustrated—I was downright mad. The local boys thought their artwork was more pleasing to the eye than our plain white paint on the masonry block walls of the church. I knew the kids who did it but could never catch them in the act. Then I remembered something in my younger days as an assistant boys dean. The head dean and I were painting the halls of the dorm and the paint wouldn't stick—it simply peeled off. "What is up with this paint?" we wondered aloud. The guy at the paint store gave us the answer: epoxy paint. The only thing that will stick to epoxy paint is epoxy paint. Amazing stuff, it is one part paint and one part glue. The stuff will not come off.

When I remembered my previous experience with the substance, the deacons and I painted the side of the church with a serious coat of epoxy paint and waited. After a week or so, I parked my car on the other side of the street and watched for the vandals to do their sinful work. They never came. So I went looking for them in the neighborhood. I found them all hanging out on someone's front yard looking bored and mischievous. Jumping out of the car, I yelled, "You guys got to come to the church and see what someone did to the walls!" Then I muttered a prayer for them to follow me on their bikes and skateboards back to the church. I waited there by myself, staring at the bright white walls. They snickered as they rode up. (Suckers.)

"Do you see this wall?" I announced proudly. "Doesn't it look great?" Their grins broadened as they looked at each other like a bunch of vultures perched over a dying animal. They must have thought that I had lost my mind or was a complete idiot. I had them.

"Yeah, man. That's a really nice paint job," they all chuckled.

"Thanks," I replied proudly. "I did it myself."

"Hope nobody tries to mess it up, man," the ringleader mentioned with a total lack of sincerity.

The others snickered. "Yeah, that would be a real tragedy, dude, someone coming and messin' it all up," another added.

I put on my most shocked look. "You really think someone might try that?" I said with a genuine note of concern.

They smirked. "I don't know. It is a rough neighborhood and all," the ringleader said.

At that moment I grabbed a can of spray paint I had waiting in the front seat of the car. "You mean like this?" After shaking the can, I began frantically spraying black enamel on my armored walls of epoxy-treated paint. They watched me in shock and amazement. I began my assault quietly, then exploded with a roar of power that Elijah would have been proud of. "I suppose someone could try to paint over these lovely walls . . . but then it wouldn't stick to the super-treated, God-inspired, Spirit-protected, sin-resistant, Satan-repellent walls of this great and God-fearing church!" My eyes were wild with frenzy.

They stared at me in fear. With a smile I said, "No paint will stick to these walls, boys. Go ahead and give it a try yourself." Then I handed the can of paint to them. No one took it. "Well, boys, gotta go back to work," I told them politely. "Maybe I'll see you around. Huh?" Then I walked into the side door of the church, punched my fist in the air, and said, "Yes!"

Jesus is noted to have burned with frustration a few times. In one particular instance it had to do with something very precious: His Sabbath.

Much more important than the walls of my church were to me, the Sabbath is Christ's connection to people. Shut down the connection—and He gets hot under the collar. Not out of selfishness, but from a heart that beats with a mighty love for His creation, and anything that gets in the way is liable to free His anger. Take a look at the bold way He makes clear the importance of real Sabbathkeeping.

> The passage to focus on in the **Life of Christ** section is "He looked around at them in anger and, deeply distressed at their stubborn hearts, said to the man, 'Stretch out your hand.' He stretched it out, and his hand was completely restored." Ask the students: "Why was Jesus so angry? How do you feel about a Savior that gets angry like this? What does this say about how important it is for us to have the right frame of mind for Sabbath?"

Life of Christ

Mark 3:1-5

"Another time he went into the synagogue, and a man with a shriveled hand was there. Some of them were looking for a reason to accuse Jesus, so they watched him closely to see if he would heal him on the Sabbath. Jesus said to the man with the shriveled hand, 'Stand up in front of everyone.' Then Jesus asked them, 'Which is lawful on the Sabbath: to do good or to do evil, to save life or to kill?' But they remained silent. He looked around at them in anger and, deeply distressed at their stubborn hearts, said to the man, 'Stretch out your hand.' He stretched it out, and his hand was completely restored."

> Have the students read the belief statement and share any questions or comments they have with their partners. As they paraphrase the passages below and chain-reference them in their Bibles, they should share with their partners what they think God is trying to say to them.

We Believe

The Sabbath

"The beneficent Creator, after the six days of Creation, rested on the seventh day and instituted the Sabbath for all people as a memorial of Creation. The fourth commandment of God's unchangeable law requires the observance of this seventh-day Sabbath as the day of rest, worship, and ministry in harmony with the teaching and practice of Jesus, the Lord of the Sabbath. The Sabbath is a day of delightful communion with God and one another. It is a symbol of our redemption in Christ, a sign of our sanctification, a token of our allegiance, and a foretaste of our eternal future in God's kingdom. The Sabbath is God's perpetual sign of His eternal covenant between Him and His people. Joyful observance of this holy time from evening to evening, sunset to sunset, is a celebration of God's creative and redemptive acts."[13]

    a. Genesis 2:1-3

    b. Exodus 20:8-11

    c. Deuteronomy 5:12-15

    d. Exodus 31:13-17

    e. Luke 4:16

    f. Ezekiel 20:12, 20

    g. Matthew 12:1-12

    h. Isaiah 58:13, 14

    i. Isaiah 56:5, 6

Which verse speaks to you the most about this topic?

What do you think God would want us to be doing, thinking, and experiencing on the Sabbath? Why?

Way to Pray

As you pray this week, begin by talking to God openly and honestly about your Sabbath experience. Whether it has been meaningful or a struggle, you should discuss with the Lord of the Sabbath the gift He has given you. Make the joy and beauty of the Sabbath hours something you pray about this week so that it might be a blessing to you and to God.

More Than Words

Look up the word "Sabbath" in an exhaustive concordance and focus on the passages in the four Gospels that describe what Jesus did on it. Begin planning with your partner, group, or family to do on the next Sabbath the kind of things Jesus did. You might have to reorganize your day a bit.

Interview someone who you think has a joyful walk with God on the Sabbath. Ask them:

In your own words, share what you think the Sabbath day is all about.

Describe the Sabbath day that has been the most memorable for you. What happened? What did you do? Why is this a good memory for you?

What passage or story from the Bible most demonstrates the importance of the Sabbath to you?

In the Mirror

Think about the attitudes and feelings you have about the Sabbath and write some of your thoughts down about what you hope for in your walk with God—especially on the Sabbath.

Lesson 9
The Life, Death, and Resurrection of Christ

Have the students reflect on the activities they participated in on Sabbath and share how they felt about the interviews they did. What did they learn?

Objective: Students will immerse themselves in stories that depict the significance of Christ's life, death, and resurrection, and determine how they will respond to the claims of Christ.

The **Opening Story** is a discussion about the horror of abandoned children. Christ felt abandoned on Calvary, and the experience was sheer hell. As a matter of fact, hell, the second death, is what happens when people choose to utterly reject Christ.

Opening Story

Abandonment. The only question more pressing than "Why?" is "How?" How can a mother and father leave a newborn baby in a dumpster?

"A few hours after giving birth in March in a Fairfax motel room, Abigail Caliboso left her baby, wrapped in a cotton towel, on the floor of a portable toilet at a construction site in Delaware. The 19-year-old nursing student from Woodbridge and the baby's father, Jose Ocampo, 18, of Chantilly, were too frightened to tell their families that they had had a child."[14]

How does this happen? The Washington *Post* article indicated abandonments are often acts of fear because those who do them are typically "good kids." They have good grades, good jobs, and are good athletes—just good people from good families who made a tragic mistake. In desperation they abandon their baby because the shame is too great. Why? How? Here is what some think:

"Some researchers believe that during childbirth a psychotic reaction can occur that is similar to what can happen in other severely stressful situations—for example, soldiers under fire—and that that reaction can compel a woman to try to rid herself of the newborn. Others contend that abandonment or neonaticide is the act of an emotionally immature, self-centered woman who may be distraught over the effect a baby will have on her life."[15]

Jesus on Calvary cried, "My God, My God, why have You forsaken Me?" Forsaken—the anguish of being abandoned. Was God, like the researchers say, experiencing "a psychotic reaction"? While it may be that those who abandon their children are not in their "right mind," the experience of having your Father abandon you to death on a cross was not a reaction, but God's planned action: "The reason my Father loves me is that I lay down my life—only to take it up again. No one takes it from me, but I lay it down of my own accord. I have authority to lay it down and authority to take it up again. This command I received from my Father" (John 10:17, 18).

Planned, premeditated, intentional abandonment. But God is no criminal here—He's a champion! He did it not out of self-protection or fear, but out of sacrifice and love for lost humanity. What Christ came to do He did with a clear mind.

> The phrase to focus on for the **Life of Christ** section is "My God, my God, why have you forsaken me?" The life of Christ may have been only a few years of earth's history, and Calvary only a matter of moments, but for what would we trade those moments?

Life of Christ

Matthew 27:45-51

"From the sixth hour until the ninth hour darkness came over all the land. About the ninth hour Jesus cried out in a loud voice, 'Eloi, Eloi, lama sabachthani?'—which means,

'My God, my God, why have you forsaken me?' When some of those standing there heard this, they said, 'He's calling Elijah.' Immediately one of them ran and got a sponge. He filled it with wine vinegar, put it on a stick, and offered it to Jesus to drink. The rest said, 'Now leave him alone. Let's see if Elijah comes to save him.' And when Jesus had cried out again in a loud voice, he gave up his spirit. At that moment the curtain of the temple was torn in two from top to bottom. The earth shook and the rocks split."

> Have the students read the belief statement and share any questions or comments they have with their partners. As they paraphrase the passages below and chain-reference them in their Bibles, they should share with their partners what they think God is trying to say to them.
>
> In *The Desire of Ages* Ellen White suggests that we spend a thoughtful hour each day on the life of Christ, especially its final moments. Ask the students: "What do you think would change about you personally if you did this?"

We Believe

The Life, Death, and Resurrection of Christ

"In Christ's life of perfect obedience to God's will, His suffering, death, and resurrection, God provided the only means of atonement for human sin, so that those who by faith accept this atonement may have eternal life, and the whole creation may better understand the infinite and holy love of the Creator. This perfect atonement vindicates the righteousness of God's law and the graciousness of His character; for it both condemns our sin and provides for our forgiveness. The death of Christ is substitutionary and expiatory, reconciling and transforming. The resurrection of Christ proclaims God's triumph over the forces of evil, and for those who accept the atonement assures their final victory over sin and death. It declares the Lordship of Jesus Christ, before whom every knee in heaven and on earth will bow." [16]

    a. John 3:16
    b. Isaiah 53
    c. 1 Peter 2:21, 22
    d. 1 John 2:2; 4:10
    e. Colossians 2:15
    f. Philippians 2:6-11

Which verse above speaks most to you personally about the meaning of the life of Christ?

In your own words, describe the significance of Jesus' life, death, and resurrection?

Way to Pray

Before you pray this week, browse through the four Gospels and scan through the stories. Imagine the stories as they unfold, then talk to God about what you see.

More Than Words

Interview someone who is familiar with the life of Jesus. Ask them:

If you had to choose three stories from the life of Christ to show someone what Jesus' life was about, which ones would you choose and why?

In the Mirror

Think about the final moments of Christ's life and present your thoughts, ideas, feelings, and wonderings in any way you like: pictures, phrases, words to a song, etc.

Lesson 10
The Lord's Supper

Have the students take a few moments to share a few insights they gained from their interviews (make sure they are writing these details down in their books).

God intends the Lord's Supper to be a great celebration of God's grace and the hope-inspiring vision of the second coming of Christ.

Objective: Students will understand the importance of symbols that remind of and renew faith as well as discover the sacred joy that believers experience as they celebrate grace with others.

The **Open Question** seeks to get the students to share incidents when life surprised them.

Open Questions

When have you had your whole world turned upside down in a matter of seconds? What happened?

> The **Opening Story** will describe how life surprised the disciples on a number of occasions.

Opening Story

"Do you understand what I have done for you?" It is kind of hard to answer that question, isn't it? Especially if you are Peter or any one of the other disciples, because you have seen ordinary moments turn into eternal monuments in just a matter of seconds.

It was just your average bad day at the lake fishing—then *Bam!* Jesus turns it into the most net-ripping, phenomenal fish catch in the history of Galilee.

One minute you're listening to Jesus teach in the Temple when BAM!, you witness the scandal, the showdown, the finger writing in the dirt, the rocks dropping to the ground, and one by one the accusers vanish and grace wins.

"We were just going for a hike up the mountain," one of the disciples remembers, "then all of a sudden the sky splits open, we're blinded by light, we see Moses and Elijah, and I heard God's voice! What is going on here?"

"He was just doing the Scripture reading in church," another disciple comments, "saying, 'Today this is fulfilled,' and the next thing I see is the whole church trying to toss Him over a cliff."

"One day we pulled over to the side of the road to respectfully let a funeral go by," still another disciple recounts. "I was watching Jesus. He took one look at that grieving mother's face, and all of a sudden He's in the middle of the road with His hand held up like a traffic cop, saying, 'Stop right here!' In just a few seconds the dead boy was talking! Man, I will never forget that moment when Jesus put the boy that had died right in front of the mom like a Mother's Day present just waiting to be opened. I will never, ever forget that day."

It can happen in a moment. If you've been with Jesus, you know that anything can happen in the flicker of a second. The bread and the juice, the water and the washing of the feet. In a moment the disciples saw what history had been waiting for: the sacrifice and the servant. The One who would come and redeem by the shedding of blood and restore all by making everything new with water. And Jesus wanted to know if they were paying attention. He used the Communion service to declare, "This is our flag. When you see it, remember what it stands for." As you look at the life of Christ, notice how important it is to Jesus that we "get it" and how precious this service is to the church when He is gone.

> The phrase to focus on is "Do you understand what I have done for you?" Jesus recognized that His disciples didn't really get it. But He knew they would eventually. The foot washing and the Last Supper became a monumental institution in Christianity for celebrating the gift of salvation on Calvary.

Life of Christ

John 13:1-12

"It was just before the Passover Feast. Jesus knew that the time had come for him to leave this world and go to the Father. Having loved his own who were in the world, he now showed them the full extent of his love. The evening meal was being served, and the devil had already prompted Judas Iscariot, son of Simon, to betray Jesus. Jesus knew that the Father had put all things under his power, and that he had come from God and was returning to God; so he got up from the meal, took off his outer clothing, and wrapped a towel around his waist. After that, he poured water into a basin and began to wash his disciples' feet, drying them with the towel that was wrapped around him. He came to Simon Peter, who said to him, 'Lord, are you going to wash my feet?' Jesus replied, 'You do not realize now what I am doing, but later you will understand.' 'No,' said Peter, 'you shall never wash my feet.' Jesus answered, 'Unless I wash you, you have no part with me.' 'Then, Lord,' Simon Peter replied, 'not just my feet but my hands and my head as well!' Jesus answered, 'A person who has had a bath needs only to wash his feet; his whole body is clean. And you are clean, though not every one of you.' For he knew who was going to betray him, and that was why he said not every one was clean. When he had finished washing their feet, he put on his clothes and returned to his place. 'Do you understand what I have done for you?' he asked them."

> Have the students read the belief statement and share any questions or comments they have with their partners. As they paraphrase the passages below and chain-reference them in their Bibles, they should share with their partners what they think God is trying to say to them.
> Ask them: "How would you teach a 4-year-old the significance of this celebration?"

We Believe

The Lord's Supper

"The Lord's Supper is a participation in the emblems of the body and blood of Jesus as an expression of faith in Him, our Lord and Saviour. In this experience of Communion Christ is present to meet and strengthen His people. As we partake, we joyfully proclaim the Lord's death until He comes again. Preparation for the Supper includes self-examination, repentance, and confession. The Master ordained the service of foot washing to signify renewed cleansing, to express a willingness to serve one another in Christlike humility, and to unite our hearts in love. The Communion service is open to all believing Christians." [17]

a. 1 Corinthians 10:16, 17; 11:23-30

b. Matthew 26:17-30

c. Revelation 3:20

d. John 6:48-63

e. John 13:1-17

Which verse speaks to you the most about this topic?

Way to Pray

Write a prayer to God this week that emphasizes what you want to remember as you take Communion. You can start the prayer like this: "Dear God, when I have Communion I want to remember . . ." Be specific, because the more specific our thoughts are, the more we remember.

More Than Words

Find out when the next Communion service is scheduled in your church and plan a week ahead of time (write it in your calendar or whatever you use to keep track of important events) to remind yourself of what you want to remember as you participate. Interview an elder, deacon, or deaconess in the church and ask them to respond to the following questions:

What Communion service was most memorable for you? Why?

Why do you think this service is so important to each individual in the church? Why is it vital to the church as an entire congregation?

What do you think about when you wash the other person's feet? How do you feel when someone is washing yours?

What's going on in your heart and mind when you eat the bread and drink the juice?

In the Mirror

Think about and write down what you have observed about the Communion service already and what you want to experience in the future.

Lesson 11
Spiritual Gifts

Before they start the lesson on spiritual gifts, have the students share the thoughts and memories of those they interviewed and the thoughtful insights they gained from listening to them.

Part of this lesson is studying about spiritual gifts, but a good portion of the study will consist of doing the "What's in the Box?" spiritual gifts inventory. Make sure the students have plenty of time to fill out the inventory and debrief each other about the results.

Objective: Students will seek to interact with God about their spiritual gifts and their identity and purpose as Christians as they learn to serve God by His Spirit.

Open Questions

On the continuum below, indicate what you think represents your church family in the area of active participation and responsibility:

1—Almost everyone (90-100 percent of the members) is doing the work of the church.

5—Only a few (10-20 percent of the members) are doing the entire work of the church.

1	2	3	4	5
Almost everyone				Only a few

Why do you think this is the case in your church? What would you like to see happen in your church when it comes to getting people involved?

The **Opening Story** contains a plan almost too simple, but it works. So does God's plan for bringing His message of the Bible to the world.

Opening Story

Nothing breeds competition like the game "Capture the Flag." Unfortunately, when I learned to play it I was at the age when the girls had already grown a bit faster than the boys. The girls on my block were stronger, faster, and meaner, and probably more vicious than kickboxers. Needless to say, they beat us every time.

This time would be different, though. Matt had a plan. At least that's why we huddled together in a tight circle of preteen camaraderie. His face was intense. "OK, guys, we have to win this time. I hate losing to those girls. I have a plan!"

The others chimed in, "Yeah, that's what we need. A plan!"

Two years younger than the rest of the boys, I eagerly watched as everyone became silent and attentive. "Here's what we are going to do," he began. Someone popped their head out of the huddle to see if the girls were inching their way closer to hear what our plan was. But they weren't.

"Everyone is going to stand around the field and pretend they are guarding a flag," Matt continued. All eyes focused on him as we waited for the rest of the plan. Matt just stared back at us as if he had just shared a national security secret.

William piped up in a high-pitched voice, "That's your plan? Stand around and pretend we're guarding a flag? You call that a plan?"

Matt was crushed. Then, regaining his composure, he said, "Yes, we have to pretend we know something."

"But we don't," Freddie said, admitting the obvious.

"That's right," Matt replied with a grin. "But while the girls are wondering what we are up to, Troy is going to sneak around the back of the park and get the flag!"

At first mutiny flared up. "Troy can't make it past the girls' guard," one of my brother's friends mentioned painfully.

"Yeah," everyone agreed.

Matt, like a true captain, settled his crew down and said, "The girls won't even notice Troy! They never notice Troy!" (I was a little offended by that.) But then the brilliance of his plan began to sink in like milk into a cookie.

"Yeah," they chanted in a whisper. "They'll be watching us, and when we're not at-

169

tacking, they'll be thinking about where our flag is instead of watching their own."

We broke from the huddle and concentrated on the plan. Meanwhile, scared to death, I unobtrusively made my way around the trees to the back of the girls' domain. Now behind enemy lines, I had never made it this close before. The flag was only yards away, and just as Matt said, no girls were guarding it. They were in fact huddling together to figure out which boy was guarding the boys' flag. When I looked for Matt, he gave me the nod. My heart felt like bursting through my 10-year-old chest as I leaped out from behind the trees and raced for the flag. The rest was a blur to me. I reached the flag, and still no girls noticed what I was doing. Clutching the white T-shirt (flag) from the top of a picnic table (the girls were so confident they didn't even need to hide it) I raced for the line of safety. At that point the boys darted far into the danger zone to distract the girls from seeing me, but for some reason I began to laugh out loud as I ran. It mixed a bit of scoffing with an element of celebration. Perhaps it was a little too soon to be laughing, but I couldn't help myself. Still, the girls figured out the plan a little too late to catch me. As I crossed the goal line, the boys were waiting for me and piled atop me with shouts of victory. We did a few "in your face" dances in front of the dumbstruck girls because we knew that it would probably be the only time we'd ever get away with the stunt—so we milked it for all it was worth. What a day. At least that's how I remembered it.

"That's your plan?"

"You call that a plan?"

Imagine the scene—a whole countrysideful of people coming to Jesus with diseases, questions, demons, and doubts and fears. As they spread out before Him like a sea of misery, Jesus reveals His plan to fix the whole mess. You want to hear it? Check it out. It doesn't sound like much of a plan, but give it a chance—let it sink in, and you may see Jesus not as a crazy dreamer, but as a wise general whose plan just may work.

> The passage to focus on is "He called his twelve disciples to him and gave them authority . . ." Authority for what? What did the disciples do? What was the result?

Life of Christ

Matthew 9:35–10:1

"Jesus went through all the towns and villages, teaching in their synagogues, preaching the good news of the kingdom and healing every disease and sickness. When he saw the crowds, he had compassion on them, because they were harassed and helpless, like sheep without a shepherd. Then he said to his disciples, 'The harvest is plentiful but the workers are few. Ask the Lord of the harvest, therefore, to send out workers into his harvest field.' He called his twelve disciples to him and gave them authority to drive out evil spirits and to heal every disease and sickness."

What's the plan?

> Have the students read the belief statement and share any questions or comments they have with their partners. As they paraphrase the passages below and chain-reference them in their Bibles, they should share with their partners what they think God is trying to say to them.

We Believe

Spiritual Gifts

"God bestows upon all members of His church in every age spiritual gifts which each member is to employ in loving ministry for the common good of the church and of humanity. Given by the agency of the Holy Spirit, who apportions to each member as He wills, the gifts provide all abilities and ministries needed by the church to fulfill its divinely ordained functions. According to the Scriptures, these gifts include such ministries as faith, healing, prophecy, proclamation, teaching, administration, reconciliation, compassion, and self-sacrificing service and charity for the help and encouragement of people. Some members are called of God and endowed by the Spirit for functions recognized by the church in pastoral, evangelistic, apostolic, and teaching ministries particularly needed to equip the members for service, to build up the church to spiritual maturity, and to foster unity of the faith and knowledge of God. When members employ these spiritual gifts as faithful stewards of God's varied grace, the church is protected from the destructive influence of false doctrine, grows with a growth that is from God, and is built up in faith and love." [18]

    a. Romans 12:4-8
    b. 1 Corinthians 12:9-11, 27, 28
    c. Ephesians 4:8, 11-16
    d. Acts 6:1-7
    e. 1 Timothy 3:1-13
    f. 1 Peter 4:10, 11

Which verse speaks to you the most about this topic?

Way to Pray

Warning! The way you pray from here on out is dangerous! If you do this, be fore-warned, it could change your life drastically.

As you take the spiritual gifts survey, begin to ask God to create opportunities for you to discover your spiritual gifts. Ask God to confirm what others say about you, what you feel God is asking you to do as a member of His church.

More Than Words

Take the Spiritual Gifts Survey at the back of this book. After you find out where your strengths seem to lie, then pick three people you trust to be honest with you and who know you pretty well (a teacher, pastor, parent, older friend, grandparent, church leader, etc.). Ask them to comment on the results of your survey and to answer the following questions:

Have you seen these qualities or gifts in me? How? When?

Are there other qualities you feel God has gifted me with that I need to consider as well?

How do you think I can best make a difference in the work of the church? Be specific.

You and your partner/group should share with each other the insights you have gained from the survey and the interviews and then commit yourselves to do some activities together to practice and experience work relating to your potential spiritual gift. It is the only way you can be sure this is what God is calling you to do.

Write a letter to your pastor or church board, or go in person to either, and share with them your results and experience and ask for a place to serve in the church.

In the Mirror

Think about and write out how you feel about being a player in God's work. What kind of impact do you want to have in the mission of the Seventh-day Adventist Church?

Lesson 12
The Church

Activity: Mix several flavors of juice together and take a sip. Have the students see if they can taste all the flavors at once. Then have them take another sip to find out if they can detect each particular juice. I have used this activity to describe the relationship between the gifts to the work of the church. While it is possible to detect individual flavors, ultimately the end product (fruit punch) is what you taste—the combined work of many to create something greater.

Objective: Students will deepen their sense of understanding of what church members are in light of the biblical descriptions of the church and church life.

Both answers can be true. Have the students share with their partners how they think both can be true.

Open Questions

Either/Or

The purpose of the church is to foster the spiritual growth of believers, or to serve the community in Christian love. From your perspective, which would you choose and why?

Does the church need modern agents of change or the faithful pioneers of old? Why did you answer the way you did?

We compare the classic analogy of the wild-geese V formation to the independence and competition of the seagull.

Opening Story

Think of the ways people have used to portray the church: As a body. A family. A hospital. A team. A flock of geese. A company of ants. A hive of bees. A chain. The list goes on with countless analogies that describe what the nature and purpose of the church is about. Here is yet another story that describes the church.

"There is a legend of a village in Southern Europe that boasted of a church called 'The House of Many Lamps.' When it was built in the sixteenth century, the architect provided for no light except for a receptacle at every seat for the placing of a lamp. Each Sunday night, as the people gathered, they would bring their lanterns and slip them into their bracket at their seat. When someone stayed away, the darkness became greater for the whole. It was the regular presence of each person that lit up the church." [19]

The problem with analogies is that they all break down at some point. They give some help, but all symbols are only partial and incomplete. Still, sometimes it is enough. If you were to describe the ideal church, what symbol, story, or analogy would you use?

I don't need to tell you this, but only in a perfect world will you have a perfect church. But I saw a perfect picture of church in the life of Christ the other day. Check it out and see if you can "catch a church in the act" in this glimpse into the life of Christ. Discuss it with your partner and compare what you see to what you believe should be the perfect church.

> The phrase to focus on in the **Life of Christ** section is "When Jesus saw their faith." Have the students and their partners answer one or all of the following questions: "Whose faith did Jesus see? Why are these special? How is their activity and behavior a good example for what church life should be like?"
>
> Hopefully, the communities we live in will say about our church, "We have never seen anything like this!"

Life of Christ

Mark 2:1-12

"A few days later, when Jesus again entered Capernaum, the people heard that he had come home. So many gathered that there was no room left, not even outside the door, and he preached the word to them. Some men came, bringing to him a paralytic, carried by four of them. Since they could not get him to Jesus because of the crowd, they made an opening in the roof above Jesus and, after digging through it, lowered the mat the paralyzed man was lying on. When Jesus saw their faith, he said to the paralytic, 'Son, your sins are forgiven.' Now some teachers of the law were sitting there, thinking to themselves, 'Why does this fellow talk like that? He's blaspheming! Who can forgive sins but God alone?' Immediately Jesus knew in his spirit that this was what they were thinking in their hearts, and he said to them, 'Why are you thinking these things? Which is easier: to say to the paralytic, "Your sins are forgiven," or to say, "Get up, take your mat and walk"? But that you may know that the Son of Man has authority on earth to forgive sins. . . .' He said to the paralytic, 'I tell you, get up, take your mat and go home.' He got up, took his mat and walked out in full view of them all. This amazed everyone and they praised God, saying, 'We have never seen anything like this!'"

> Have the students read the belief statement and share any questions or comments they have with their partners. As they paraphrase the passages below and chain-reference them in their Bibles, they should share with their partners what they think God is trying to say to them.
>
> Have the students look up the words "church," "assembly," and "believers" in the concordance and see what the Bible says about life in the New Testament church.

We Believe

The Church

"The church is the community of believers who confess Jesus Christ as Lord and Saviour. In continuity with the people of God in Old Testament times, we are called out from the world; and we join together for worship, for fellowship, for instruction in the Word, for the celebration of the Lord's Supper, for service to all mankind, and for the worldwide proclamation of the gospel. The church derives its authority from Christ, who is the incarnate Word, and from the Scriptures, which are the written Word. The church is God's family; adopted by Him as children, its members live on the basis of the new covenant. The church is the body of Christ, a community of faith of which Christ Himself is the Head. The church is the bride for whom Christ died that He might sanctify and cleanse her. At His return in triumph, He will present her to Himself a glorious church, the faithful of all the ages, the purchase of His blood, not having spot or wrinkle, but holy and without blemish." [20]

 a. Genesis 12:3
 b. Acts 7:38
 c. Ephesians 4:11-15; 3:8-11
 d. Matthew 28:19, 20
 e. Matthew 16:13-20; 18:17
 f. Ephesians 2:19-22, 1:22, 23; 5:23-27
 g. Colossians 1:17, 18

Which passage really speaks to you the most about a church? Why?

Way to Pray

As you pray this week, invite God to speak to you about what you can do to live as a member of the body of Christ. Share with Him what you hope for and then claim responsibility for your part in fulfilling the mission.

Pray for specific missionaries around the world who may be far away but are still part of the same body of Christ.

More Than Words

Interview: Invite someone who has seen many decades of church life to respond to the following questions:

How do you think the church has changed through the years? How is it still the same?

What would you say is the primary purpose for the Seventh-day Adventist Church as a whole? What do you think we should be devoting ourselves to?

What do you think will need to happen in our churches for us to become successful in our mission?

What specifically would you like to see young people do to "be a light" in this community?

In the Mirror

Think and write about your hopes and fears for your local church. Consider what you might do to be an "agent of change" or a "pioneer of old."

Lesson 13
Death and Resurrection

Before they continue with this new section, have the students reflect and share with their partners some of the insights they learned from their interviews.

The next four lessons deal with the final moments of earth's history and the new world that Christ died to secure for us.

Objective: Students will integrate the biblical view of death and resurrection into a hopeful and confident trust in Christ.

The **Opening Story** addresses the need to understand death in the context of birth and resurrection.

Opening Story

An old adage about skydiving declares that "it's not the fall that kills you as much as it is the ground." Death is something that few people want to experience. Rarely do people volunteer joyfully for the experience, save a few misguided or severely hurting people.

What is death? Is it another step into a different existence? Do we get reincarnated? And is it instant bliss for the do-gooders and flaming terror for the bad people? What trips most people up in a conversation about death is that they are talking about the middle of a conversation instead of the whole.

Janet, an academy student of mine, walked around the corner of the hallway at school and overheard part of a conversation. "I walked into the office and Frank was drinking; can you believe it?" one girl said to another as they stood in front of their lockers. Concerned for Frank, who obviously had a drinking problem and was doomed to life as an alcoholic for sure if we didn't intervene immediately, she hurried to my office.

"How do you know this, Janet?" I said, a little suspicious, after she told me what the girl had said.

"I heard some girls talking about it in the hall. No mistaking it, Pastor Troy, we need to do something," she pleaded.

I called up Frank, but he was not at home. So I went to talk with the principal to see if he knew where Frank was. "Frank should be going into surgery about now," he told me with a smile. "He was supposed to have knee surgery early in the morning, but apparently they postponed it a bit because he forgot about the 'no fluids' rule and drank about a quart of water."

Glad I asked, I thought to myself.

If Janet had heard the beginning of the conversation and the end, she would have discovered more than she could have from just the middle. The same is true as we look at the topic of death. When we talk about death, it is not safe or wise to leave out birth or the resurrection. As you study this glimpse into the mind of Christ, notice that Jesus is mostly interested in discussing the resurrection day. Some questions you may need to ask to help balance your study of this topic include: What is a human being? What does it mean to be alive? What does it mean to be dead? What is the resurrection, and who will be resurrected and for what purpose? Is death the end of us, or will there be an end to death?

> The passage to focus on in the **Life of Christ** section is "And this is the will of him who sent me, that I shall lose none of all that he has given me, but raise them up at the last day. For my Father's will is that everyone who looks to the Son and believes in him shall have eternal life, and I will raise him up at the last day."
>
> Ask the students: "How is the heart of God displayed in this section of the gospels?"

Life of Christ

John 6:30-40

"So they asked him, 'What miraculous sign then will you give that we may see it and believe you? What will you do? Our forefathers ate the manna in the desert; as it is written: "He gave them bread from heaven to eat."' Jesus said to them, 'I tell you the truth, it is not Moses who has given you the bread from heaven, but it is my Father who gives you the true bread from heaven. For the bread of God is he who comes down from heaven and gives life to the world.' 'Sir,' they said, 'from now on give us this bread.' Then Jesus declared, 'I am the bread of life. He who comes to me will never go hungry, and he who believes in me will never be thirsty. But as I told you, you have seen me and still you do not believe. All that the Father gives me will come to me, and whoever comes to me I will never drive away. For I have come down from heaven not to do my will but to do the will of him who sent me. And this is the will of him who sent me, that I shall lose none of all that he has given me, but raise them up at the last day. For my Father's will is that everyone who looks to the Son and believes in him shall have eternal life, and I will raise him up at the last day.'"

Have the students read the belief statement and share any questions or comments they have with their partners. As they paraphrase the passages below and chain-reference them in their Bibles, they should share with their partners what they think God is trying to say to them.

As the students work through the passages on this topic, make sure they have the opportunity to ask questions of each other. The study of death and resurrection is powerful, especially today when people have so much uncertainty about the hereafter.

We Believe

Death and Resurrection

"The wages of sin is death. But God, who alone is immortal, will grant eternal life to His redeemed. Until that day death is an unconscious state for all people. When Christ, who is our life, appears, the resurrected righteous and the living righteous will be glorified and caught up to meet their Lord. The second resurrection, the resurrection of the unrighteous, will take place a thousand years later." [21]

a. Romans 6:23
b. 1 Timothy 6:15, 16
c. Ecclesiastes 9:5, 6
d. Psalm 146:3, 4
e. John 11:11-14
f. Colossians 3:4
g. 1 Corinthians 15:51-54
h. 1 Thessalonians 4:13-17
i. John 5:28, 29
j. Revelation 20:1-10

Which verse speaks to you the most about this topic?

If someone were to ask you what you believe about death, how would you respond?

Way to Pray

As you pray, think about the different aspects of life, death, and resurrection you might have questions about. Invite God to give you understanding, comfort, hope, and courage.

Think about asking God for an opportunity to be a source of comfort to someone who may be suffering from the loss of a loved one.

More Than Words

Interview someone you know pretty well in the church who has lost someone close to them. (First, though, make sure they feel comfortable talking about it.) Ask them:

What stories or passages from Scripture first brought you the most comfort? What stories or passages bring you the most comfort today? If someone were to ask you about what happens at death, how would you respond to them, given what you know?

(Be sure to thank them and mention how this helps you personally.)

In the Mirror

Think and write about the resurrection day. What do you believe it will be like?

Lesson 14
The Second Coming

Have the students briefly share what they learned most from their interviews for the previous lesson.

Objective: Students will understand the attributes of the second coming of Christ and experience the personal assurance that believers can enjoy as they watch and work for the approaching day.

Open Questions

Agree/Disagree

Most people who are alive at the second coming of Christ will be fully aware of the events and their significance.

The **Opening Story** amplifies the need for the truth to penetrate beyond the superficial layers of our lives.

Opening Story

"Limited Processing." She looked at me just seething with anger.

"Huh?" I mumbled, a bit shocked by her explosive glare.

"You are a 'limited processor,'" she replied coolly.

I have been called many things in my life, some which I deserve, but most of the time I had at least an idea what the other person meant. Now, though, I was utterly clueless about being a "limited processor" and frankly, a little unsure whether it was good or bad. From my student's attitude I guessed being a "limited processor" was a bad thing. Because I had sought to teach my students that we should be honest with each other, I used the direct approach. "You're mad at me, aren't you?"

"Yes, I am," she erupted. "I was working on the research project you assigned, and that's when I came across this article that says that you're a . . ."

"A limited processor?" I finished.

"Yes," she said, handing me the article. "You made us do a paper on a social issue. I chose the environment crisis. You are constantly doing irresponsible things to the environment. You don't process the issues! That makes you a . . ."

"OK," I said before she could call me that name again. "Show me what you are talking about." She pointed to a portion of an article in *Psychology Today* that focused on the behavior of people on Earth Day. Here is the quote that labeled me a "limited processor."

"Ignorance. Robyn Dawes, Ph.D., a professor at Carnegie Mellon University, blames 'limited processing': People simply don't place their daily behaviors in an environmental context, their decisions are literally thoughtless." [22]

I looked at her, waiting for her to explain further. I was still a little slow with this one. "You use all the lights in the classroom and we need only half of them," she said. "Flip one switch instead of all of them. Like this." She looked as if she were trying to explain something to a child. Then going to the garbage can, she removed my empty plastic water bottle, which I tossed into the trash can at the end of class every day. "And this is abominable. Do you know how long this will take to decompose?" I didn't answer. "Please recycle your plastic bottles! And paper. Why can't we e-mail our assignments and save paper? We have all this paper stuff, and we don't need it." Finally she finished her tirade. It took me awhile, but I finally got it.

Debbie's frustration was real and, for the most part, true. I know the issues that surround the problem of our environment, but I'd never let them sink in deep enough to change the way I lived each day. To a certain degree, we are all "limited processors," and even Jesus would agree with Debbie about her frustration as she watched me day by day in the full knowledge of "the truth" about throwaway bottles, paper, and electricity. Jesus mirrored that frustration because of the resistance to His message. He warned the people of His time about the day of destruction (Jerusalem destroyed in A.D. 70), but they didn't see it. Before He returns, many people will have heard that Christ is coming, many will have seen the signs and known the facts, but the message will have never penetrated. The key for us is to see, hear, and know, but most of all, let it sink in deep enough to change the way we live.

> The passage to focus on from the **Life of Christ** section is "If you, even you, had only known on this day what would bring you peace." The triumphal entry marks a moment in the life of Jesus in which we can see images of the Second Coming. The crowds and the thrill go away quickly, and those who cheer for Christ will soon call for Him to be crucified. But in Luke 19:44 Jesus is troubled by Jerusalem because they did not recognize the time of God's coming.

Life of Christ

Luke 19:37-44

"When he came near the place where the road goes down the Mount of Olives, the whole crowd of disciples began joyfully to praise God in loud voices for all the miracles they had seen: 'Blessed is the king who comes in the name of the Lord!' 'Peace in heaven and glory in the highest!' Some of the Pharisees in the crowd said to Jesus, 'Teacher, rebuke your disciples!' 'I tell you,' he replied, 'if they keep quiet, the stones will cry out.' As he approached Jerusalem and saw the city, he wept over it and said, 'If you, even you, had only known on this day what would bring you peace—but now it is hidden from your eyes. The days will come upon you when your enemies will build an embankment against you and encircle you and hem you in on every side. They will dash you to the ground, you and the children within your walls. They will not leave one stone on another, because you did not recognize the time of God's coming to you.'"

How is this story of Jerusalem's destruction descriptive of the scene of the Second Coming?

Have the students read the belief statement and share any questions or comments they have with their partners. As they paraphrase the passages below and chain-reference them in their Bibles, they should share with their partners what they think God is trying to say to them.

Scripture describes the Second Coming as "the day," "The blessed hope," "The day of our Lord's appearing." The New Testament contains many references to the coming of Christ. As the students study the passages that describe how Jesus will return, have them ask their partner to share their insights on the nearness of Christ's return.

We Believe

The Second Coming

"The second coming of Christ is the blessed hope of the church, the grand climax of the gospel. The Saviour's coming will be literal, personal, visible, and worldwide. When He returns, the righteous dead will be resurrected, and together with the righteous living will be glorified and taken to heaven, but the unrighteous will die. The almost complete fulfillment of most lines of prophecy, together with the present condition of the world, indicates that Christ's coming is imminent. The time of that event has not been revealed, and we are therefore exhorted to be ready at all times."[23]

   a. Revelation 1:7
   b. Matthew 24:43, 44
   c. 1 Thessalonians 4:13-18
   d. 1 Corinthians 15:51-54
   e. 2 Thessalonians 1:7-10; 2:8
   f. Revelation 14:14-20
   g. Revelation 19:11-21
   h. Matthew 24
   i. 2 Timothy 3:1-5
   j. 1 Thessalonians 5:1-6

Which verse speaks to you the most about this topic?

Way to Pray

Take some time to think about the things you get complacent over. Ask God to give you this week a love for the Second Coming, so you can say with John in Revelation, "Even so, Lord, come!"

More Than Words

Interview someone over the age of 20 with the following questions:

When in your life have you thought that God would come right away?

How do you make the reality that Jesus is coming something you can experience every day?

What is your favorite passage or story from the Bible about the second coming of Christ and why?

In the Mirror

Think and write about the confidence you want to have in the last days.

Lesson 15
The Millennium and
the End of Sin

Before the students begin this study, have them spend a few moments sharing the insights they gained from their interviews.

Objective: Students will see the compassion and justice of God as He finally eradicates sin.

The coming of Christ and the beginning of the millennium has a sense of finality about it. People will have already made their choices about where they will spend eternity. It is done. The **Opening Story** describes games in which one side has overwhelmingly won, but time still remains on the clock. Ask: "With what attitude do we live while waiting for the clock to run out?"

Opening Story

You can see it at the end of blowout basketball games. One team has a 20-point lead, 39 seconds remain to play, and the game continues, but the teams are walking around. The winners are smiling, the losers aren't, and everyone kills time just waiting out the clock.

It's over, but the clock still has to tick away. On the cross Jesus' final words were "It is finished!" That phrase sealed Satan's doom and the end of death. Sin had been conquered, Satan had lost. It was over. You can bounce the ball around all you want, but one reality will not change—Satan is done for and sin and death will never reappear again. It seems hard to imagine such a thing when we see how sin still affects everything. But remember what Paul said:

"When the perishable has been clothed with the imperishable, and the mortal with immortality, then the saying that is written will come true: 'Death has been swallowed up in victory.' 'Where, O death, is your victory? Where, O death, is your sting?'" (1 Corinthians 15:54, 55).

"It is finished!" It is the cry of One who has already won. And no matter what Satan tries—even the worst scenarios of destruction you can think of—it still will not change the fact that Jesus has won, the believer will be resurrected, and Satan, sin, and their pet dog, "death," will be no more. It was this notion that fired up the early church. No torture, no persecution, no threat could shake them. Why? Because the game has been won, and now it's all about the countdown of the seconds remaining.

The battle between Christ and Satan is over. But you and I still have to choose which team we want to finish with. It doesn't seem right, I know, but imagine you are watching the NBA finals, and at the last minute you and your friends get to join the winning team. It has a 50-point lead. The choice is a no-brainer—at least you'd think so. Notice the book of Revelation talks about this (underline the phrases and words that help you understand what will happen at the end).

"Blessed and holy are those who have part in the first resurrection. The second death has no power over them, but they will be priests of God and of Christ and will reign with him for a thousand years" (Revelation 20:6).

"He who has an ear, let him hear what the Spirit says to the churches. He who overcomes will not be hurt at all by the second death" (Revelation 2:11).

"But the cowardly, the unbelieving, the vile, the murderers, the sexually immoral, those who practice magic arts, the idolaters and all liars—their place will be in the fiery lake of burning sulfur. This is the second death" (Revelation 21:8).

"Then death and Hades were thrown into the lake of fire. The lake of fire is the second death" (Revelation 20:14).

You can choose to die the second death or to allow Christ to die it for you. He already has, and it worked. How much more do you need to decide which team to join? It's a no-brainer, but why is it that so few seem to see it that way? I know the clock is still ticking, but I'm thinking there's only a few seconds left.

> The phrase to focus on is "It is finished." Ask the students: "What was finished on Calvary? What do you think Jesus meant when He said these words?" Once a dentist told me, "I'm finished." I relaxed because the torture was finally over. His fingers and tools lingered in my mouth. "OK, I think we've got it taken care of." Then he added, "I'm all through; I just have to . . ." Enough already. When you are through, say it, but most of all, mean it. In a way, this is a lot like the words Christ spoke. The final work takes place at the end when we hear the words echo from Calvary, "It is finished." The fire comes down, and the earth is cleansed; and finally it will be done.

Life of Christ

John 19:25-30

"Near the cross of Jesus stood his mother, his mother's sister, Mary the wife of Clopas, and Mary Magdalene. When Jesus saw his mother there, and the disciple whom he loved standing nearby, he said to his mother, "Dear woman, here is your son,' and to the disciple, 'Here is your mother.' From that time on, this disciple took her into his home. Later, knowing that all was now completed, and so that the Scripture would be fulfilled, Jesus said, 'I am thirsty.' A jar of wine vinegar was there, so they soaked a sponge in it, put the sponge on a stalk of the hyssop plant, and lifted it to Jesus' lips. When he had received the drink, Jesus said, 'It is finished.' With that, he bowed his head and gave up his spirit."

> Have the students read the belief statement and share any questions or comments they have with their partners. As they paraphrase the passages below and chain-reference them in their Bibles, they should share with their partners what they think God is trying to say to them.
>
> Point out that God can and will destroy the wicked by fire. That in the end, we will have no question, no doubt, no fear of God or His ways, only an eternally abiding love for His relentless pursuit of people to save them. The people who are lost will have rejected God fully. But they will be the first to acknowledge, "You were right, just, and good." When the destruction of the wicked takes place, we will not only agree with what God does, but it will make sense. It will be a merciful end. Ask the students: "How is the destruction of the wicked a merciful act?"

We Believe

The Millennium and the End of Sin

"The millennium is the thousand-year reign of Christ with His saints in heaven between the first and second resurrections. During this time the wicked dead will be judged; the earth will be utterly desolate, without living human inhabitants, but occupied by Satan and his angels. At its close Christ with His saints and the Holy City will descend from heaven to earth. The unrighteous dead will then be resurrected, and with Satan and his angels surround the city; but fire from God will consume them and cleanse the earth. The universe will thus be freed of sin and sinners forever." [24]

  a. Revelation 20
  b. 1 Corinthians 6:2, 3
  c. Jeremiah 4:23-26
  d. Revelation 21:1-5
  e. Malachi 4:1
  f. Ezekiel 28:18, 19

Which verse speaks to you the most about this topic?

As you understand the events of the end of time and the end of Satan's existence, draw out a little time line indicating what you think will happen and when.

Way to Pray

Think about the verses you have just studied. God has given you enough information to make you confident about where you stand both now and in the days to come. Pray this week in thankfulness for what God has already done and what He promises to do in the last days.

More Than Words

Interview someone with the following questions:

How do you explain how a God of love could destroy the world by fire? Doesn't that seem harsh to you?

What story or passage from the Bible gives you the most confidence and assurance that your life is safe in God's hands?

In the Mirror

Think and write about God's character as you see it—both His amazing grace and the fact that He will punish the wicked by fire. How does that all fit together for you?

Lesson 16
The New Earth

As they begin the lesson on the new earth, have the students take a moment to reflect and share the details and the helpful ideas that came from their interviews.

Objective: Students will discover the marvelous plan of God for restoring and re-creating the earth and seek to create ways in which they can foster the reality of a place called Paradise.

Sometimes I think we do a disservice to God's plan for the new earth by trying to guess what it will be like. On the other hand, it brings hope and help in troubled times to imagine a life better than we can conceive of. I don't know what life on the new earth will be like—I tend to want to let God surprise me. Ask the students: "Would you prefer to know more about it so you can look forward to it, or would you rather trust God completely with His plans, knowing that you won't be disappointed?"

Opening Story

Joe is a friend of mine. I love him, but he's . . . well . . . cheap. I hate to say it like that, but since his wife, Jenny, came right out with it, I guess I can too. Joe makes enough money to buy his wife a new car, but he won't. Now, I'm not going to share all the conversations we have had about this topic, but needless to say Joe finally broke down, and we went shopping for a new car for his wife.

Although Joe almost had a nervous breakdown haggling with the dealer, we finally purchased the car (I say we because I had to literally force his hand to sign the check). He wanted it to be a surprise, so we parked the car beforehand at a restaurant. They had a wonderful dinner together. Then, as they were beginning to leave, he said, "Jenny, I have a present for you, but I want it to be a surprise, so I'm going to blindfold you."

Jenny rarely received surprises from him, so she didn't want to ruin her chances by asking too many questions. He led her out to the new car, unlocked it with the remote key, and opened the door. A smile crept across her face and blossomed into laughter as she sat down in the brand-new car.

"I can't believe you bought me a brand-new car," she said, not taking the blindfold off.

"How do you know it is a new car, Jenny? You haven't even seen it," Joe said in shock. "You have never had a new car before, so how can you tell?"

"I can tell it's new because it smells new," she cooed.

Joe left it at that. And so should we. I have heard too many questions about what we will eat, what we will do and not do, or whom we will be married to or not married to in heaven. It is all fascinating, but I know only two things for sure:

1. Heaven will be new.
2. I will not argue or be disappointed in whatever the arrangements are.

Take the passages you find in God's Word and let them give you the basic idea and then you can dream on. Many will ask questions and make claims about heaven, but don't miss the point, as did the Pharisees and Sadducees in Christ's day. They weren't interested in heaven—they wanted the head of Jesus. Consider this story as you study about heaven and the new earth.

> The passage to focus on is "No one who has left home or brothers or sisters or mother or father or children or fields for me and the gospel will fail to receive a hundred times as much in this present age (homes, brothers, sisters, mothers, children and fields—and with them, persecutions) and in the age to come, eternal life." Not only will God not fail us, but He will abundantly reward us. But notice the cost in this section.

Life of Christ

Mark 10:17-31

"As Jesus started on his way, a man ran up to him and fell on his knees before him. 'Good teacher,' he asked, 'what must I do to inherit eternal life?' 'Why do you call me good?' Jesus answered. 'No one is good—except God alone. You know the commandments: "Do not murder, do not commit adultery, do not steal, do not give false testimony, do not defraud, honor your father and mother.'" 'Teacher,' he declared, 'all these I have kept since I was a boy.' Jesus looked at him and loved him. 'One thing you lack,' he said. 'Go, sell everything you have and give to the poor, and you will have treasure in heaven. Then come, follow me.' At this the man's face fell. He went away sad, because he had great wealth. Jesus looked around and said to his disciples, 'How hard it is for the rich to enter the kingdom of God!' The disciples were amazed at his words. But Jesus said again, 'Children, how hard it is to enter the kingdom of God! It is easier for a camel to go through the eye of a needle than for a rich man to enter the kingdom of God.' The disciples were even more amazed, and said to each other, 'Who then can be saved?' Jesus looked at them and said, 'With man this is impossible, but not with God; all things are possible with God.' Peter said to him, 'We have left everything to follow you!' 'I tell you the truth,' Jesus replied, 'no one who has left home or brothers or sisters or mother or father or children or fields for me and the gospel will fail to receive a hundred times as much in this present age (homes, brothers, sisters, mothers, children and fields—and with them, persecutions) and in the age to come, eternal life. But many who are first will be last, and the last first.'"

> Have the students read the belief statement and share any questions or comments they have with their partners. As they paraphrase the passages below and chain-reference them in their Bibles, they should share with their partners what they think God is trying to say to them.
>
> After the students look at the following passages, have them describe in a paragraph or two how they envision an average day of life in the new earth. Have them share their paragraphs with their partners.

We Believe

The New Earth

"On the new earth, in which righteousness dwells, God will provide an eternal home for the redeemed and a perfect environment for everlasting life, love, joy, and learning in His presence. For here God Himself will dwell with His people, and suffering and death will have passed away. The great controversy will be ended, and sin will be no more. All things, animate and inanimate, will declare that God is love; and He shall reign forever. Amen."[25]

   a. 2 Peter 3:13
   b. Isaiah 35

c. Isaiah 65:17-25
d. Matthew 5:5
e. Revelation 21:1-7; 22:1-5; 11:15

In your own words, share how you would explain the heaven and the new earth to a child in kindergarten.

Way to Pray

As you pray this week, ask God to keep you focused on living in the mind-set of the new earth.

More Than Words

Interview someone with the following questions:
What are you looking forward to about the new earth the most?
What promise from Scripture best helps you understand what heaven will be like?

In the Mirror

Think and write about what you imagine the earth will be like when Christ makes it new all over again.

Lesson 17
Stewardship

As you move toward the lessons that demonstrate our love and loyalty to God, have the students reflect and share some of the insights they gained from their interviews.

Objective: Students will deepen their understanding of the way God calls believers to a complete surrender of their lives, resources, and hearts for the work and glory of His kingdom.

The **Open Questions** may seem the same, but they are not. What God wants and what demonstrates our commitment could be different. For instance, does God really need or want my money? No, not as much as my mind and my heart. But I can demonstrate the state of my heart best by the way I love my stuff the least. As the students debrief on the questions, ask them: "Why did you choose this order?"

Open Questions

Rank the following in order of importance to you, 1 being the most and 5 being the least. What God wants most from us?

___ Time
___ Service
___ Money and Resources
___ Talents
___ Mind and Heart

Why?

Rank what you think demonstrates our commitment to God the most:

___ Time
___ Service
___ Money and Resources
___ Talents
___ Mind and Heart

Why?

The **Opening Story** addresses the issue of ownership. In a world that seeks to own as much as it can get its hands on, how does knowing that it all belongs to God reshape the way we live?

Opening Story

"Get off of my property!" the girl screamed.

"The sidewalk is not your property; it's government property, so there!" the boy said.

The argument raged on while I raked up the leaves on the lawn next door to the battle. I realized that I used to participate in arguments almost identical to this, but my patience for such belligerence now wore thin. Although I don't want to be known in the neighborhood for being the mean dad, I had had enough. What I did to stifle the arrogant stubbornness of the trespasser may have been somewhat dubious. But while I don't make a practice of it, still it was more than a little fun.

I went inside and called a friend of mine and made arrangements for the boy outside to speak directly to the government about whose property he was standing on. Then returning outside, I continued to rake leaves while the girl screamed, "It's my property! Get off!"

"I can stand here on the sidewalk and do whatever I want because it's government property," the boy replied.

My cell phone rang. After answering the phone, I assumed a convincing expression of concern and mentioned the boy's name with a questioning look on my face. "Billy? Yeah, he's right here." I think it was the first time anyone had ever called him on a cell phone. "Billy, it's for you."

"Me?" he replied in disbelief. I handed him the phone and watched, barely able to keep from bursting into laughter. "Hello," Billy said, puzzled. He was silent as he listened, but looked around as if some unseen watcher were observing him. Then without another word he handed me the phone and walked quickly back to his home, glancing around as though someone were watching him. Every once in a while Billy still paused in the middle of playing to see if he could spot the unseen watcher.

The issue of ownership rights to the sidewalk is still under way in many neighborhoods. But for every believer in Christ, the Lord is sole owner of not only our stuff, but also us. Paul said, "Do you not know that you belong to Christ?"

In our world people struggle to acquire and own things. *Our resources, our own lives, belong to me,* we think. "It's my life!" says the average person today. But the Christian at baptism declares, "It's not my life." You no longer live, but Christ lives within you.

The kind of selfless giving that grows out of an attitude of knowing who owns everything enables us to contribute to God's cause instead of our own interests.

Notice how Jesus emphasizes selflessness in giving.

Ask the students how they can tell if their motivation for giving, volunteering, etc. results from a pure selfless spirit. Suggest the following test: have them and their partners privately pray and think of something to give or do for someone else. It needs to be a sacrifice. Then have them do their act of kindness or give their gift—but do it secretly in the full knowledge that only the Father in heaven will ever know or see what they have done. If the idea excites them, then they are giving with the right heart. If they can keep from letting it slip—even the slightest hint—then I would question why it is so important for others to know.

Life of Christ

Matthew 6:1-4

"Be careful not to do your 'acts of righteousness' before men, to be seen by them. If you do, you will have no reward from your Father in heaven. So when you give to the needy, do not announce it with trumpets, as the hypocrites do in the synagogues and on the streets, to be honored by men. I tell you the truth, they have received their reward in full. But when you give to the needy, do not let your left hand know what your right hand is doing, so that your giving may be in secret. Then your Father, who sees what is done in secret, will reward you."

Have the students read the belief statement and share any questions or comments they have with their partners. As they paraphrase the passages below and chain-reference them in their Bibles, they should share with their partners what they think God is trying to say to them.

Here is a good place to go back to the lessons on "the church" and spiritual gifts and consider the purpose of the church before the students study this section. Why? Because the concept of stewardship is directly tied to our mission as a church. Our money, resources, time, and energy are not working for our personal goals, but the goals of the church. Love the church and its mission. Then we will love spending ourselves for it.

Have the students ask their partners: "What kinds of tired make you feel good?" (For me, the best tired I feel is when I'm on a plane returning from a mission trip. I'm exhausted—but for purposes that will last forever.)

We Believe

Stewardship

"We are God's stewards, entrusted by Him with time and opportunities, abilities and possessions, and the blessings of the earth and its resources. We are responsible to Him for their proper use. We acknowledge God's ownership by faithful service to Him and our fellowmen, and by returning tithes and giving offerings for the proclamation of His gospel and the support and growth of His church. Stewardship is a privilege given to us by God for nurture in love and the victory over selfishness and covetousness. The steward rejoices in the blessings that come to others as a result of his faithfulness." [26]

a. Genesis 1:26-28; 2:15
b. 1 Chronicles 29:14
c. Haggai 1:3-11
d. Malachi 3:8-12
e. 1 Corinthians 9:9-14
f. Matthew 23:23
g. 2 Corinthians 8:1-15
h. Romans 15:26, 27

Which verse speaks to you the most about this topic?

How would you teach the concept of stewardship to a fourth grader?

Way to Pray

Write a letter to God that gives Him all of the stuff you tend to desperately hold on to. Pray regularly this week for a sense that God is the owner and you are the trusted manager.

More Than Words

Interview someone who has children who are in college or older. Ask the following questions:

When in your life has God come through miraculously for you as a result of your faithful giving?

Why do you think it is hard for us to think of our "things" or even "time" as belonging to God and not to ourselves?

What words of wisdom do you have for someone my age about giving and working in the church?

In the Mirror

Think and write about your desire to make your giving and your serving a regular part of your walk with God.

Lesson 18
Christian Behavior

Ask the students if as they interviewed parents of older children last week, they felt inspired by the visions of giving they encountered. What else did they learn from their interviews?

Objective: Students will understand the importance of living their lives by the principles that God has given to His children in order to experience the abundant life.

The **Open Question** is not a trick one, but simply requires the students to determine what they mean by "standing out in the world." The process is important. Ask them to explain why they answered the way they did.

Open Questions

Agree/Disagree

Christians should stand out in our world because of their dress, entertainment, and health principles.

Why did you answer the way you did?

The **Opening Story** is about how our commitments to a cause are sometimes short-lived when we finally see what they involve.

Opening Story

I read this story and thought it would be a great start to our study on the Christian lifestyle.

"There is a story about two New York men who had never been out of the city. They decided that they had had it with city living, so they bought a ranch down in Texas in order to live off the land like their ancestors.

"The first thing they decided they needed was a mule. So they went to a neighboring rancher and asked him if he had a mule to sell. The rancher answered, 'No, I'm afraid not.'

"They were disappointed, but as they visited with the rancher for a few moments one of them saw some honeydew melons stacked against the barn and asked, 'What are those?' The rancher, seeing that they were hopeless city slickers, decided to have some fun. 'Oh,' he answered, 'those are mule eggs. You take one of those eggs home and wait for it to hatch, and you'll have a mule.' The city slickers were overjoyed at this, so they bought one of the melons and headed down the bumpy country road toward their ranch. Suddenly they hit an especially treacherous bump, and the honeydew melon bounced out of the back of the pickup truck, hit the road, and burst open. Now, seeing in his rearview mirror what had happened, the driver turned his truck around and drove back to see if he could retrieve his mule egg.

"Meanwhile a big old Texas jackrabbit came hopping by and saw this honeydew melon burst in the road. He hopped over to it, and standing in the middle of that mess he began to eat. Now here came the two city slickers. They spied their mule egg burst open and this long-eared creature in the middle of it. One of the men shouted, 'Our mule egg has hatched! Let's get our mule.'

"But seeing those two men coming toward it, the jackrabbit took off, hopping in every direction with the two city fellows in hot pursuit. The two men from New York gave everything they had to catch him, but finally they could go no farther. Both men fell wearily on the ground gasping for air while the jackrabbit hopped off into the distance. Rising up on his elbow, one of the men said to the other, 'Well, I guess we lost our mule.' The other man nodded grimly. 'Yes, but you know,' he said, 'I'm not sure I wanted to plow that fast anyway.' " [27]

When you make a decision to follow Christ, it is a commitment. Being a Christian today will involve your giving up things that others pursue, doing things others would never think to do, and living a life that stands out as different in our world. Is it worth it? Not if your commitment is only part time or only part of your life or part of your habits or part of your relationships or part of your lifestyle. It just isn't worth it. But full surrender, full commitment, will bring about a life that is full. Count on it.

The passage to focus on in the **Life of Christ** section is "By their fruit you will recognize them. Do people pick grapes from thornbushes, or figs from thistles? Likewise every good tree bears good fruit, but a bad tree bears bad fruit. A good tree cannot bear bad fruit, and a bad tree cannot bear good fruit." As my pastor says, "Call me old-fashioned, but I still believe that if you have faith, your life should demonstrate it." Ask the students how this passage shapes the way they think about their lifestyle right now.

Life of Christ

Matthew 7:15-29

"'Watch out for false prophets. They come to you in sheep's clothing, but inwardly they are ferocious wolves. By their fruit you will recognize them. Do people pick grapes from thornbushes, or figs from thistles? Likewise every good tree bears good fruit, but a bad tree bears bad fruit. A good tree cannot bear bad fruit, and a bad tree cannot bear good fruit. Every tree that does not bear good fruit is cut down and thrown into the fire. Thus, by their fruit you will recognize them. Not everyone who says to me, "Lord, Lord," will enter the kingdom of heaven, but only he who does the will of my Father who is in heaven. Many will say to me on that day, "Lord, Lord, did we not prophesy in your name, and in your name drive out demons and perform many miracles?" Then I will tell them plainly, "I never knew you. Away from me, you evildoers!" Therefore everyone who hears these words of mine and puts them into practice is like a wise man who built his house on the rock. The rain came down, the streams rose, and the winds blew and beat against that house; yet it did not fall, because it had its foundation on the rock. But everyone who hears these words of mine and does not put them into practice is like a foolish man who built his house on sand. The rain came down, the streams rose, and the winds blew and beat against that house, and it fell with a great crash.' When Jesus had finished saying these things, the crowds were amazed at his teaching, because he taught as one who had authority, and not as their teachers of the law."

Have the students read the belief statement and share any questions or comments they have with their partners. As they paraphrase the passages below and chain-reference them in their Bibles, they should share with their partners what they think God is trying to say to them.

The difference between personal standards and biblical principles is big. A principle is a timeless truth that applies to all people, all places, at all times. It is a guide by which people make choices about their lifestyles. Standards are specific goals and behaviors that they choose to accomplish their goals or live within their principles. The topic is touchy. Ask the students what they think about this concept: Instead of becoming focused on what we can and can't do as a Christian, we should immerse ourselves in what a Christian must be doing. What would some of those "must do" things look like? What would some of the "can or can't do" things look like?

We Believe

Christian Behavior

"We are called to be a godly people who think, feel, and act in harmony with the principles of heaven. For the Spirit to re-create in us the character of our Lord we involve ourselves only in those things which will produce Christlike purity, health, and joy in our lives. This means that our amusement and entertainment should meet the highest standards of Christian taste and beauty. While recognizing cultural differences, our dress is to be simple, modest, and neat, befitting those whose true beauty does not consist of outward adornment but in the imperishable ornament of a gentle and quiet spirit. It also means because our bodies are the temples of the Holy Spirit, we are to care for them intelligently. Along with adequate exercise and rest, we are to adopt the most healthful diet possible and abstain from the unclean foods identified in the Scriptures. Since alcoholic beverages, tobacco, and the irresponsible use of drugs and narcotics are harmful to our bodies, we are to abstain from them as well. Instead, we are to engage in whatever brings our thoughts and bodies into the discipline of Christ, who desires our wholesomeness, joy, and goodness." [28]

    a. Romans 12:1, 2
    b. 1 John 2:6
    c. Ephesians 5:16-26
    d. Philippians 4:8
    e. 1 Peter 3:1-4
    f. 1 Corinthians 6:19, 20
    g. Leviticus 11
    h. 3 John 2

What do you think these passages are saying about how we should live as followers of Christ?

Which passage speaks to you the most about your lifestyle? Why?

Way to Pray

Make a list of the areas of your life that you want God to guide the most.

As you pray this week, begin each day with a prayer that focuses on a particular part of your personal life and in it ask for His help and guidance in making choices.

More Than Words

What adjustments or commitments do you want to make in order to put your life in harmony with the great plan God has for you? What changes will you make? What will you do that you're not doing now?

Interview a college student or someone older and ask the following questions:

What are the big choices you have had to make about your personal standards as a Christian?

What stories or passages from Scripture are guides for what you choose to eat, wear, listen to, and participate in?

What Bible character would you most like to pattern your life after? Why?

In the Mirror

What things last forever, and what things tend to fade away? Think and write about how you relate to temporary things as opposed to eternal things.

Lesson 19
Marriage and Family

Before the students start the lesson on marriage and the family, have them share the insights that came from their interviews with a college student (or young adult).

Objective: Students will discuss God's original plan for the family and the reason for the brokenness that plagues families today. Also, they will set goals for their lives based on Scripture.

Open and value questions are useful only if you ask why the students answered the way they did.

Open Questions

Rank in order of importance the elements you think are necessary in a successful marriage, 1 being the most important and 5 being the least important of the suggestions listed.

___ Communication
___ Personal and physical attraction
___ Mutual respect
___ United in spiritual goals
___ Common interests and activities

Why?

Opening Story

The retirement home was buzzing with junior high students. They wanted to visit and to sing and to bring some encouragement to the elderly people living in the home. I went to one room where a man named Henry lived. In addition to a number of ailments he was suffering from, he could no longer see.

"I've been blind for so long I don't remember what anything looks like anymore," he told me. (I thought about that for a moment. I can imagine how difficult it would be to have been born blind and not have any way to identify the things that people talk about. But what of those who had seen clearly before they went blind? Can they still remember and visualize in their mind those images? I don't know.) "Do you remember what your favorite scenery looks like?" I asked.

"Nope," he replied quickly. "In my mind I can remember only two things: the sunrise on my daddy's wheat field and Sue Betty Lou Bender's face. She was the most beautiful girl I ever . . ."

My attention drifted as I thought to myself, *Who on earth would name their child . . . ?* Anyway, he remembered two things before his world grew dark—the sunrise and that girl. Two things.

Most humans can't even imagine a world without sin. Sin is so much a part of our world we use the phrase "the world" to describe the totality of what is sinful. However, we still have two things that remind us about the perfect world God created: the Sabbath and marriage. They are precious to God because they are about His relationship to us. The Sabbath reminds us who created us and whom we belong to. And marriage is the experience two people have that can reflect the relationship God wants to have with us. While the marriage relationship is far from what it used to be, it still holds the same place in God's heart as it did in Eden. Notice that the opening of John's Gospel of Jesus begins with a wedding in the second chapter. As you study about God's love for marriage, take a look at "what can be" instead of what is.

> The passage to focus on in this story is "this, the first of his miraculous signs, Jesus performed at Cana in Galilee. He thus revealed his glory, and his disciples put their faith in him." Of all the Gospels, only John mentions the miracle at the wedding. Why do you suppose John included this story in his Gospel? No other writer even mentions the incident. Have the students share with their partners what it is about this story that prompts John to put it in the Gospel record.

Life of Christ

John 2:1-12

"On the third day a wedding took place at Cana in Galilee. Jesus' mother was there, and Jesus and his disciples had also been invited to the wedding. When the wine was gone, Jesus' mother said to him, 'They have no more wine.' 'Dear woman, why do you involve me?' Jesus replied. 'My time has not yet come.' His mother said to the servants, 'Do whatever he tells you.' Nearby stood six stone water jars, the kind used by the Jews for ceremonial washing, each holding from twenty to thirty gallons. Jesus said to the servants, 'Fill the jars with water'; so they filled them to the brim. Then he told them, 'Now draw some out and take it to the master of the banquet.' They did so, and the master of the banquet tasted the water that had been turned into wine. He did not realize where it had come from, though the servants who had drawn the water knew. Then he called the bridegroom aside and said, 'Everyone brings out the choice wine first and then the cheaper wine after the guests have had too much to drink; but you have saved the best till now.' This, the first of his miraculous signs, Jesus performed at Cana in Galilee. He thus revealed his glory, and his disciples put their faith in him. After this he went down to Capernaum with his mother and brothers and his disciples. There they stayed for a few days."

> Have the students read the belief statement and share any questions or comments they have with their partners. As they paraphrase the passages below and chain-reference them in their Bibles, they should share with their partners what they think God is trying to say to them.
>
> Before they move into the study, have the students think about this question: If God gave the Sabbath and marriage before sin, when God restores the earth made new, will marriage be a part of that world as well? Why or why not?

We Believe

Marriage and Family

"Marriage was divinely established in Eden and affirmed by Jesus to be a lifelong union between a man and a woman in loving companionship. For the Christian, a marriage commitment is to God as well as to the spouse, and should be entered into only between partners who share a common faith. Mutual love, honor, respect, and responsibility are the fabric of this relationship, which is to reflect the love, sanctity, closeness, and permanence of the relationship between Christ and His church. Regarding divorce, Jesus taught that the person who divorces a spouse, except for fornication, and marries another, commits adultery. Although some family relationships may fall short of the ideal, marriage partners who fully commit themselves to each other in Christ may achieve loving unity through the guidance of the Spirit and the nurture of the church. God blesses the family and intends that its members shall assist each other toward complete maturity. Parents are to bring up their children to love and obey the Lord. By their example and their words they are to teach them that Christ is a loving disciplinarian, ever tender and caring, who wants them to become members of His body, the family of God. Increasing family closeness is one of the earmarks of the final gospel message."[29]

a. Genesis 2:18-25

b. Matthew 19:3-9

c. 2 Corinthians 6:14

d. Ephesians 5:21-33

e. Matthew 5:31, 32

f. Exodus 20:12

g. Ephesians 6:1-4

h. Proverbs 22:6

Which verse speaks to you the most about this topic?

Way to Pray

Pray this week to God about your present family and ask God to help you become a team player in it.

More Than Words

Interview someone, other than your own parents, who you think honors the marriage relationship:

What do you think are the most important skills to have as a spouse? Why do you think they are essential?

What passage or story from Scripture reminds you of your relationship with God and your spouse?

What advice would you give someone my age about marriage (other than "wait until you're a little older")?

In the Mirror

Why do you think God set up the whole system of families? Do you think it was by accident or intentional? What do you think God really wants families to be like?

Lesson 20
Christ's Ministry in the Heavenly Sanctuary

Ask the students what insights they gained from their interviews.

Objective: Students will survey the meaning and purpose of the sanctuary (on earth and in heaven) and discover the incredible significance of the events that mark the beginning of the Adventist movement.

Open Questions

When has someone distracted you from communicating to someone else? What was that like? How did you respond?

The **Opening Story** is a transition to what Jesus does to the Temple.

Opening Story

My friend teaches art to children. With her ability, she could easily do well in the world of art. However, she chooses to teach art to children—children who are blind. She instructs them in the basic skills of pottery, an art form in which her students can create things and express themselves even though they cannot see.

I stopped by to observe her class one time, but her students were not busy at work. Instead, they were sitting quietly on their stools, apparently waiting for Mrs. Robbins. "Is Mrs. Robbins here?" I asked sheepishly.

"No, she's taking care of the bad guys," a girl said, turning her head my direction. "She'll be back soon."

Bad guys? I thought. *In an art class?* Stepping outside, I could see Mrs. Robbins in the distance speaking to a police officer. "What happened?" I asked afterward.

"Some high school boys have been disrupting my art class by making noise and banging on the windows and running away. They have been at it for a week now, and I finally got them." She punched her fist into the air victoriously.

"What did you do?"

"I just called my friend at the police station, and three cars came down and rounded up the boys and took them back to the high school. I made arrangements for their bikes and skateboards to be impounded as well," she said with a smile.

"Isn't that a bit harsh?" Even as the words fell from my mouth I knew I had made a mistake.

"Do you have any idea how hard it is to teach art to blind children? Not to mention how much more complicated it gets when I have boys outside scaring these children to death?" I didn't think she really wanted me to answer that. "For some of these kids my class is the only opportunity for them to create anything," she continued, "so I'm not going to let a bunch of disrespectful, mindless teenagers get in the way of the best part of their day." Needless to say, I felt my hair singed. Quickly agreeing with her measures, I got away while I could.

After thinking about it, I concluded her response was appropriate. It reminds me of the passion God had for His people:

"Then have them make a sanctuary for me, and I will dwell among them" (Exodus 25:8).

"Then I will dwell among the Israelites and be their God. They will know that I am the Lord their God, who brought them out of Egypt so that I might dwell among them. I am the Lord their God" (Exodus 29:45, 46).

God's passion is to be close to us. He wants us to know Him, especially how He plans to save us. He doesn't want anyone or anything to get in the way! The sanctuary wasn't just an oversized tent for mindless rituals to keep people busy with religious activity. The awe, the blood, the sounds, the smell of incense, the solemn prayers, the light, the sense that God was behind the next door, gave the children of Israel an opportunity to live with God. But don't get in the way when people want to come and be with God! Just like my zealous friend who teaches art, God will not tolerate people distracting others from His great purpose for their lives. Take a look at Jesus in the Temple.

The Temple was *the place* where people could come to worship, make a sacrifice, and serve God. But some had turned it into a three-ring circus of hucksters, crooks, and political gamers busily haggling that kept people from seeing God. Notice the zeal Jesus had for the place where God and humanity were supposed to meet together.

> In addition to bartering and selling the sacrificial animals for the highest prices possible, people did other terrible things in the Temple. The eastern entrance was busy with travelers who were interested in the business district or the markets. The Temple was, well . . . in the way, and the most efficient route to the markets was through the Temple courts. This would have been unthinkable in David's time, not to mention during the Exodus. People would pay to pass through. The Temple became a tollbooth for traffic. Those who wanted to see God in the Temple service couldn't.

Life of Christ

John 2:13-22

"When it was almost time for the Jewish Passover, Jesus went up to Jerusalem. In the temple courts he found men selling cattle, sheep and doves, and others sitting at tables exchanging money. So he made a whip out of cords, and drove all from the temple area, both sheep and cattle; he scattered the coins of the money changers and overturned their tables. To those who sold doves he said, 'Get these out of here! How dare you turn my Father's house into a market!' His disciples remembered that it is written: 'Zeal for your house will consume me.' Then the Jews demanded of him, 'What miraculous sign can you show us to prove your authority to do all this?' Jesus answered them, 'Destroy this temple, and I will raise it again in three days.' The Jews replied, 'It has taken forty-six years to build this temple, and you are going to raise it in three days?' But the temple he had spoken of was his body. After he was raised from the dead, his disciples recalled what he had said. Then they believed the Scripture and the words that Jesus had spoken."

The elements of the sanctuary show us Christ's ministry to us, not only at Calvary but today in heaven. Ultimately, the sanctuary was then, and still is, about Jesus.

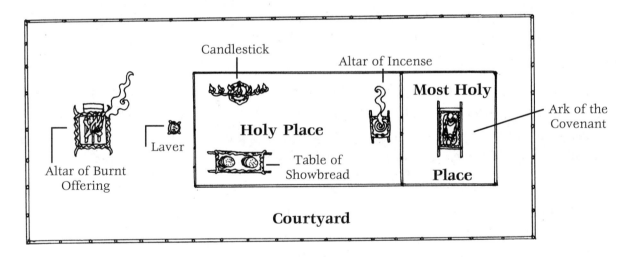

What is the sanctuary?

The courtyard: the altar of burnt offering and the laver. The tent of the sanctuary had two parts: the holy place and the Most Holy Place. The holy place housed the seven-branched candlestick (lampstand), the table of showbread, and the altar of incense.

The Most Holy Place held the ark of the covenant, which contained the Ten Commandments written by God on two tables of stone. Two golden cherubim stood facing each other, and in the middle of the covering was the mercy seat.

What took place at the sanctuary?

As a sinner, you would bring a sacrifice (usually a lamb) and place your hands on the innocent animal. The animal was killed as you confessed your sins, thus in a way placing them on the victim. The priest sprinkled the animal's blood on the altar of burnt offering or in the Holy Place. Every day people transferred their sins to the sanctuary, a practice called the daily sacrifice. Anyone who confessed their sins walked away forgiven.

Because the sanctuary now had the sins of the sinner, it would need to be cleansed once a year. Scripture calls it the Day of Atonement. Essentially, it was a day of judgment in which everyone who had confessed sins throughout the year was judged. It was a moment of awe and solemn reverence. The Levites brought the high priest two goats on the Day of Atonement. The one goat he would sacrifice was called the Lord's goat, while the other was the scapegoat. The high priest sacrificed the Lord's goat and took the blood into the Most Holy Place. The high priest entered this room once a year on this special day and sprinkled the blood on the mercy seat. Then he returned to the holy place and spattered blood on the altar of incense. Next he moved into the courtyard, where he spattered the blood on the altar of burnt offering.

Afterward, the high priest placed his hands on the head of the other goat (the scapegoat) and confessed the sins for a whole year of all the people of Israel and symbolically placed them on the scapegoat. The Levites then sent the scapegoat into the wilderness to wander around until it died with the sins of Israel.

What does it mean?

God showed Moses the sanctuary in heaven, and the one that Moses then built was a model of the one in heaven. The parts of the sanctuary have tremendous meaning and purpose. The sanctuary service demonstrates the two parts of the ministry of Christ (the work of intercession and the work of judgment).

The First Part (the Courtyard and the Holy Place)

When people confessed their sin over the lamb and it was killed and placed on the altar, the act portrayed the sacrifice of Christ as He died on Calvary. (Remember, John the Baptist said, "Behold the Lamb of God who takes away the sins of the world.")

The laver, filled with water, illustrates baptism and the forgiveness of sins as the water washes away the old person of sin.

In the holy place, the table of showbread demonstrates Christ, who is the Bread of life (John 6:35). The candlestick symbolizes that Jesus was the light of the world (John 8:12). The altar of incense depicts the way Christ intercedes for sinners (John 17).

The Second Part (the Most Holy Place)

The ministry of the second compartment involves judgment. The truth about sin is that even though there is forgiveness for sin, someone has to pay. The ark of the covenant is a timeless symbol of God's unchanging law of righteousness. It is important to remember that what makes the sacrifice and the blood and death necessary is God's law. Sin (transgression of the law) brings death. The ark represents God's throne, where His justice calls for an answer to the sin problem.

The scapegoat stands for Satan, who is banished from the sanctuary with the sins of the people. Justice is served, because sin, death, and shame die with the one who is ultimately responsible for them.

The sanctuary is not a sick ritual ordered by an angry God who wants blood. No, quite the opposite, it is a moment to participate in and witness a loving and just God who deals with the sin problem by becoming the payment for sin Himself. Scripture has many wonderful stories of God's love that are warm and fuzzy. But the sanctuary service is not warm and fuzzy—it is God's love conquering the cold, cruel effects of sin. While it is not pretty, it does save.

As you read the passages that describe the heavenly sanctuary and God's plan of salvation also read chapters 23 and 24 in *The Great Controversy* for a more thorough explanation on the work of the sanctuary and Christ's ministry in the sanctuary.

> Have the students read the belief statement and share any questions or comments they have with their partners. As they paraphrase the passages below and chain-reference them in their Bibles, they should share with their partners what they think God is trying to say to them.

We Believe

Christ's Ministry in the Heavenly Sanctuary

"There is a sanctuary in heaven, the true tabernacle which the Lord set up and not man. In it Christ ministers on our behalf, making available to believers the benefits of His atoning sacrifice offered once for all on the cross. He was inaugurated as our great High Priest and began His intercessory ministry at the time of His ascension. In 1844, at the end of the prophetic period of 2300 days, He entered the second and last phase of His atoning ministry. It is a work of investigative judgment, which is part of the ultimate disposition of all sin, typified by the cleansing of the ancient Hebrew sanctuary on the Day of Atonement. In that typical service the sanctuary was cleansed with the blood of animal sacrifices, but the heavenly things are purified with the perfect sacrifice of the blood of Jesus. The investigative judgment reveals to heavenly intelligences who among the dead are asleep in Christ and therefore, in Him, are deemed worthy to have part in the first resurrection. It also makes manifest who among the living are abiding in Christ, keeping the commandments of God and the faith of Jesus, and in Him, therefore, are ready for translation into His everlasting kingdom. This judgment vindicates the justice of God in saving those who believe in Jesus. It declares that those who have remained loyal to God shall receive the kingdom. The completion of this ministry of Christ will mark the close of human probation before the Second Advent." [30]

    a. Hebrews 8:1-5; 4:14-16

    b. Daniel 7:9-27; 8:13, 14; 9:24-27

    c. Numbers 14:34

    d. Ezekiel 4:6

    e. Leviticus 16

    f. Revelation 14:6, 7; 20:12; 14:12; 22:12

Which verse speaks to you the most about this topic?

What did you learn about the plan of salvation that you may not have heard or understood before?

Way to Pray

As you pray, picture Jesus—your High Priest—praying for you and taking your prayers to the Father as a perfect mediator. Think about what He is doing for you now—judging you by His goodness—and then pray with the joy and confidence of His finished work for you.

More Than Words

Interview a pastor, teacher, elder, or someone who you think has a pretty good knowledge of the meaning and purpose of the sanctuary. Ask the following questions:

What do you think is the most significant feature of the sanctuary service?

What story or passage from Scripture reminds you most of God's great work of salvation?

What do you think the sanctuary in heaven is all about?

In the Mirror

As you reflect on this study, what part of the study do you think was the most meaningful part?

Lesson 21
The Remnant and
Mission of the Church

Have the students reflect on the interviews they have done during the past few weeks. Which interview made the biggest impact on them and why? What part of their study helped them to grow the most?

As they study the remnant church and its mission, at some point have them pray with their partners to devote themselves fully to the cause.

Objective: Students will discover the wonderful and sacred responsibility of inviting people to know the Savior and unite together to communicate the truth of the gospel to the world.

Opening Story

The end of the book of Revelation contains a challenge to faithfulness. The people of God at the end of time will have several marks that distinguish them from others. Those marks, according to the Bible, will be clear. Notice the emphasis Revelation puts on the faithful:

"This calls for patient endurance on the part of the saints who obey God's commandments and remain faithful to Jesus" (Revelation 14:12).

"Do not be afraid of what you are about to suffer. I tell you, the devil will put some of you in prison to test you, and you will suffer persecution for ten days. Be faithful, even to the point of death, and I will give you the crown of life" (Revelation 2:10).

"They will make war against the Lamb, but the Lamb will overcome them because he is Lord of lords and King of kings—and with him will be his called, chosen and faithful followers" (Revelation 17:14).

It is clear that at the end of time God's people will have certain attributes:

1. They keep God's commandments.

2. They will be persecuted for their faith.

3. Their faith will be a deep, abiding love for Jesus and His Word.

The following illustration reminds me of God's remnant people at the end:

"When Pompei was destroyed by the eruption of Mount Vesuvius, there were many people buried in the ruins. Some were found in cellars, as if they had gone there for security. Some were found in the upper rooms of buildings. But where was the Roman sentinel found? Standing at the city gate where he had been placed by the captain, with his hands still grasping his weapon. There, while the earth shook beneath him—there, while the floods of ashes and cinders covered him—he had stood his post. And there, after a thousand years, was this faithful man still to be found." [31]

Jesus spoke to the disciples about being a true follower. As you read the statement below, notice the struggle between the faithful followers and those who are mistaken. Make your choice today about being part of God's faithful followers.

> This story sums up the difference between the true remnant and those who desperately think they are the remnant by right of birth. The passage to focus on is "If you hold to my teaching, you are really my disciples." The phrase "hold to my teaching" means more than believing. It involves "to do or to obey." As the students look at this encounter, ask them what parallels they see in the Pharisees' mind-set to the way some think today.

Life of Christ

John 8:30-37

"Even as he spoke, many put their faith in him. To the Jews who had believed him, Jesus said, 'If you hold to my teaching, you are really my disciples. Then you will know the truth, and the truth will set you free.' They answered him, 'We are Abraham's descendants and have never been slaves of anyone. How can you say that we shall be set free?' Jesus replied, 'I tell you the truth, everyone who sins is a slave to sin. Now a slave has no permanent place in the family, but a son belongs to it forever. So if the Son sets you free, you will be free indeed. I know you are Abraham's descendants. Yet you are ready to kill me, because you have no room for my word.'"

> Have the students read the belief statement and share any questions or comments they have with their partners. As they paraphrase the passages below and chain-reference them in their Bibles, they should share with their partners what they think God is trying to say to them.
>
> After the students go through the passages about the remnant, have them obtain a copy of the *Seventh-day Adventist Yearbook.* It is a directory of all the Adventist organizations around the world divided by geographical locations. Have them get a map and a globe and just look through the book and pray for different people, schools, hospitals, missions, and unions around the world. Ask them what

they would want others to be praying for for them.

We Believe

The Remnant and the Mission of the Church

"The universal church is composed of all who truly believe in Christ, but in the last days, a time of widespread apostasy, a remnant has been called out to keep the commandments of God and the faith of Jesus. This remnant announces the arrival of the judgment hour, proclaims salvation through Christ, and heralds the approach of His second advent. This proclamation is symbolized by the three angels of Revelation 14; it coincides with the work of judgment in heaven and results in a work of repentance and reform on earth. Every believer is called to have a personal part in this worldwide witness." [32]

a. Revelation 12:17; 14:6-12; 18:1-4
b. 2 Corinthians 5:10
c. Jude 3, 14
d. 1 Peter 1:16-19
e. 1 Peter 3:10-14
f. Revelation 21:1-14

Way to Pray

As you pray to God this week, make a list of seven areas of your spiritual life that you want to become more faithful in, and then pray about each one each day this week.

More Than Words

Choose a person in your church who you believe is a faithful follower of Christ and ask the following questions:

From your understanding of the Bible, describe what you think the remnant in the last days is like.

Think of a person you believe can be characterized as a faithful follower of Christ. What are some of their qualities and commitments?

In the Mirror

Think about the final moments of earth's history, as you imagine they will be like, and write your hopes and expectations as the old world passes away and the new enters in.

[1] *Seventh-day Adventists Believe*, p. 4

[2] *Transworld Skateboarding*, p. 78.

[3] *Seventh-day Adventists Believe*, p. 16.

[4] *Ibid.*, p. 28.

[5] *Ibid.*, p. 36.

[6] *Ibid.*, p. 58.

[7] Erwin Lutzer, *Ten Lies About God*, p. 1.

[8] *Seventh-day Adventists Believe*, p. 98.

[9] *Ibid.*, p. 118.

[10] *Ibid.*, p. 180.

[11] *Ibid.*, p. 68.

[12] *Ibid.*, p. 232.

[13] *Ibid.*, p. 248.

[14] Washington *Post*, Oct. 20, 2000.

[15] *Ibid.*

[16] *Seventh-day Adventists Believe*, p. 106.

[17] *Ibid.*, p. 194.

[18] *Ibid.*, p. 206.

[19] *Nelson's Complete Book of Stories*, p. 127.

[20] *Seventh-day Adventists Believe*, p. 134.

[21] *Ibid.*, p. 348.

[22] "Why We Are Destroying the Earth," *Psychology Today*, March-April 2000, p. 49

[23] *Seventh-day Adventists Believe*, p. 332.

[24] *Ibid.*, p. 362.

[25] *Ibid.*, p. 374.

[26] *Ibid.*, p. 268.

[27] James S. Hewett, *Illustrations Unlimited*, pp. 98, 99.

[28] *Seventh-day Adventists Believe*, p. 278.

[29] *Ibid.*, p. 294.

[30] *Ibid.*, p. 312.

[31] Michael Green, *1500 Illustrations for Biblical Preaching*, p. 143.

[32] *Seventh-day Adventists Believe*, p. 152.

ChristWise: Youth
Lesson 1
The Scriptures

Objective: Students will discover the authority of God's Word and its purpose and power in the life of the believer.

The **Open Questions** seek to show how difficult it can be to communicate with people. If you have only a minute or two to send a message, what will its nature be? Probably only what is absolutely necessary.

Have the students share their responses with their partners. Why did they choose to communicate what they wrote? What do they think communicating with humans is like from God's perspective?

Open Questions

Have you ever had to send a message to another person but been unable to do so because of a communication mess-up? How did you feel? Share the story.

Suppose you have a 12-year-old child. You have two minutes to pass on to him or her information that will be most helpful for their future survival and happiness. What will you say? (Write out your advice.)

The **Opening Story** targets Scripture's role in our everyday life. Especially in youth, beliefs, faith, and convictions often exist in a separate part of their lives than their actions, habits, and deeds. The major task for youth is to shape their lives so the two go together. From the start, we need to decide how this Book will relate to our lives and how we will reorder our lives to live by its message.

Opening Story

I'm not a sensational guy when I speak to young people. One time, though, I couldn't resist the urge to be edgy. As I began the sermon I announced, "Enough of this—this is so ridiculous! What are we all doing here, anyway? What does this book have to say that's relevant to us?" I began ripping random pages out of my Bible, crumpling them roughly and throwing them to the ground. I even had the guts to stomp irreverently on a few crumpled pages beneath my feet.

Talk about getting their attention! Gasps exploded through the chapel like gunshots on a battlefield. Students gazed at me in horror, amazed by my blasphemous treatment of the Sacred Scriptures. Older adults in the back of the room began murmuring about how to get rid of me before I inflicted any further damage on innocent young minds.

"Relax," I said finally. "Anyone who knows me knows I would never tear up a Bible. I simply took a cheap Harlequin romance novel and put an old Bible cover on it." (I have no problem defacing romance novels.) The tension eased a little, but before I lost the crowd's attention, I posed a question to the squirming group: "Which is worse—openly defacing God's Word or quietly ignoring it day by day?"

It is a shocking way to approach the Scriptures, but think about the words John penned years ago. The Bible writers chose the sayings and stories of the Bible because they communicate what is vital to know about God.

> The passage to focus on in this passage is "Jesus did many other miraculous signs in the presence of his disciples, which are not recorded in this book. But these are written that you may believe that Jesus is the Christ, the Son of God, and that by believing you may have life in his name." Just as with the two-minute letter the students wrote earlier, the words of Scripture are given to equip us with what we need. According to the Bible, what is it that John hopes this will accomplish?

Life of Christ

John 20:24-31

"Now Thomas (called Didymus), one of the Twelve, was not with the disciples when Jesus came. So the other disciples told him, 'We have seen the Lord!' But he said to them, 'Unless I see the nail marks in his hands and put my finger where the nails were, and put my hand into his side, I will not believe it.' A week later his disciples were in the house again, and Thomas was with them. Though the doors were locked, Jesus came and stood among them and said, 'Peace be with you!' Then he said to Thomas, 'Put your finger here; see my hands. Reach out your hand and put it into my side. Stop doubting and believe.' Thomas said to him, 'My Lord and my God!' Then Jesus told him, 'Because you have seen me, you have believed; blessed are those who have not seen and yet have believed.' Jesus did many other miraculous signs in the presence of his disciples, which are not recorded in this book. But these are written that you may believe that Jesus is the Christ, the Son of God, and that by believing you may have life in his name."

The section **We Believe** succinctly states the fundamental belief. The beauty of the Adventist faith is its commitment to God's Word, even if it means saying, "This is something we never saw before." As the students read the statements, have them consider how other religions or denominations might be different.

We Believe

The Scriptures

"The Holy Scriptures . . . are the written Word of God, given by divine inspiration through holy men of God who spoke and wrote as they were moved by the Holy Spirit."[1] Everything we need for salvation is available in the Bible. The Bible is really about God revealing to us who He is and who we are in relation to Him. It reveals a trustworthy picture of God and becomes the authoritative guide for people as they follow Him.

Have the students read the statement below that summarizes what the Seventh-day Adventist Church believes about the Holy Scriptures. Then have them read each verse and write what they think it means as they chain-reference the verses in their Bibles.

As the students look up each verse, they will be doing two things at once: paraphrasing (writing in their own words what they think it means) and making a chain reference as they mark their Bibles (making a topical reference guide in the front of their Bible so they can refer to passages later on).

Make sure they understand how to mark their Bible. If you begin to mark your Bible with them, it will be easier for them to follow you. Put the name of the study and the first text of the study in the front of their Bible: "1—The Scriptures a. 2 Peter 1:20, 21," then go to 2 Peter 1:20, 21, read the verse, and write in your study guide a short paraphrase of that verse in simple everyday language. Have the students do the same. Highlight the verse in your Bible (you can use colored pencils and have each study color-coded, or just use a pen and a ruler—whatever you choose to do) and at the end of the verse or in the margin next to it write the next verse in the study: "1b. 2 Timothy 3:16." Continue the process of looking up the passage, paraphrasing it in your own words, then chain-reference the verses. After the students repeat this a few times they will find that it will go faster and easier.

Read the following verses and briefly paraphrase them in your own words. Don't use the same words or phrases as the text—be creative!

a. 2 Peter 1:20, 21

    b. 2 Timothy 3:16

    c. Hebrews 1:1, 2

    d. Hebrews 4:12

    e. John 5:39

    f. Psalm 119:105

    g. Proverbs 30:5

    h. 1 Thessalonians 2:13

    i. James 1:22-25

Which verses above especially speak to you about God's Word in your life? Why?

> As the students study with their partners, have them share the verse or passage that really spoke to them and explain why they think it is significant to them now.
>
> For youth the process of summarizing or communicating the essence of their belief is an important exercise. At the end of the chain-reference section invite them to say it in their own words.
>
> Ask them: Which verses above especially speak to you about God's Word in your life?
>
> **I Believe:** (Have them write what they believe about the Bible, based on their study so far.

I Believe

Write what you believe about the Bible, based on your study so far.

Way to Pray

"Your word is a lamp to my feet and a light for my path" (Psalm 119:105).

Write a prayer to God about a part of your life that really needs insight and guidance from His Word.

> Personal interviews enable a variety of people to interact with the student, instead of just one person. Such interviews are relatively easy to do and not very time-consuming. The key is selecting the right person to interview. It is not always a good idea for them to choose someone they know very well. Much better for them is to talk and interact with people they don't know. Either way, the goal is to ask thoughtful questions.

More Than Words

Interview someone you know about his or her experience in trusting God's Word. Here are a few questions to ask them:

1. When in your life did you come to trust the Bible as God's Word for you?
2. When has the Bible been a real source of strength to you? Have you had times when you had doubts about God's Word?
3. If you could tell only one story from Scripture, which one would you choose to help a friend know God? Why?

Soil Check

What soil represents your life the most (Matthew 13:3-8; 18-23)? How can you make the soil of your heart more receptive to God's Word in your life?

The journaling section will feature a variety of prompts. It is a good idea to get the student into the habit of journaling early in the study even if it doesn't seem to be their favorite activity. The long-term impact of thoughtful reflection will be well worth it.

In the Mirror

If God has only two minutes to get a message through to you on paper, write what you think He might say to you—keeping in mind what you know about the purpose, person, and power of His Word.

Lesson 2
The Trinity

The lesson on the Holy Scriptures is something that develops over the whole series. Experiencing God's Word is a process, and during the coming weeks it is likely that the students' outlook and love for God's Word will grow.

Objective: Students will encounter the mystery and marvelous relationship of the Trinity and see how an unfathomable God becomes real to people.

The Trinity is a tough topic in many ways. One problem has to do with the limitations of human knowledge and experience. We know only what God has revealed to us. Unfortunately, for centuries we have struggled with how to describe and define the Godhead. "How do you explain one God with three names?" Or "It is one God with three personalities." Or how about this one: "One God that functions in three different ways"? If we apply what we discovered in John's Gospel last week, although we don't have every story and every truth, we know enough to believe. The key is not to try to explain or to define the Trinity; rather, the task for the Christian is to know the Trinity.

The two **Open Questions** below seek to engage the students and their partners to think about the notion that we know people (and God) to the degree that they reveal themselves to us.

Open Questions

Which member of the Trinity (Father, Son, Holy Spirit) do you relate to the most? Why?

How do you think your best friend would describe you? How well do you think they know you? On the continuum below, indicate the degree at which the person who knows you the best really understands you.

1—Knows very little of the real you
5—Knows you completely

1	2	3	4	5

Knows very little   **Knows you completely**

How would you like to be Moses and get this response from God?

"Moses said to God, 'Suppose I go to the Israelites and say to them, "The God of your fathers has sent me to you," and they ask me, "What is his name?" Then what shall I tell them?' God said to Moses, 'I AM WHO I AM. This is what you are to say to the Israelites: "I AM has sent me to you"'" (Exodus 3:13, 14).

"I AM." What kind of answer is that? Why does this have to be such a mystery? *Just give me a nice, neat definition of who You are and what I should call You and we'll be OK,* you may be thinking to yourself. But God reveals not only what we *need* to know but what we *can* know. Why the mystery? It is not because God is hiding. He is using every way possible to make His character clear to us. In looking at who God is, it is important to note two facts: 1. God has revealed Himself plainly enough that we can love and serve Him. 2. God's desire is to reveal more of Him to us personally each day.

Opening Story

When a group of us were in Africa holding meetings and conducting a free medical clinic, Jaci prayed a remarkable prayer. Exhausted from the constant drain on her strength and her spirit, she begged, "God, I don't feel like I have anything to give today. Father, lend me Your heart today, and I will give that away."

While Jaci doesn't claim to know all about God, she knew enough about Him to recognize that she needed Him at that moment. Maybe all she knew was that God was the great "I AM"—and that would be enough. For the rest of the day her service to others mattered more than her own comfort, more than her inner cares and conflicting emotions. If you had asked her, she would not have claimed to know everything about God, nor would she have said she was always close to Him. But she knew enough about God to know what He is like: selfless, compassionate, and heartbroken at the sight of suffering people. The list of His traits could go on and on. Why? Because God is still revealing who He is to us. But for the moment, compassion and selfless service can become the way to live. Jaci has never been the same since that experience.

The Trinity is a word to describe God—the Father, Son, and Holy Spirit. Like us, God has personality. He has a character. But all we can know about Him is what He reveals to us. The problem with understanding the Trinity comes when we try to define or completely explain or describe the nature, personality, and person of God. Instead of "figuring it out," try letting God reveal Himself to you through His Word. Let Him show His heart to you. You will be confused if you focus on the "what" of the Trinity, but you will find yourself changed when you see the who of the Trinity.

The phrases to focus on in this part of the **Life of Christ** are the names of the Father, Son, and Holy Spirit. We tend to relate to Jesus the most, because of His humanness. Once we become parents, we can identify with the Father somewhat— but the Spirit? Many think the Holy Spirit is some force, power, or ethereal conscience. Christ gives away the secret of the Holy Spirit when He mentions that "I am with you always." When you get to the list of texts on the Holy Spirit it will be hard to track whether Jesus is referring to the Spirit or Himself.

Life of Christ

Matthew 28:18-20

"Then Jesus came to them and said, 'All authority in heaven and on earth has been given to me. Therefore go and make disciples of all nations, baptizing them in the name of the Father and of the Son and of the Holy Spirit, and teaching them to obey everything I have commanded you. And surely I am with you always, to the very end of the age.'"

We Believe

The Trinity

"There is one God: Father, Son, and Holy Spirit, a unity of co-eternal Persons. God is immortal, all-powerful, all-knowing, above all, and ever present. He is infinite and beyond human comprehension, yet known through His self-revelation. He is forever worthy of worship, adoration, and service by the whole creation."[2]

Read the following verses and briefly paraphrase them in your own words. Think about what they say about who God is and what we can know about Him.

a. Deuteronomy 6:4

b. Matthew 28:19, 20

c. 2 Corinthians 13:14

The Father

"God the Eternal Father is the Creator, Source, Sustainer, and Sovereign of all creation. He is just and holy, merciful and gracious, slow to anger, and abounding in steadfast love and faithfulness. The qualities and powers exhibited in the Son and the Holy Spirit are also revelations of the Father."[3]

Read the following verses and briefly paraphrase their meaning in your own words. How does God's Word describe the Father?

a. Genesis 1:1

b. John 3:16

c. John 14:8-11

As you have read and marked the verses in your Bible, what three characteristics of God the Father are most meaningful to you right now? Which passages describe those qualities?

The Son

"God the Eternal Son became incarnate in Jesus Christ. Through Him all things were created, the character of God is revealed, the salvation of humanity is accomplished, and the world is judged. Forever truly God, He became also truly man, Jesus the Christ. He was conceived of the Holy Spirit and born of the virgin Mary. He lived and experienced temptation as a human being, but perfectly exemplified the righteousness and love of God. By His miracles He manifested God's power and was attested as God's promised Messiah. He suffered and died voluntarily on the cross for our sins and in our place, was raised from the dead, and ascended to minister in the heavenly sanctuary in our behalf. He will come again in glory for the final deliverance of His people and the restoration of all things."[4]

    a. John 1:1-3, 14

    b. Luke 1:35

    c. Colossians 1:13-20

    d. John 10:30

As you have read and marked the verses in your Bible, which three characteristics of God the Son are most meaningful to you right now? Which passages best describe those qualities?

The Holy Spirit

"God the eternal Spirit was active with the Father and the Son in Creation, incarnation, and redemption. He inspired the writers of Scripture. He filled Christ's life with power. He draws and convicts human beings; and those who respond He renews and transforms into the image of God. Sent by the Father and the Son to be always with His children, He extends spiritual gifts to the church, empowers it to bear witness to Christ, and in harmony with the Scriptures leads it into all truth."[5]

    a. Genesis 1:1, 2

    b. John 14:16-18, 26

    c. Acts 1:8

    d. Ephesians 4:11, 12

As you have read and marked the verses in your Bible, which three characteristics of God the Holy Spirit are most meaningful to you? Now note which passages describe those qualities.

Think about how you would describe the person and the work of the Holy Spirit to a child. What illustrations or analogies would you use?

Way to Pray

Write a prayer to each person of the Trinity based upon what you know about Them. Ask God to reveal Himself more fully to you this week.

> If student partners need help finding someone to interview, have them do the first interview with each other. Whoever the person is, always choose someone in the church who will appreciate the opportunity to share.

More Than Words

Interview: Invite someone you know who has thought and studied about the Trinity to share with you in a short interview. Ask them:

How do you describe the different members of the Trinity? What other ways might you explain Their relationship? Why do you think the Bible describes God in these three ways/personalities?

In the Mirror

Take a few moments to reflect on what you discovered this week about the Trinity that you had not understood before. What do you want to say to God today about who you think He is?

Lesson 3
The Great Controversy

As the students begin their time together, have them share with each other how their interviews went and what kind of response they gained from the activity.

Objective: Students will observe the nature of evil and the core issues of how people can better understand such characteristics of God as freedom, will, love, and war.

Open Questions

Would people characterize you as a strong-willed person, or are you more laid-back and easygoing? What do you think are some strengths and weaknesses of both personality types?

1—I live each day aware of the war between good and evil.

5—I rarely consider the reality of supernatural warfare taking place.

1	2	3	4	5
Aware				**Rarely think about it**

If you have ever traveled to countries in which people live on the brink of war you will find a constant tension. People live their lives aware that the enemy is near. Americans rarely wondered about their safety and security in this way until September 11, 2001. As terrorism attacked the United States, it became clear that it had an enemy close by.

One of our goals in this lesson is to accept the reality that this is a war, and like it or not, we are a part of it. The **Opening Story** describes the playful approach to good guys and bad guys on the playground. But the **Life of Christ** section has four places where the battle is quite real. As you look at those stories, consider the following questions: "What is Satan's angle? What is he trying to do to Jesus? How will these skirmishes affect Christ's life and ministry?"

Opening Story

My son looked back over his shoulder to the kids screaming and chasing each other on the playground. He came to report the current status of the battle that raged between two groups on the playground. "The girls are trying to get us," my son proudly sputtered, "and I'm a bad guy!" Then he watched to see my reaction to his self-proclaimed status as a bad boy.

I smiled. "Go get 'em, bad guy!" He was already off to the war. Immediately three girls captured and placed him in "jail." But he didn't seem to mind, and I didn't blame him. It was a game. Being the "bad guy" was part of the game. After all, it is only a game, right? Good girls and bad guys?

My son always wants to be the bad guy. I'll be honest with you—that worries me a bit. Why? Bad guys are, well, bad. Real life isn't a playground. As we go through our daily routine, there is an all-out war raging all around us, with real people and real casualties. At the end of the day it is not as easy as shaking off the dust of the playground and going home to have a sandwich and a "tubby." Probably the most dangerous attitude to have in a time of war is the misguided notion that there is no war, no danger, and no side on which to take a stand.

Jesus entered the war zone when He was born. But His visit to the wilderness to prepare for His ministry is a special point at which the battle between Christ and Satan intensified. Look at the great controversy between Christ and Satan in the desert wilderness, and consider what this war is about as you watch the two armies clash.

> The phrase to focus on is "If you worship me, it will all be yours." In the following verses Satan tempts Jesus to avoid Calvary—to choose another way rather than the Father's way.

Life of Christ

Luke 4:1-13

"Jesus, full of the Holy Spirit, returned from the Jordan and was led by the Spirit in the desert, where for forty days he was tempted by the devil. He ate nothing during those days, and at the end of them he was hungry. The devil said to him, 'If you are the Son of God, tell this stone to become bread.' Jesus answered, 'It is written: "Man does not live on bread alone."' The devil led him up to a high place and showed him in an instant all the kingdoms of the world. And he said to him, 'I will give you all their authority and splendor, for it has been given to me, and I can give it to anyone I want to. So if you worship me, it will all be yours.' Jesus answered, 'It is written: "Worship the Lord your God and serve him only."' The devil led him to Jerusalem and had him stand on the highest point of the temple. 'If you are the Son of God,' he said, 'throw yourself down from here. For it is written: "He will command his angels concerning you to guard you carefully; they will lift you up in their hands, so that you will not strike your foot against a stone."' Jesus answered, 'It says: "Do not put the Lord your God to the test."' When the devil had finished all this tempting, he left him until an opportune time."

> The passage to focus on in this story is "He [Jesus] began to teach them that the Son of Man must suffer many things. . . . And Peter . . . began to rebuke him. . . . 'Get behind me, Satan!' he [Jesus] said." Peter can't imagine Jesus being killed. The conflict involves God's way versus humanity's way.

Mark 8:27-33

"Jesus and his disciples went on to the villages around Caesarea Philippi. On the way he asked them, 'Who do people say I am?' They replied, 'Some say John the Baptist; others say Elijah; and still others, one of the prophets.' 'But what about you?' he asked. 'Who do you say I am?' Peter answered, 'You are the Christ.' Jesus warned them not to tell anyone about him. He then began to teach them that the Son of Man must suffer many things and be rejected by the elders, chief priests and teachers of the law, and that he must be killed and after three days rise again. He spoke plainly about this, and Peter took him aside and began to rebuke him. But when Jesus turned and looked at his disciples, he rebuked Peter. 'Get behind me, Satan!' he said. 'You do not have in mind the things of God, but the things of men.'"

> The phrase to focus on in this story is in the prayer in which Jesus begs the Father to "take this cup from me. Yet not what I will, but what you will." The weight of sin is oppressive. Jesus accepts His Father's will—and Satan is again defeated.

Mark 14:32-38

"They went to a place called Gethsemane, and Jesus said to his disciples, 'Sit here while I pray.' He took Peter, James and John along with him, and he began to be deeply distressed and troubled. 'My soul is overwhelmed with sorrow to the point of death,' he said to them. 'Stay here and keep watch.' Going a little farther, he fell to the ground and prayed that if possible the hour might pass from him. 'Abba, Father,' he said, 'everything is possible for you. Take this cup from me. Yet not what I will, but what you will.' Then he returned to his disciples and found them sleeping. 'Simon,' he said to Peter, 'are you asleep? Could you not keep watch for one hour? Watch and pray so that you will not fall into temptation. The spirit is willing, but the body is weak.'"

> The phrase to focus on at the scene of Calvary is "Come down from the cross, if you are the Son of God!" Could Christ have done it? Our salvation depends on Him refusing to save Himself. The great controversy between Christ and Satan goes back a long way, but the essence of the fight is between the will of the Father and the will of self.

Matthew 27:39-43

"Those who passed by hurled insults at him, shaking their heads and saying, 'You who are going to destroy the temple and build it in three days, save yourself! Come down from the cross, if you are the Son of God!' In the same way the chief priests, the teachers of the law and the elders mocked him. 'He saved others,' they said, 'but he can't save himself! He's the King of Israel! Let him come down now from the cross, and we will believe in him. He trusts in God. Let God rescue him now if he wants him, for he said, "I am the Son of God."'"

Divide this study between you and your partner. Each of you should take a story and ask the following questions:

1. Underline or circle the verse you think is key to understanding this story.
2. Describe the struggle taking place in this story.
3. How is the adversary at war with Jesus? What is Satan seeking to accomplish?
4. How does Jesus respond, and why do you think He responds this way?
5. How do these stories depict the great controversy? According to these stories, what is the great controversy really about? (Restrict your answer to a sentence.)

Share responses to the questions, then work on the following questions together:

1. What temptation does Satan constantly throw at Jesus?
2. How would you describe Jesus' response to these dilemmas? What is His attitude?
3. In a sentence or two, tell what God's will was in the garden when Jesus said, "Not My will, but Yours . . ."
4. What do you think it will take for us (you) to be able to offer that prayer in any situation? Under what circumstance is it most difficult for you to surrender your will to God's?

Have the students read the statement below that summarizes what the Seventh-day Adventist Church believes about the great controversy. Then have them read each verse and write what they think it means as they chain-reference the verses in their Bibles.

One of the greatest attributes of the Adventist message is the big picture it provides of the origin of sin and the plan of redemption.

We Believe

The Great Controversy

The great controversy juts out of the landscape of the life of Christ like giant rocks thrusting from the ground. The war between Christ and Satan is and always will be about self versus selflessness. It's a war of the wills—your will versus the will of God.

"All humanity is now involved in a great controversy between Christ and Satan regarding the character of God, His law, and His sovereignty over the universe. This conflict originated in heaven when a created being, endowed with freedom of choice, in self-exaltation became Satan, God's adversary, and led into rebellion a portion of the angels. He introduced the spirit of rebellion into this world when he led Adam and Eve into sin. This human sin resulted in the distortion of the image of God in humanity, the disordering of the created world, and its eventual devastation at the time of the worldwide flood. Observed by the whole creation, this world became the arena of the universal conflict, out of which the God of love will ultimately be vindicated. To assist His people in this controversy, Christ sends the Holy Spirit and the loyal angels to guide, protect, and sustain them in the way of salvation."[6]

- **a.** Revelation 12:4-9
- **b.** Isaiah 14:12-14
- **c.** Ezekiel 28:12-18
- **d.** Genesis 3
- **e.** Genesis 6–8
- **f.** 2 Peter 3:6
- **g.** 1 Corinthians 4:9

Which verse spoke to you most profoundly about the conflict between Christ and Satan? Why?

As you mark (chain-reference) your Bible with these passages, what one word do you find that best describes the problem of the great controversy?

Whether they do the practical exercises **(Way to Pray, More Than Words, In the Mirror)** together or privately throughout the week, have the students take a few moments to debrief and share some of their experiences with their partners.

I Believe

How would you answer someone who asks, "How can I believe or serve a God who allows the innocent to suffer and the guilty to go unpunished?"

As you look at what Scripture says about how sin began and how God chooses to deal with it, how would you explain what you find to someone who doesn't know much about the Bible?

Way to Pray

When you pray "Father, Your will be done, not mine," be specific with God about the things that seem to be His will and the things that you want.

More Than Words

Jesus chose to do His Father's will and His Father's way—alone in the desert, in conflict with a close friend, in the heat of a big decision, in front of the world at Calvary. Alone. Among friends. Facing big decisions. As you consider the decisions and struggles you will have to face in your life, think of tangible ways to remind yourself that you are caught in a spiritual war. Keep them visible and practical. I'm putting bright-blue tape on the tips of my running shoes so when I jog (alone) I'll be reminded of My Father's will for my life. By my phone (where I make decisions) I have taped to the desk: "Not my will, but Yours." You can create your own reminders. The Old Testament is filled with symbols that stayed in the memories of believers so they would not forget.

Interview: Ask someone how they would deal with this dilemma:

Many people have a difficult time relating to a God who seems either unwilling or unable to respond to the bad things that happen to innocent people in the world. How do you explain a loving God to people when so many innocent people suffer? How do I relate to a God who seems far away or distant?

In the Mirror

In what ways do you see the great controversy at work in your life? in those around you? Reflect on either how oblivious or aware you are of this struggle between good and evil, of the war between human will and God's will.

Lesson 4
The Experience
of Salvation

Much of the war between Christ and Satan rages over the people that God calls "His children." Before you continue with the next lesson, have the students take a moment to review or share the experiences from their interviews.

Objective: Students will enter the lives of those who were lost, found, and restored in order to experience the power of God's saving grace in their own lives.

The focal point of this lesson is not to sort out all the issues and questions of salvation, but to respond to what Scripture does tell us.

The story about Sabrina makes the truth of God's amazing grace clear. God's grace does more than forgive—it restores. At some point toward the end of their study session, have the students kneel down with their partners and receive this gift together.

Open Questions

When in your life have you felt as if you were the furthest away from God? What helped you draw close to Him in those moments?

Opening Story

"That's life." It was one of her favorite sayings, a common phrase when things turned out less desirable than she wanted or expected. I knew her only from the little statements she made in front of her friends in the ice-cream shop I worked in while I was in high school. Sabrina was a few years younger than I was, but she still scared me. Always dressed in black, her dyed black hair hung like a greasy curtain covering her eyes. Although she rarely spoke, when she did, her words displayed what her hair tried to hide—her life was empty, even hopeless.

I would try to avoid being the one to say to Sabrina, "May I help you?" Although I managed to dodge that experience several times during the summer, on one occasion I did get stuck with her. She ordered her ice cream—two scoops of Black Forest chocolate. When I handed the ice-cream cone to her I stared at her wrists as she reached for the ice cream. Her long sleeves slid back to reveal a tattoo on the inside of each forearm—a razor blade. Who would tattoo a razor blade on their wrists? Sabrina would and did. Instinctively I jumped, the ice-cream cone tipped, and the awkward, terrible moment continued as I had to remake her ice cream.

Later in the year I was able to actually have a conversation with her. As the store was closing one night, I asked her about her tattoos. "I don't know," she said. "I think about killing myself a lot, but I don't have the guts—so I got a tattoo instead. My life hasn't been so great. That's life, I guess."

I wish I could say that I prayed for her, or with her. But I didn't. I was just as lost as she was—I just didn't know it. I returned to the ice-cream shop two years later while visiting in my hometown. As I studied the familiar tubs of ice cream in the window I heard that familiar phrase: "May I help you?" I looked up—it was Sabrina. But not the one I used to know. For the first time ever I think I saw her eyes. I almost didn't believe it was she. We talked as she prepared my ice-cream sundae. "Sabrina, what happened?" I had to ask. She described how she met Christ through a friend, and now she was trying to put her life back together. When I glanced at her arms I saw that they bore the evidence of the painful surgery to remove the tattoos. She smiled. "Did it hurt?"

"Yeah, but that's life." She said it with a sense of peace this time, making me believe that the phrase meant something different. As I left the store with a new confidence in God's power to completely restore someone's life, I began thinking about having Him transform mine.

Many times Jesus describes the gift of salvation as "life." Scripture describes the experience of conversion as a birth:

"Yet to all who received him, to those who believed in his name, he gave the right to become children of God—children born not of natural descent, nor of human decision or a husband's will, but born of God" (John 1:12, 13).

Such a birth is usually the result of the power of God's message of salvation through His Word:

"For you have been born again, not of perishable seed, but of imperishable, through the living and enduring word of God" (1 Peter 1:23).

"He chose to give us birth through the word of truth, that we might be a kind of first-fruits of all he created" (James 1:18).

"That's life." Or "Now, that's *the* life." Apply these two expressions about life to this story from the life of Christ in which Jesus demonstrates in a marvelous way the experience of salvation in the restoration of a man dying with leprosy.

> No story seems to capture sin's effects as does the healing of the leper. The account is filled with phrases to focus on. The students can choose their own example.

Life of Christ

Mark 1:40-45

"A man with leprosy came to him and begged him on his knees, 'If you are willing, you can make me clean.' Filled with compassion, Jesus reached out his hand and touched the man. 'I am willing,' he said. 'Be clean!' Immediately the leprosy left him and he was cured. Jesus sent him away at once with a strong warning: 'See that you don't tell this to anyone. But go, show yourself to the priest and offer the sacrifices that Moses commanded for your cleansing, as a testimony to them.' Instead he went out and began to talk freely, spreading the news. As a result, Jesus could no longer enter a town openly but stayed outside in lonely places. Yet the people still came to him from everywhere."

How is the leper's experience with leprosy and healing like our experience with sin and salvation?

> Have the students read the statement below that summarizes what the Seventh-day Adventist Church believes about how a person can come to experience the gift of salvation. Then have them read each verse and write what they think it means as they chain-reference the verses in their Bibles.
>
> While many denominations believe in righteousness by faith, I have yet to find a summary of it more thoughtful than the following:

We Believe

The Experience of Salvation

"In infinite love and mercy God made Christ, who knew no sin, to be sin for us, so that in Him we might be made the righteousness of God. Led by the Holy Spirit we sense our need, acknowledge our sinfulness, repent of our transgressions, and exercise faith in Jesus as Lord and Christ, as Substitute and Example. This faith, which receives salvation, comes through the divine power of the Word and is the gift of God's grace. Through Christ we are justified, adopted as God's sons and daughters, and delivered from the lordship of sin. Through the Spirit we are born again and sanctified; the Spirit renews our minds, writes God's law of love in our hearts, and we are given the power to live a holy life. Abiding in Him we become partakers of the divine nature and have the assurance of salvation now and in the judgment."[7]

What do these passages say about the experience of salvation?

a. John 3:16
b. Romans 3:21
c. 2 Corinthians 5:17-21
d. Galatians 4:4-7
e. Titus 3:3-7
f. Romans 8:14-17
g. Romans 10:17
h. Galatians 3:2
i. Romans 8:1-4
j. Romans 12:2

Which passages above spoke to you the most about God's saving power? How would you describe the experience of salvation to another person? What is it, and how do you get it?

Way to Pray

Read 1 John 5:13, 14. As you pray, focus on thanking God with confidence for giving you the gift of salvation. You can write out your prayer if you want.

More Than Words

Interview: Invite someone to share their story of conversion with you. Ask them:
How did you come to give your life to Christ? What were the circumstances of your salvation experience? How do you live in a world of sin with the confidence that you are

saved? How do you remind yourself of this experience?

Read Mark 5:18-20.

Tell another person this week about the certainty and the joy you have as someone who is "saved."

In the Mirror

Take a few moments to reflect. Why do you think it is difficult to experience the gift of salvation in our world today? What are the obstacles? What can we do to enable people to receive the free gift of God's grace in our busy world?

Lesson 5
Baptism

Before you move into the study on baptism, have the students take a moment to share any insights they gained from the interviews or other applications they participated in this week.

Have the students discuss their partners' baptism, if they haven't already.

Objective: Students understand the nature, purpose, and awesome privilege of baptism.

In this study we describe our relationship with the Father through the different relationships we experience on earth: birth, adoption, and marriage. The experience of baptism is in many ways like adoption. It has a formal, legal ring to the event that is similar to adoption. But when God calls us to Him by adoption, the relationship becomes more direct than any human counterpart.

Open Questions

Agree or Disagree:

Baptism is required for those who want to be saved.

Opening Story

Birth (the experience of salvation), adoption (baptism), and marriage (the law of God) help us to understand what it means to live in a relationship with God. When we are born, we receive life. God's Word, His message of salvation, comes to us and we believe and receive it. When we are born, it is usually into a family. Since we are born sinners, we call our spiritual rebirth experience "being born again." The Bible uses the idea of adoption to describe our newfound life in God's family. (In the next lesson we will discuss marriage. Through it we begin a new family—and, I might add, become part of another.)

The Bible uses these three experiences to describe how believers relate to God and His family. This lesson is about the life-changing experience of baptism.

"After his grandmother's funeral, Gary was leafing through his grandma's well-worn Bible, and he found his name on the family register page. He expected to see his name there, but what he didn't expect to see was the word written next to his name—ADOPTED. Gary was bewildered, hurt, and not a little angry that nobody had ever told him. It wasn't the best way for him to find out how he got into the family."[8]

Adoption. I used the analogy in a sermon I gave to some young people at a retreat. A young man came to me after the closing song and said, "Thanks for the talk. But when you spoke about being God's children through adoption you never really mentioned much about what it feels like to be chosen." He was right. I missed it entirely. "I'm adopted," he continued, "and for me the best thing about being adopted is that, although my biological parents wouldn't keep me, someone did choose me. Do you understand how important it is to really experience what it is like to be chosen?" I didn't, but that night Neal helped me.

I went to the Scriptures and found this:

"For he chose us in him before the creation of the world to be holy and blameless in his sight. In love he predestined us to be adopted as his sons through Jesus Christ, in accordance with his pleasure and will—to the praise of his glorious grace, which he has freely given us in the One he loves" (Ephesians 1:4-6).

Chosen. In our sinful, fallen world, Christ uses adoption to describe our entrance into a new life in His family. He chose you. Christ declared:

"You did not choose me, but I chose you and appointed you to go and bear fruit—fruit that will last. Then the Father will give you whatever you ask in my name" (John 15:16).

Christ "chose us" before we even dreamed of choosing Him. But notice that we show our acceptance of this grace by "receiving" and "believing." John describes this experience in the context of John the Baptist inviting people to respond to the Savior by being born into the family of God. Talk with your partner about the significance of "believing and receiving" and also the "right to be called children of God."

> The passage to focus on in this selection is "to all who received him, to those who believed in his name, he gave the right to become children of God—children born not of natural descent, nor of human decision or a husband's will, but born of God." This describes the rights we now have as full-fledged children by believing and receiving Christ.

Life of Christ

John 1:10-13

"He was in the world, and though the world was made through him, the world did not recognize him. He came to that which was his own, but his own did not receive him. Yet to all who received him, to those who believed in his name, he gave the right to become children of God—children born not of natural descent, nor of human decision or a husband's will, but born of God."

As you consider your own baptism, how does the idea of adoption and entering into a new family shape the way you think of baptism?

> Have the students read the statement below that summarizes what the Seventh-day Adventist Church believes about baptism. Then have them read each verse and write what they think it means as they chain-reference the verses in their Bibles.

We Believe

Baptism

"By baptism we confess our faith in the death and resurrection of Jesus Christ, and testify of our death to sin and of our purpose to walk in newness of life. Thus we acknowledge Christ as Lord and Saviour, and become His people, and are received as members by His church. Baptism is a symbol of our union with Christ, the forgiveness of our sins, and our reception of the Holy Spirit. It is by immersion in water and is contingent on an affirmation of faith in Jesus and evidence of repentance of sin. It follows instruction in the Holy Scriptures and acceptance of their teachings."[9]

    a. Romans 6:1-6

    b. Acts 2:38

    c. Acts 16:30-33

    d. Acts 22:16

    e. Colossians 2:12, 13

    f. Matthew 28:19, 20

    g. 1 Corinthians 12:13

What is your own statement of belief about baptism?

Way to Pray

Read the prayer that Jesus offers to His Father in John 17. Think about what Christ asked for as He prayed for Himself, His disciples, and for everyone who would become His disciples over time. You are one of those He prayed for 2,000 years ago. Talk to Christ in prayer about His prayer for you and consider asking for some of the same things He prayed for you as you pray this week.

More Than Words

Decide how you want your baptism to be memorable. Plan the event in such a way that it will be a meaningful statement to God and other believers about your decision: What are some things you want to happen, to be said, and to be experienced during this time?

Interview: Invite someone to share with you the significance of their baptism.

What motivated them to make the decision to be baptized?

What happened at their baptism that they will never forget?

How do they remind themselves of the meaning of their baptism?

In the Mirror

Part of baptism is entry into a church family. How do you see yourself becoming a part of the family? What do you want to do to serve as a member of God's family in your church? What will you bring to the church family that you think might be helpful to its mission?

Lesson 6
Creation

Before you begin the study on Creation, have the students ask their partners which part of the studies has been most helpful for them.

Objective: Students will discuss the significance of Christ as the Creator and embrace His re-creative work in their lives.

The *ChristWise* lessons seek to draw every believer into a deep and abiding relationship with Jesus and His church. Creation is a powerful part of that goal because Jesus Christ, the Son of God, is personally responsible for Creation. What too often seems to get lost in discussions of Creation is its crowning work—people. I'm all for beautiful beaches and mountain surprises, but God's heart leaped as the human heart beat for the very first time. Why? It seems mysterious to us, but I think the answer is hidden in the meaning of the phrase "Created in His image." What do you think that means? Take time to answer this question when it comes up.

Opening Story

Lost in the preschool's maze of proudly displayed construction paper portraits, I scanned the room for my son's creative handiwork. The pictures lining the walls were great. Their jagged lines and shocking colors spoke of passion and individual tonal integrity. Or something like that—I'm not exactly what you'd call an art expert. I am, however, an expert at spotting my son's work. The trademark of his artistic brilliance is a simple sticker added to the pictures that he draws and colors. No artistic endeavor is complete without one. It may be a flower, bug, or bear, but that crowning touch is inevitable—"The Sticker."

Quickly I recognized the picture that had to be my son's. In the top left-hand corner of an unidentifiable watercolor creation was a small black-and-red ladybug sticker. "Do you see mine, Daddy?" he asked eagerly.

With the pride of Van Gogh's dad I replied, "Of course I do. What a beautiful sticker!"

With nonchalant confidence my son replied, "I know."

Enhancing the beauty of God's creation is the signature mark of His handiwork, the pride of His creative masterpiece—a man and a woman. They have names, faces, and identities—just as you and I do. Humanity stands out like a vibrant sticker on an already beautiful creation, signaling God's proudest thoughts: *This is Mine, and this is good.* What a creation! What a Creator! Look at the story:

"So God created man in his own image, in the image of God he created him; male and female he created them" (Genesis 1:27).

"This is the written account of Adam's line. When God created man, he made him in the likeness of God. He created them male and female and blessed them. And when they were created, he called them 'man'" (Genesis 5:1, 2).

Why are people such a vital part of creation? The Creator makes man and woman in His image—in His likeness. We are the sticker on His creation. Forget for a moment what we may be like today. Picture God's face (if you can) full of pride when He made Adam and Eve and thought it was *really* good. Who is this God who creates creatures in His image—like Him?

"For he has rescued us from the dominion of darkness and brought us into the kingdom of the Son he loves, in whom we have redemption, the forgiveness of sins. He is the image of the invisible God, the firstborn over all creation. For by him all things were created: things in heaven and on earth, visible and invisible, whether thrones or powers or rulers or authorities; all things were created by him and for him" (Colossians 1:13-16).

Did you see it? Look at another verse:

"In the past God spoke to our forefathers through the prophets at many times and in various ways, but in these last days he has spoken to us by his Son, whom he appointed heir of all things, and through whom he made the universe" (Hebrews 1:1, 2).

The Creator, the one who stamps the world with a picture of Him in the form of humanity, is the Son, Jesus Christ. As wonderful as the reality of God's creative work is, even more so is the reality of His commitment to restore His precious creatures (us) to life, as He becomes one of us.

> The phrase to focus on in the **Life of Christ** is "Without him, nothing was made that has been made." While John's language is philosophical, the fact that Jesus is the active agent at Creation amplifies His commitment to the human race. The Creator becomes one of His own creation.

Life of Christ

John 1:1-14

"In the beginning was the Word, and the Word was with God, and the Word was God.

He was with God in the beginning. Through him all things were made; without him nothing was made that has been made. In him was life, and that life was the light of men. . . . The Word became flesh and made his dwelling among us. We have seen his glory, the glory of the One and Only, who came from the Father, full of grace and truth."

We live in a world that often makes it difficult to see the beauty of the Creator and His creation. Some argue that there is no Creator, that only chance began the existence of life on earth millions of years ago. But those who believe the Bible's account of our beginnings stand in awe of the Creator, asking, "Who is the amazing God who called this world to be by His own breath?"

Open Questions

What do you think it means to be "made in the image of God"? What glimpses of God can you still see in others?

> Have the students read the statement below that summarizes what the Seventh-day Adventist Church believes about Creation. Then have them read each verse and write what they think it means as they chain-reference the verses in their Bibles.
>
> As they chain-reference the Creation stories in Genesis 1 and 2, they might want to highlight or underline the key phrases instead of the entire first two chapters of Genesis. It is much easier to see the outline of Creation week if they just highlight the parts that describe either what was created or the day it was created on.

We Believe

Creation

"God is Creator of all things, and has revealed in Scripture the authentic account of His creative activity. In six days the Lord made 'the heaven and the earth' and all living things upon the earth, and rested on the seventh day of that first week. Thus He established the Sabbath as a perpetual memorial of His completed creative work. The first man and woman were made in the image of God as the crowning work of Creation, given dominion over the world, and charged with responsibility to care for it. When the world was finished it was 'very good,' declaring the glory of God." [10]

a. Genesis 1
b. Genesis 2
c. Exodus 20:8-11

d. Psalm 19:1-6
e. Psalm 33:6, 9
f. Psalm 104
g. Hebrews 11:3

I Believe

Write your own statement of belief about the glory of Creation. You may choose to focus on the beauty, uniqueness, and meaning of this event, or you may decide to write about your beliefs in light of the current ideas about evolution.

Way to Pray

In your prayers to God this week, converse with Him about the Creation event. You may want to read about it in Genesis 1 and meditate and talk to God about what happened each day of Creation. Ultimately, in light of the wonder of God's creative power, practice praising God this week for His creative ability.

More Than Words

God's creative genius reveals itself in a variety of ways. How can you demonstrate God's glory in the natural world or in the way you personally live your life as the crowning work of Creation? Think of some tangible ways to do this.

Interview: Ask someone:

What place on earth reminds you most of God's creative power and why? What experience or event in your life causes you to think of Creation? Have you ever had a conversation with someone who does not believe in God as the Creator? Describe the conversation and what you talked about.

In the Mirror

Write some of your thoughts down as you reflect on our world's creation, especially God's crowning event of making people. How do we glorify God with our lives today as His sticker on Creation? The first of the three angels' messages in Revelation speaks of worshiping the Creator. Reflect on this passage and write your thoughts and perspective.

Revelation 14:7

"He said in a loud voice, 'Fear God and give him glory, because the hour of his judgment has come. Worship him who made the heavens, the earth, the sea and the springs of water.'"

Lesson 7
The Law of God

As you begin the study on God's law, have the students discuss the interview they had this week and any insights they gained or thought were helpful.

Objective: Students will discover the primary principle of God's government (love) and determine how the rules of God's kingdom work.

The opening illustration connects the legal language and the attitudes of "in-laws." But such a relationship is doomed from the start if the only connection is a legal one.

Opening Story

I've heard all the jokes, especially in the setting of weddings, about the dreaded "in-laws." In-laws are people you become family to through the act of marrying one of their family members. (That's my personal definition.) So when I married Julie, Julie's mother became my "mother-in-law." While it's not a hard concept to get, I don't like the term *in-law*. While many may have uncomfortable or awkward feelings about their "in-laws," I happen to love my "in-laws" so much that I don't even use the term *law* to describe the relationship. Love describes my relationship to Julie—and her family. I don't love them just because I'm legally attached to them. I'm proud to be associated with them because of who they are as persons. It would stifle the relationship if it were solely a legal association. Two points are important in the in-law relationship: (1) the marriage—obviously vital, and (2) the new family mentality. Now I belong to a bigger group who love the same people I do.

Look at the way Scripture uses the analogy of marriage to describe the way we relate to God:

"As a young man marries a maiden, so will your sons marry you; as a bridegroom rejoices over his bride, so will your God rejoice over you" (Isaiah 62:5).

Love pours out of this analogy. We glimpse how God feels about us, His children. In Jeremiah He recalls the obedience of the children of Israel with the same attitude of deep devotion and marital bliss:

"Go and proclaim in the hearing of Jerusalem: 'I remember the devotion of your youth, how as a bride you loved me and followed me through the desert, through a land not sown'" (Jeremiah 2:2).

As you study the law of God, watch Jesus as He tries to show that the motivation, the basis of the law, is a response of total love and devotion. It's not a list of rules to manage your life, but merely the expression of the way we honor the ones we love. As we approach life in God's family it is not with an attitude of being an "in-law," but one who is "in-love" with the Father.

According to Scripture, "the Law" was more than the Ten Commandments. It was the first five books of Moses, the prophets, the Psalms, the whole Old Testament, as we know it, as well as an oral tradition.

Look at the scene in the passage below and share your insights about how God wants us to relate to the law and how to make it meaningful and practical.

> The phrase to focus on in this section of the **Life of Christ** is "Love the Lord your God with all your heart and with all your soul and with all your mind." Love is the legal word.

Life of Christ

Matthew 22:34-40

"Hearing that Jesus had silenced the Sadducees, the Pharisees got together. One of them, an expert in the law, tested him with this question: 'Teacher, which is the greatest commandment in the Law?' Jesus replied: '"Love the Lord your God with all your heart and with all your soul and with all your mind." This is the first and greatest commandment. And the second is like it: "Love your neighbor as yourself." All the Law and the Prophets hang on these two commandments.'"

Many people today ignore God's Ten Commandments as outdated rules that really don't apply anymore. As you read the Ten Commandments, ask yourself, "What would this world be like if we shelved the Ten Commandments?" How close do you think we are to that moment? Do you think we will ever get there? If so, what will take the place of God's law?

> One of the misunderstandings others have had about Adventism is that we teach legalism. The Adventist Church may have legalists and people who practice legalism, but what it teaches about the relationship between the law and grace is clear, biblical, and meaningful to believers.
>
> Have the students read the statement below that summarizes what the Seventh-day Adventist Church believes about God's law. Then have them read each verse and write what they think it means as they chain-reference the verses in their Bibles.

We Believe

The Law of God

"The great principles of God's law are embodied in the Ten Commandments and exemplified in the life of Christ. They express God's love, will, and purposes concerning human conduct and relationships and are binding upon all people in every age. These precepts are the basis of God's covenant with His people and the standard in God's judgment. Through the agency of the Holy Spirit they point out sin and awaken a sense of need for a Saviour. Salvation is all of grace and not of works, but its fruitage is obedience to the Commandments. This obedience develops Christian character and results in a sense of well-being. It is an evidence of our love for the Lord and our concern for our fellow men. The obedience of faith demonstrates the power of Christ to transform lives, and therefore strengthens Christian witness."[11] (Chain-reference the following verses and paraphrase them in your own words.)

a. Exodus 20:1-17
b. Psalm 40:7, 8
c. Matthew 22:36-40
d. Deuteronomy 28:1-14
e. Matthew 5:17-20
f. John 15:7-10
g. 1 John 5:3
h. Psalm 19:7-14

In your own words, how do you think the law relates to those who are saved by God's grace and enter into His family?

Way to Pray

As you pray, consider how keeping God's law would change your life today. If you were to decide to keep His commandments, what would you need to do? What would you need to stop doing?

Write a prayer to God about the commitments you will have to make with each commandment and how it will make your life better. Each day choose a different commandment to reflect and pray about.

More Than Words

Interview: Invite someone to share a response to the following interview questions:

How do you explain the balance between being saved by God's grace and being obedient to God's law?

How does keeping the Ten Commandments affect the quality of your daily life?

Which commandment do you think would change the world most significantly if everyone were to be convicted of it and start keeping it?

Character Search

Try to get to know someone this week you didn't really know very well before. Ask questions that will get at the heart of who they really are, such as "What do you really enjoy doing?" "What do you want to become?" As you get to know that certain individual, think about how you might begin to know God more fully.

Make a list of some things you want to know about God's character, who He is and what He is like. Read and reflect on Philip's famous plea, "Show us the Father" (John 14:6-10).

In the Mirror

How has this study helped you see God's character more clearly? In what ways does God's law reveal what He is like?

Lesson 8
The Sabbath

Have the students continue to share the insights they discovered from their interviews or the other exercises they participated in last week.

Objective: Students will explore the beauty and promise that exist in keeping the Sabbath as a permanent reminder of God's claim on humanity.

The **Open/Values Question** will enable you to focus on the aspect of the Sabbath that you feel needs emphasis. For instance, you can focus the study on clarifying when, how, or why Sabbath should be kept.

Open Questions

Rank in order of importance to you (1—most important, 5—least important)
The Sabbath is primarily about:

___ Serving others in love

___ Resting from physical work

___ Worshiping together with other believers

___ Being with family

___ Stopping normal activities to commune personally with God

Opening Story

It is a well-known fact that students do not all learn the same way. Some learn visually, some through music, and others by active use of their hands. This day turned out to be one of those moments in college classrooms in which everyone learned, especially the teacher.

The class consisted almost exclusively of college freshmen, taking a course on the life and ministry of Christ. As the teacher, I had devised a variety of ways to engage them in an active discovery of gospel themes. Still, I could never—not in a million years—have devised a lesson plan so powerful that every student would leave the room a different person.

It was Veterans Day. Usually I would plan a discussion in which students could say something to affirm the veterans in their life. But I had forgotten entirely about the holiday. What is even more difficult to imagine is that the only student who was not a freshman had served in Vietnam. John's papers, describing some of the horror of war in the jungles—friends killed, villages decimated—thoughtfully wove the beautiful truths of the Savior into his traumatic experience. He shared his overwhelming shock and anger as he returned home, only to be mistreated by the country he had risked his life to protect. How could I have missed it this day?

I realized it in the first few minutes of class. As the students took a quiz, I glanced at the calendar—Veterans Day. By the time they turned in their papers I thought I could salvage the moment. "How many of you knew when you came to class that it was Veterans Day?" I asked. They looked at me with blank stares. John quietly stared at his desk, not wishing to look up.

"That's right; other colleges don't have to come to class today!" one student observed.

Another student chimed in, "I know, this college is constantly robbing us of legitimate days off." The others murmured in agreement, and the air became alive with the hope that I would dismiss class. By now I wanted to crawl under the desk.

"We need a day off."

"I have so much to study for."

"It is a national holiday, right—like Labor Day?"

"We should be camping."

I glanced at John as the students stared at me. His face was red, with either embarrassment or anger—I could not tell. The classroom grew quiet. The gravity of the moment began to dawn on several students as they recalled the first day of class when we had all introduced ourselves. John had mentioned that he was in college on a scholarship from his service in the Marines.

Realizing that I couldn't avoid the tension or dismiss it, I took responsibility for my part in forgetting this day. Apologizing personally to John, I mentioned to the rest of the class that he had served in Vietnam. One thoughtful student on the front row asked him in a quiet voice, "What was it like?"

Never had anyone in my class asked a question that demanded everyone's attention like that one. John, although quite embarrassed, mentioned briefly the more rudimentary details of war in Vietnam—the weather, the people, the terrain, and the conditions. The class was quiet again. "Did you lose any friends in battle?" someone said. The questions and answers continued for the rest of the period. At the end of class everyone gave a spontaneous round of applause for John. Veterans Day had become what it was meant to be.

The Sabbath had lost its beauty and honor for many in the time of Christ. Rules and stipulations hid its intended purpose. Here again we see Jesus seeking to shake people from their unthinking religion and awaken an experience that demonstrates God's grace and His mighty power in the lives of His created beings.

> The passage to focus on appears at the end of the story where Jesus blisters the Pharisees for their hypocrisy by saying, "Doesn't each of you on the Sabbath untie his ox or donkey from the stall and lead it out to give it water? Then should not this woman, a daughter of Abraham, whom Satan has kept bound for eighteen long years, be set free on the Sabbath day from what bound her?" Don't miss the target of Sabbath's significance—the woman. Sabbath is about her and her Creator. The very heart of Sabbath observance must have more to do with people than with anything else.

Life of Christ

Luke 13:10-16

"On a Sabbath Jesus was teaching in one of the synagogues, and a woman was there who had been crippled by a spirit for eighteen years. She was bent over and could not straighten up at all. When Jesus saw her, he called her forward and said to her, 'Woman, you are set free from your infirmity.' Then he put his hands on her, and immediately she straightened up and praised God. Indignant because Jesus had healed on the Sabbath, the synagogue ruler said to the people, 'There are six days for work. So come and be healed on those days, not on the Sabbath.' The Lord answered him, 'You hypocrites! Doesn't each of you on the Sabbath untie his ox or donkey from the stall and lead it out to give it water? Then should not this woman, a daughter of Abraham, whom Satan has kept bound for eighteen long years, be set free on the Sabbath day from what bound her?'"

As you study the truth of the seventh-day Sabbath, consider some of the following questions:

What is the purpose of the Sabbath?

How did Jesus model Sabbathkeeping?

How can we honor God by our time on the seventh day of the week?

> Have the students read the statement below that summarizes what the Seventh-day Adventist Church believes about the Sabbath. Then have them read each verse and write what they think it means as they chain-reference the verses in their Bibles.
> We have all heard many reasons for keeping the first day of the week holy instead of the Jewish Sabbath. I remember reading a commentary on Genesis that claimed God rested on the seventh day, but that He did not command everyone else to do

this. For many denominations, there is simply too much at stake to even imagine observing the seventh-day Sabbath.

We Believe

The Sabbath

"The beneficent Creator, after the six days of Creation, rested on the seventh day and instituted the Sabbath for all people as a memorial of Creation. The fourth commandment of God's unchangeable law requires the observance of this seventh-day Sabbath as the day of rest, worship, and ministry in harmony with the teaching and practice of Jesus, the Lord of the Sabbath. The Sabbath is a day of delightful communion with God and one another. It is a symbol of our redemption in Christ, a sign of our sanctification, a token of our allegiance, and a foretaste of our eternal future in God's kingdom. The Sabbath is God's perpetual sign of His eternal covenant between Him and His people. Joyful observance of this holy time from evening to evening, sunset to sunset, is a celebration of God's creative and redemptive acts."[12] (Chain-reference these verses in your Bible and be sure to mark or write notes about them that have particular meaning or raise questions you would like to talk about.)

a. Genesis 2:1-3
b. Exodus 20:8-11
c. Deuteronomy 5:12-15
d. Exodus 31:13-17
e. Luke 4:16
f. Ezekiel 20:12, 20
g. Matthew 12:1-12
h. Isaiah 58:13, 14
i. Isaiah 56:5, 6

Way to Pray

Talk to God about what you really love about the Sabbath day as well as what frustrates or confuses you.

More Than Words

Interview: Invite someone to share with you their perspective on the Sabbath experience. Ask them:

Describe the most meaningful Sabbath you have ever had.

What is the main reason you keep the Sabbath? How does it shape your relationship with God?

On what principles or criteria do you make choices about what to do on the Sabbath day?

As you finish this study, you may want to look at the passages from the life of Christ and plan your next Sabbath after the pattern of how He kept it. Do it with other believers who have the same desire to remember who God is and why He wants us to pause to remember His creation. (Write out the things you want to do and share them with your partner and friends.)

In the Mirror

Reflect on the following statement: "Keeping the Bible Sabbath can be an invasion into your life." How does the Sabbath intrude on our way of living?

Reflect on how the Sabbath can reorient your priorities, relationships, and spiritual experience.

What is going to change about your life now that you understand the purpose of Sabbath and the joy that awaits you?

Lesson 9
The Life, Death, and
Resurrection of Christ

Before you begin the next study, have the students share the major insights and ideas they have gained from their interviews.

Objective: Students will immerse themselves in stories that depict the significance of Christ's life, death, and resurrection, and then they will have to determine how they will respond to the claims of Christ.

Opening Story

"During hard times in the darkness of winter in an Alaskan Eskimo village a young man of unequaled courage might go out into the bitter cold in search of food for his people. Armed only with a pointed stick and his compassion for his starving village, he would wander, anticipating the attack of a polar bear. Having no natural fear of humans, a polar bear will stalk and eat a man. In the attack the Eskimo hunter would wave his hands and spear to anger the bear and make him rise up on his hind legs to over ten feet in height; and then, with the spear braced on his foot, the hunter would aim for the heart as the weight of the bear came down upon his spear. With the heart pierced, the bear might live long enough to maim or kill this noble hunter. Loving family and friends would then follow his tracks out of the village and find food for their survival and evidence of profound courage." [13]

The illustration wonderfully describes courage, commitment to family and friends, and willingness to lay down one's life for loved ones. But such analogies have problems.

One involves the fact that the bold hunter risks his life for the survival of his loved ones. The problem? I know a lot of godless people who would risk their lives for their family, especially their children. No question—I would. If it came down to me or my sandy-haired boy with that disarming grin, I'd give my life for him. I'm certain that even those who claim to be skeptics or atheists would as well. The Eskimo does what anyone would do for the ones they love. Wouldn't you? The difference is that Christ faced the bear (so to speak) for everyone—anyone. Whether they returned His love or not. Romans 5:8 says that "while we were still sinners, Christ died for us." That is, while we were His enemies: hateful, rebellious, indifferent, ungrateful, inconsistent, unpopular, psychotic, sexually perverted, insane, undeserving. The truth is that while I would unquestioningly lay down my life for my son, I doubt I would die for my enemy. But Jesus did.

The other problem raised in this illustration is the notion that the brave Eskimo may or may not live. There was a chance he would survive, perhaps with a few scars or even the loss of a limb. We take risks all the time. But when Christ became a baby, He became destined for death—death on a cross. He had no other choice, no other way that He could save you and me. In Gethsemane it was clear to Jesus that the Father's will was the way of the cross. He would, in fact, experience an ugly separation from His Father. The Holy God would regard Him as sinful so that you and I might be "the righteousness of God." It was a sure thing. He would die. And it would be terrible.

One final problem concerns those in the igloo—that's us. You and I would follow the footsteps of the brave Eskimo into the unknown because it might mean our survival. Unfortunately, many stay in the igloo and never make the journey to Calvary to receive the saving grace that comes from the sacrificed Son. We think we can survive the winter on our own. It's too cold out there to leave the igloo. We don't have the right shoes or are too busy decorating the inside of the igloo. It's crazy, I know. But that's who we are.

C. S. Lewis made an interesting point when he wrote, "A man who was merely a man and said the sort of things Jesus said wouldn't be a great moral teacher. He'd either be a lunatic—on the level with a man who says he's a poached egg—or else he'd be the devil of hell. You must make your choice. Either this man was, and is, the Son of God, or else a madman or something worse." [14]

Only rarely did Jesus ever mention why He came. But in each conversation we catch a glimpse of God's purpose in sending His Son into the world. Notice what He said about Himself and reflect on each statement as to what His mission means to you as you surrender all of yourself to Him.

> As the students read the following sections from the **Life of Christ** section, have them highlight or underline the phrase that demonstrates the mission and purpose of Christ's life.

Life of Christ

Matthew 9:11-13

"When the Pharisees saw this, they asked his disciples, 'Why does your teacher eat with tax collectors and "sinners"?' On hearing this, Jesus said, 'It is not the healthy who need a doctor, but the sick. But go and learn what this means: "I desire mercy, not sacrifice." For I have not come to call the righteous, but sinners.'"

Matthew 20:20-28

"Then the mother of Zebedee's sons came to Jesus with her sons and, kneeling down, asked a favor of him. 'What is it you want?' he asked. She said, 'Grant that one of these two sons of mine may sit at your right and the other at your left in your kingdom.' 'You don't know what you are asking,' Jesus said to them. 'Can you drink the cup I am going to drink?' 'We can,' they answered. Jesus said to them, 'You will indeed drink from my cup, but to sit at my right or left is not for me to grant. These places belong to those for whom they have been prepared by my Father.' When the ten heard about this, they were indignant with the two brothers. Jesus called them together and said, 'You know that the rulers of the Gentiles lord it over them, and their high officials exercise authority over them. Not so with you. Instead, whoever wants to become great among you must be your servant, and whoever wants to be first must be your slave—just as the Son of Man did not come to be served, but to serve, and to give his life as a ransom for many.'"

Luke 19:5-10

"When Jesus reached the spot, he looked up and said to him, 'Zacchaeus, come down immediately. I must stay at your house today.' So he came down at once and welcomed him gladly. All the people saw this and began to mutter, 'He has gone to be the guest of a "sinner."' But Zacchaeus stood up and said to the Lord, 'Look, Lord! Here and now I give half of my possessions to the poor, and if I have cheated anybody out of anything, I will pay back four times the amount.' Jesus said to him, 'Today salvation has come to this house, because this man, too, is a son of Abraham. For the Son of Man came to seek and to save what was lost.'"

Matthew 5:17, 18

"Do not think that I have come to abolish the Law or the Prophets; I have not come to abolish them but to fulfill them. I tell you the truth, until heaven and earth disappear, not the smallest letter, not the least stroke of a pen, will by any means disappear from the Law until everything is accomplished."

Have the students read the statement below that summarizes what the Seventh-day Adventist Church believes about the life, death, and resurrection of Christ. Then have them read each verse and write what they think it means as they chain-reference the verses in their Bibles.

Consider this quote from *The Desire of Ages:* "It would be well for us to spend a thoughtful hour each day in contemplation of the **Life of Christ**. We should take it point by point, and let the imagination grasp each scene, especially the closing ones. As we thus dwell upon His great sacrifice for us, our confidence in Him will be more constant, our love will be quickened, and we shall be more deeply imbued with His spirit. If we would be saved at last, we must learn the lesson of penitence and humiliation at the foot of the cross" (p. 83).

Ask the students what they think would change about their day if it were to start this way. Be specific.

We Believe

The Life, Death, and Resurrection of Christ

"In Christ's life of perfect obedience to God's will, His suffering, death, and resurrection, God provided the only means of atonement for human sin, so that those who by faith accept this atonement may have eternal life, and the whole creation may better understand the infinite and holy love of the Creator. This perfect atonement vindicates the righteousness of God's law and the graciousness of His character; for it both condemns our sin and provides for our forgiveness. The death of Christ is substitutionary and expiatory, reconciling and transforming. The resurrection of Christ proclaims God's triumph over the forces of evil, and for those who accept the atonement assures their final victory over sin and death. It declares the Lordship of Jesus Christ, before whom every knee in heaven and on earth will bow."[15]

(Chain-reference the following passages in your Bible and comment on what each says to you about where you are at in your life today.)

    a. John 3:16
    b. Isaiah 53
    c. 1 Peter 2:21, 22
    d. 1 John 2:2; 4:10
    e. Colossians 2:15
    f. Philippians 2:6-11

Way to Pray

Imagine the final moments of Christ's life on Calvary. As you picture the scene, hear the voices, feel the hatred in the air. After you meditate on the cross, say to God whatever you feel you need to tell Him. If God were to speak to you in the light of Calvary, what do you think He would say about your life right now?

More Than Words

Interview: Ask someone you know to be spiritually thoughtful to respond to the following interview questions:

If you had only three stories or events to share from the life of Christ, which ones would you choose and why?

What do you think is the most important saying in the four Gospels?

Share an experience, story, or event from your life during which the life of Christ was especially meaningful to you. (Give them time for this question.)

In the Bible we find essential stories and sayings that make the message of Scripture real and life-changing for us. What moments in your life (choose three) have been pivotal?

In the Mirror

How has the study of the life and mission of Jesus been helpful to you? What do you wish you knew more about?

Lesson 10
The Lord's Supper

Before you continue to the lesson on the Lord's Supper, have the students take a few moments to reflect on and share last week's exercises.

Objective: Students will understand the importance of symbols that remind them of and renew their faith as well as discover the sacred joy that believers can experience as they celebrate grace with others.

Sadly, many churches report that attendance is low on those Sabbaths they celebrate the Lord's Supper. Why do you think people tend to avoid Communion Sabbath?

Opening Story

The collision was unavoidable. I was hurtling around a blind turn, and Karen, heading right toward me, was neither looking for nor expecting me to come racing around the corner. We were short of deacons on this particular Sabbath, so I was sprinting around the outside of the church, hands tightly gripping the silver tray of small grape juice goblets and thumb-sized pieces of bread I held in front of me. Even as we ran into each other I was thinking, *I hope nobody comes around this corner because if they'd . . . Crash!* Grape juice went everywhere as the toothpaste-cap-sized goblets tumbled to the ground. Karen had spatters of grape juice on her plain yellow dress. I was the last person she wanted to, or had expected to, run into—literally.

"I'm sorry!" she cried. "I guess you are wondering why I'm leaving."

"Well, actually, I'm just kind of wet right now, so I hadn't had much time to think about where you were headed. Are you leaving because it's Communion Sabbath?" (If she was, boy, I'd have given it to her.)

She nodded. "I didn't know it was today, and lately . . . I just . . . well . . . I just don't think I should take Communion right now."

I picked up the goblets and the bread and put them back in the tray. "Would you mind telling why you feel as though you shouldn't participate?"

She looked away. "I just haven't been very close to God lately, and I don't think I deserve to do this."

I thought about what she said for a moment. "Karen, I want you to know that when you are far away from God is when you are most ready for Communion. Communion is not for those who are ready; it is for those who are aware of their sinfulness and want to remember God's work of grace on Calvary for them. When you feel far away is when you need this the most. We all forget the significance of Christ's sacrifice, so we do this to remember, not to show how ready we are.

"Plus, if you don't participate in the Communion service, your pastor will chase you down and baptize you in grape juice until you straighten up!" I said with a crooked smile. She looked up and laughed. We walked back into the church, and she sat down while I went to the kitchen to get more juice.

During the testimony time in the little church Karen stood and told the congregation about her collision. "I felt like staying away. I think that what Satan wants more than anything else is to get us to leave when God's hope is that we draw closer."

The incident reminded all of us that day of God's amazing grace. "Do this to remember Me," Jesus said. "Remember Me." Sometimes we remain away from moments of remembrance because it is awkward. Other times our hesitation involves our strong awareness of sin. You couldn't run into (except perhaps in Karen's case) a better opportunity to receive grace. Communion is really only for those who know they need it.

What do you use to remind yourself of important things in your life? A list? A string around your index finger? In our fast-paced world it is so easy to forget even the most significant things. God intended the Lord's Supper to be an active reminder (much as the Sabbath is a reminder of God as our Creator) that Christ is our Redeemer and Lord. Read the following verses and notice how this supper is more than just a "last meal."

> The phrase to focus on in the study of the Lord's Supper is embedded in the heart of the service: "This is my blood of the covenant, which is poured out for many." For many? While the attendees were only a few, the experience of celebrating the Lord's Supper became one of the major characteristics of the church. Ask the students how they think a church could enrich or deepen the meaning of the service.

Life of Christ

Mark 14:17-26

"When evening came, Jesus arrived with the Twelve. While they were reclining at the table eating, he said, 'I tell you the truth, one of you will betray me—one who is eating with me.' They were saddened, and one by one they said to him, 'Surely not I?' 'It is one of the Twelve,' he replied, 'one who dips bread into the bowl with me. The Son of Man will go just as it is written about him. But woe to that man who betrays the Son of Man! It would be better for him if he had not been born.' While they were eating, Jesus took bread, gave thanks and broke it, and gave it to his disciples, saying, 'Take it; this is my body.' Then he took the cup, gave thanks and offered it to them, and they all drank from it. 'This is my blood of the covenant, which is poured out for many,' he said to them. 'I tell you the truth, I will not drink again of the fruit of the vine until that day when I drink it anew in the kingdom of God.' When they had sung a hymn, they went out to the Mount of Olives."

Luke 24:30, 31

"When he was at the table with them, he took bread, gave thanks, broke it and began to give it to them. Then their eyes were opened and they recognized him, and he disappeared from their sight."

> Have the students read the statement below that summarizes what the Seventh-day Adventist Church believes about the Lord's Supper. Then have them read each verse

and write what they think it means as they chain-reference the verses in their Bibles.

When believers participate in the Lord's Supper it is a hopeful celebration of the second coming of Christ as well. Jesus promised that He would not drink that fruit of the vine again until we were together in the kingdom. As they study the passages that describe the significance of the Lord's Supper, encourage the students to make a decisive commitment to share in this gift of remembrance.

We Believe

The Lord's Supper

"The Lord's Supper is a participation in the emblems of the body and blood of Jesus as an expression of faith in Him, our Lord and Saviour. In this experience of Communion Christ is present to meet and strengthen His people. As we partake, we joyfully proclaim the Lord's death until He comes again. Preparation for the Supper includes self-examination, repentance, and confession. The Master ordained the service of foot washing to signify renewed cleansing, to express a willingness to serve one another in Christlike humility, and to unite our hearts in love. The Communion service is open to all believing Christians."[16]

  a. 1 Corinthians 10:16, 17; 11:23-30
  b. Matthew 26:17-30
  c. Revelation 3:20
  d. John 6:48-63
  e. John 13:1-17

Way to Pray

Write a prayer to God focusing on what you remember most about Calvary and the sacrifice Christ paid for you there. Invite God to remind you in other ways about your relationship with Him.

More Than Words

Have a Communion service or participate in a memorial supper for the Lord's death. Do this with friends or your partner in this study. Reflect on the moments of Calvary and then plan the event.

Interview: Invite someone to share with you their responses to the following questions: Share with me your most memorable Communion service. Why was it so special?

How can a person experience the real significance of the Communion service and make it as meaningful as possible?

How is foot washing an important part of the Communion experience?

In the Mirror

Reflect on the parts of your relationship with God that you tend to forget about and write about some ideas you might have to remember God's work of grace in your life.

Lesson 11
Spiritual Gifts

As you begin this lesson have a special prayer that God will guide your time together.

Objective: Students will seek to interact with God about their spiritual gifts and their identity and purpose as Christians as they learn to serve God by His Spirit.

In a way, the topic of spiritual gifts can be one of the most important studies a young person can undertake. Not because the doctrine is superior, but because the need in the Adventist Church for workers is great. Roger Dudley's 10-year study to determine why Adventist youth were leaving the church discovered that about 50 percent departed by their mid-20s. Why? It has very little to do with the teachings of the church and everything with doing the work of Christ. Tell the students that whatever they do, they must follow through with discovering the gifts God has given them to spread the gospel. The body. Unity. Parts. Equality. Build. The words are all part of a powerful metaphor for church life.

Opening Story

Every time I make a major purchase I do two things: (1) buy an extended service warranty and (2) pray. I pray because if whatever I buy breaks, I don't have a mechanical bone in my body to fix it. I remember working with my dad on the car. When he asked me to hand him a Phillips screwdriver, I left the garage and made my way to Phillip's house (he lived about six houses down) to borrow his screwdriver. I had no idea why his was so special, but I just did what my father requested. Returning with Phillip's screwdriver, I handed it to my dad. "Here you go," I announced proudly.

"Where have you been?" he said as he popped his head out from under the car.

"Getting Phillip's screwdriver for you!" With a smile he then proceeded to show me the difference between a Phillips screwdriver and a regular one. While I now know the difference between a Phillips screwdriver and Phillip's screwdriver, I'm still not good at using either.

Some people are wired for certain tasks. God created us with different abilities. Some we learn and develop over time, while others are inherent in our makeup. I can force myself to learn music and play an instrument, but true musicians have music in their makeup. They are passionate about it. Whether you learn a skill or whether you are born with it, the fact remains that God needs you and your abilities. When you surrender yourself to God, you also surrender all of your abilities for the purpose of the mission of the body of Christ.

"Therefore, I urge you, brothers, in view of God's mercy, to offer your bodies as living sacrifices, holy and pleasing to God—this is your spiritual act of worship" (Romans 12:1).

This is what it means to worship God. It is not sitting in church quietly for an hour or two once a week. Worshiping God is giving all of yourself to Him. Look at how Jesus turned His disciples loose to do the work of service for God.

> *Authority.* Notice the words of Christ: "I have given you authority to trample on snakes and scorpions and to overcome all the power of the enemy." While I have no desire to tiptoe through scorpions and snakes, the message is clear: God expects us to work.

Life of Christ

Luke 10:1-20

"After this the Lord appointed seventy-two others and sent them two by two ahead of him to every town and place where he was about to go. He told them, 'The harvest is plentiful, but the workers are few. Ask the Lord of the harvest, therefore, to send out workers into his harvest field. Go! I am sending you out like lambs among wolves. Do not take a purse or bag or sandals; and do not greet anyone on the road. When you enter a house, first say, "Peace to this house." If a man of peace is there, your peace will rest on him; if not, it will return to you. Stay in that house, eating and drinking whatever they give you, for the worker deserves his wages. Do not move around from house to house. When you enter a town and are welcomed, eat what is set before you. Heal the sick who are there and tell them, "The kingdom of God is near you." But when you enter a town and are not welcomed, go into its streets and say, "Even the dust of your town that sticks to our feet we wipe off against you. Yet be sure of this: The kingdom of God is near." I tell you, it will be more bearable on that day for Sodom than for that town. Woe to you, Korazin! Woe to you, Bethsaida! For if the miracles that were performed in you had been performed in Tyre and Sidon, they would have repented long ago, sitting in sackcloth and ashes. But it will be more bearable for Tyre and Sidon at the judgment than for you. And you, Capernaum, will you be lifted up to the skies? No, you will go down to the depths. He who listens to you listens to me; he who rejects you rejects me; but he who rejects me rejects him who sent me.' The seventy-two returned with joy and said, 'Lord, even the demons submit to us in your name.' He replied, 'I saw Satan fall like lightning from heaven. I have given you authority to trample on snakes and scorpions and to overcome all the power of the enemy; nothing will harm you. However, do not rejoice that the spirits submit to you, but rejoice that your names are written in heaven.'"

Christ sent each disciple. I don't know how He paired them up. I'm not sure who went to what place. But Jesus empowered them to work. Each had a role to play. It's the same with us. Every believer has received a gift—a spiritual gift—to use for the purpose of building the kingdom of God on earth. Some have a few gifts, others have many, but each gift is valuable, and the church needs all the gifts if its mission is to succeed.

What is a spiritual gift?

When or how is it given?

How do I discover what God wants me to do?

Have the students read the statement below that summarizes what the Seventh-day Adventist Church believes about the doctrine of spiritual gifts. Then have them read each verse and write what they think it means as they chain-reference the verses in their Bibles.

As they read and mark each verse, they should be thinking of two questions: 1. What is God calling them to do? 2. What would the church look like if it fully embraced this teaching?

We Believe

Spiritual Gifts

"God bestows upon all members of His church in every age spiritual gifts which each member is to employ in loving ministry for the common good of the church and of humanity. Given by the agency of the Holy Spirit, who apportions to each member as He wills, the gifts provide all abilities and ministries needed by the church to fulfill its divinely ordained functions. According to the Scriptures, these gifts include such ministries as faith, healing, prophecy, proclamation, teaching, administration, reconciliation, compassion, and self-sacrificing service and charity for the help and encouragement of people. Some members are called of God and endowed by the Spirit for functions recognized by the church in pastoral, evangelistic, apostolic, and teaching ministries particularly needed to equip the members for service, to build up the church to spiritual maturity, and to foster unity of the faith and knowledge of God. When members employ these spiritual gifts as faithful stewards of God's varied grace, the church is protected from the destructive influence of false doctrine, grows with a growth that is from God, and is built up in faith and love." [17]

a. Romans 12:4-8

b. 1 Corinthians 12:9-11, 27, 28

c. Ephesians 4:8, 11-16

d. Acts 6:1-7

e. 1 Timothy 3:1-13

f. 1 Peter 4:10, 11

Make sure the students fill out the survey together so they can discuss the results. As with any instrument, the provided survey is a human construction. It seeks to get in touch with the students' own self-description, thus providing a basis for further consideration and experimentation. If a student scores high in the area of leadership, it doesn't mean they are scientifically proven leaders. It simply means that leadership is something they should pray about and practice, because God may have gifted them to function as a leader in the church. The only way to know the end result is to become involved. This is true for every other gift.

Have the students go through the instructions at the beginning of the survey so they can assist their partners. They may want to let their parents and the pastor or other church leaders know where they are in the study and briefly describe to them what this lesson is about so that others can be helpful in this process. The goal is to enable the students to sense their calling for ministry in the life of the church. When they have finished the survey and have the results, have them debrief with their partners what they have discovered. Ask them: "Were you surprised by the scores you have? How do you feel about the area(s) that you scored the highest in? Out of the seven gifts this survey has focused on, do you feel that the gift you scored highest on is something you have an interest in? Why/Why not? Are you willing to experiment with some of the different activities in the church to see if this might really be a gift you have?"

Another way to affirm the gifts God gives us is to ask godly people to give us insight and advice. A teacher, a relative, a Sabbath school or Pathfinder leader, or anyone who might know the student well enough can share how they feel God has gifted this particular young person. Questions to ask: "What examples can you share that demonstrate this particular gift (higher scores) in Susie's life? What other gifts (lower scores) would you recommend Susie give some prayer and attention to? Why? What specific activities would you recommend Susie participate in to help her discover her spiritual gifts?"

There is no magical formula other than allowing the Spirit to guide us and engage us in activities that build the ministry and mission of the church. An indicator of giftedness is success.

Take the spiritual gifts questionnaire (see Appendix A) and see what you think your gifts are. Compare your findings with your partner or your group and talk about how you feel about them.

Way to Pray

Prayer Focus This Week

Thank God for the specific gifts you think He has given you. Mention them by name, and ask God to affirm them in your life. (He can do that only when you start actively doing those tasks and ministries.)

More Than Words

Since God intended spiritual gifts to build up the body of Christ (the church), write a letter to your pastor and/or church board describing what you think your gifts are, and ask them to involve you in or enable you to work for the ministry of the church—or, to use the old baseball adage, "Where do you want me to play?"

For your spiritual gift, think of several specific tasks that you can do that develop your gift(s) and begin to reflect on and share what is happening to you as you become what God designed you to be.

In the Mirror

Reflect on your experiences with spiritual gifts this week. What do you hope will happen with your service to God during the next few months? What hopes do you have about how this will help you become more like Christ?

Lesson 12
The Church as the
Body of Christ

Before you begin the lesson on the church, have the students share some of their thoughts and experiences in light of their study on spiritual gifts. What do they think God is calling them to do?

Objective: Students will deepen their sense of understanding of what church members are in light of the biblical descriptions of church and church life.

Have the students share their answers to the **Open Question**s given at the beginning of this lesson and explain why they answered the way they did.

The **Opening Story** has two points that relate to church life:

1. Any revival or revolution begins with one person.

2. But it takes a team of people to serve.

Open Questions

Either/Or

Is the primary purpose of the church to provide a place for believers to grow *or* to focus on reaching unbelievers?

Show where you think your church is at on the continuum below.

1—Lively, strong, and effective

5—Broken and divided, with only a few parts working

1	2	3	4	5
Alive				**Broken**

Why do you think your church is this way?

Opening Story

Outside of recess and PE, lunchtime has few competing highlights during the school day. One day I visited my wife while she worked on developing a remedial program for students, and thus I found myself spending lunchtime in the first grade. I enjoyed watching the students rustle around the classroom with their lunch pails and small cartons of milk. One boy with bright-red curly hair, however, remained in his seat. My heart sank into my stomach as someone announced out loud what was obvious to anyone watching, "Billy doesn't have a lunch."

At first I thought the remark was cruel. But before I could react the roomful of students scurried into action. What I saw permanently engraved the most beautiful image of community into my mind. Each student began breaking off pieces of their peanut-butter-and-jelly sandwiches and placed them on a tray that they passed around the room. I never saw who started the tray around. Bags of chips popped open and littered the brown plastic cafeteria tray with samples of every flavor known to first graders across the land, plus half of a banana, tons of carrot and celery sticks, and a bounty of cookies broken in half. As someone set the tray filled with food before the hungry lad, a grin crept shyly across his sweet freckled face.

Embarrassed? A little. Tickled to death at the feast fit for five first graders looming before him like a small mountain? No question.

Actually, I had many questions. Who started the tray? When did they learn to do this? Why didn't I forget my lunch? "Where did they learn to do this?" I asked the teacher. He smiled. "It happened a few years back when one of my students would share his lunch with anyone who forgot theirs. Everyone joined in, and then it just became kind of an unspoken rule in the classroom. When someone forgets a lunch, everyone helps." The simple way the kids created community in their classroom stunned me.

Two truths strike me as I remember that day in the classroom. 1. When everyone gives, what is given is so abundant that it leaves those who are helped with a powerful experience of God's overflowing grace. 2. The revolution of "the big lunch" started with one child.

Jesus began the church when one person finally understood the purpose. What did He really mean? Was Peter the newly appointed church leader? Is Jesus talking about Himself as the rock?

I think it is safe to say that Peter had a long way to go. It is also safe to say that entrance into the church does not go through Peter. Jesus simply says, "I'm going to start with you."

The church—is it a building? an organization? The various symbols Scripture uses to describe the church are powerful windows for seeing what God is like and how He created us as people who thrive in community. Look at the following biblical story and see what you think.

> "On this rock I will build my church." For centuries Christians have battled over the meaning of "the rock." Some suggest that it is Jesus and that He is pointing to Himself as He says to Peter, "You are Peter [little stone] and on this rock [Himself] I will build my church." Another interpretation is the classical understanding that Peter is "the rock" and from him a whole tradition of church leaders will succeed each other. Still another way to view "this rock" is by what Peter just did to spark the whole conversation. Peter announced that Jesus was the Christ, the Son of God. The testimony is "the rock." And still another idea is that Jesus begins building His church one person at a time. It starts with Peter and continues with every other person who makes this same confession. What do you think "the rock" is?

Life of Christ

Matthew 16:13-18

"When Jesus came to the region of Caesarea Philippi, he asked his disciples, 'Who do people say the Son of Man is?' They replied, 'Some say John the Baptist; others say Elijah; and still others, Jeremiah or one of the prophets.' 'But what about you?' he asked. 'Who do you say I am?' Simon Peter answered, 'You are the Christ, the Son of the living God.' Jesus replied, 'Blessed are you, Simon son of Jonah, for this was not revealed to you by man, but by my Father in heaven. And I tell you that you are Peter, and on this rock I will build my church, and the gates of Hades will not overcome it.'"

> Have the students read the statement below that summarizes what the Seventh-day Adventist Church believes about the doctrine of the church. Then have them read each verse and write what they think it means as they chain-reference the verses in their Bibles.
>
> Ask the students what they think about the opening statement from *The Acts of the Apostles*: "The church is God's appointed agency for the salvation of men. It was organized for service, and its mission is to carry the gospel to the world. From the begin-

ning it has been God's plan that through His church shall be reflected to the world His fullness and His sufficiency. The members of the church, those whom He has called out of darkness into His marvelous light, are to show forth His glory. The church is the repository of the riches of the grace of Christ; and through the church will eventually be made manifest, even to 'the principalities and powers in heavenly places,' the final and full display of the love of God (Eph. 3:10)" (*The Acts of the Apostles,* p. 9).

We Believe

The Church as the Body of Christ

"The church is the community of believers who confess Jesus Christ as Lord and Saviour. In continuity with the people of God in Old Testament times, we are called out from the world; and we join together for worship, for fellowship, for instruction in the Word, for the celebration of the Lord's Supper, for service to all mankind, and for the worldwide proclamation of the gospel. The church derives its authority from Christ, who is the incarnate Word, and from the Scriptures, which are the written Word. The church is God's family; adopted by Him as children, its members live on the basis of the new covenant. The church is the body of Christ, a community of faith of which Christ Himself is the Head. The church is the bride for whom Christ died that He might sanctify and cleanse her. At His return in triumph, He will present her to Himself a glorious church, the faithful of all the ages, the purchase of His blood, not having spot or wrinkle, but holy and without blemish." [18]

a. Genesis 12:3

b. Acts 7:38

c. Ephesians 4:11-15; 3:8-11

d. Matthew 28:19, 20

e. Matthew 16:13-20; 18:17, 18

f. Ephesians 1:22, 23; 2:19-22; 5:23-27

g. Colossians 1:17, 18

What should the church be for its members and for the world around them?

How do you balance personal shortcomings with the powerful impact believers have when they come together to work for God?

Why is the church so important for spreading the gospel to the world?

Way to Pray

A vast difference exists between a gladiator and a spectator. One is active in the fight; the other simply watches. The churches in America desperately need gladiators, not spectators. Talk to God about the problem and invite God to speak to you personally about how you can change your local congregation. Ask Him about the mission He has for you.

More Than Words

Obtain a Seventh-day Adventist yearbook, flip through the pages, and read the names, places, and ministries that comprise the worldwide church. While each local church is a unit, at the same time we are all connected worldwide to others when we worship, believe, and work for the same cause. Take the yearbook and a globe, look up some of the places mentioned in the yearbook, and pray specifically for the mission of the church in an area you feel led to pray for. You may want to write a letter and ask the local leaders how things are going and what you can be praying for as you think of them.

In the Mirror

Reflect on the impact of a congregation on your life. What are some qualities you bring to it? How do you see your role as a member of Christ's body? How do you see your gifts contributing to the whole?

Lesson 13
Death and Resurrection

As you begin this study on death and resurrection, have the students take turns sharing about loved ones they have lost or funerals they have had to attend recently.

Objective: Students will integrate the biblical view of death and resurrection into a hopeful and confident trust in Christ.

The **Opening Story** is an invitation to view death in a broader perspective. Most people, when struck by the loss of a loved one, can't see the big picture as easily as others who are not going through grief.

Opening Story

"A boy and his father were traveling in a car when a bee flew in the open window. The boy was so highly allergic to beestings that both he and his father knew that his life was in danger. As the boy frantically jumped around and tried to avoid the agitated bee, the father calmly reached out and grabbed the bee. When he opened his hands, the bee began to fly again, terrorizing the boy once more. The father then said, 'Look, son,' holding up a hand with an implanted stinger, 'his stinger is gone; he can't hurt you any longer.'"[19]

The experience is the same for those who trust in Christ—the sting of death cannot hurt us. As we study the human condition in death we begin with a story in which Jesus finds Himself in the middle of the most heart-wrenching human scenario: the death of a loved one. As a matter of fact, three stories in the life of Christ describe God's reaction to death. Death is the result of sin, and sin is the enemy of the Savior. Read the three stories and discuss what each one tells you about the power of death.

The **Life of Christ** section has only a few incidents in which Jesus immediately conquers death and restores individuals back to life again. Take a look at these stories and highlight or underline what you think are the most important phrases or sentences in the three stories from the Gospels.

Life of Christ

John 11:1-44

"Now a man named Lazarus was sick. He was from Bethany, the village of Mary and her sister Martha. This Mary, whose brother Lazarus now lay sick, was the same one who poured perfume on the Lord and wiped his feet with her hair. So the sisters sent word to Jesus, 'Lord, the one you love is sick.' When he heard this, Jesus said, 'This sickness will not end in death. No, it is for God's glory so that God's Son may be glorified through it.' Jesus loved Martha and her sister and Lazarus. Yet when he heard that Lazarus was sick, he stayed where he was two more days. Then he said to his disciples, 'Let us go back to Judea.' 'But Rabbi,' they said, 'a short while ago the Jews tried to stone you, and yet you are going back there?' Jesus answered, 'Are there not twelve hours of daylight? A man who walks by day will not stumble, for he sees by this world's light. It is when he walks by night that he stumbles, for he has no light.' After he had said this, he went on to tell them, 'Our friend Lazarus has fallen asleep; but I am going there to wake him up.' His disciples replied, 'Lord, if he sleeps, he will get better.' Jesus had been speaking of his death, but his disciples thought he meant natural sleep. So then he told them plainly, 'Lazarus is dead, and for your sake I am glad I was not there, so that you may believe. But let us go to him.' Then Thomas (called Didymus) said to the rest of the disciples, 'Let us also go, that we may die with him.' On his arrival, Jesus found that Lazarus had already been in the tomb for four days. Bethany was less than two miles from Jerusalem, and many Jews had come to Martha and Mary to comfort them in the loss of their brother. When Martha heard that Jesus was coming, she went out to meet him, but Mary stayed at home. 'Lord,' Martha said to Jesus, 'if you had been here, my brother would not have died. But I know that even now God will give you whatever you ask.' Jesus said to her, 'Your brother will rise again.' Martha answered, 'I know he will rise again in the resurrection at the last day.' Jesus said to her, 'I am the resurrection and the life. He who believes in me will live, even though he dies; and whoever lives and believes in me will never die. Do you believe this?' 'Yes, Lord,' she told him, 'I believe that you are the Christ, the Son of God, who was to come into the world.' And after she had said this, she went back and called her sister Mary aside. 'The Teacher is here,' she said, 'and is asking for you.' When Mary heard this, she got up quickly and went to him. Now Jesus had not yet entered the village, but was still at the place where Martha had met him. When the Jews who had been with Mary in the house, comforting her, noticed how quickly she got up and went out, they followed her, supposing she was going to the tomb to mourn there. When Mary reached the place where Jesus was and saw him, she fell at his feet and said, 'Lord, if you had been here, my brother would not have died.' When Jesus saw her weeping, and the Jews who had come along with her also weeping, he was deeply moved in spirit and troubled. 'Where have you laid him?' he asked. 'Come and see, Lord,' they replied. Jesus wept. Then the Jews said, 'See how he loved him!' But some of them said, 'Could not he who opened the eyes of the blind man have kept this man from dying?' Jesus, once more deeply moved, came to the tomb. It was a cave with a stone laid across the entrance. 'Take away the stone,' he said. 'But, Lord,' said Martha, the sister of the dead man, 'by this time there is a bad odor, for he has been there four days.' Then Jesus said, 'Did I not tell you that if you believed, you would see the glory of God?' So they took away the stone. Then Jesus looked up and said, 'Father, I thank you that you have heard me. I knew that you always hear me, but I said this for the benefit of the people standing here, that they may believe that you sent me.' When he had said this, Jesus called in a loud voice, 'Lazarus, come out!' The dead man came out, his hands and feet wrapped with strips of linen, and a cloth around his face. Jesus said to them, 'Take off the grave clothes and let him go.'"

Mark 5:35-43

"While Jesus was still speaking, some men came from the house of Jairus, the synagogue ruler. 'Your daughter is dead,' they said. 'Why bother the teacher any more?' Ignoring what they said, Jesus told the synagogue ruler, 'Don't be afraid; just believe.' He did not let anyone follow him except Peter, James and John the brother of James. When they came to the home of the synagogue ruler, Jesus saw a commotion, with people crying and wailing loudly. He went in and said to them, 'Why all this commotion and wailing? The child is not dead but asleep.' But they laughed at him. After he put them all out, he took the child's father and mother and the disciples who were with him, and went in where the child was. He took her by the hand and said to her, *'Talitha koum!'* (which means, 'Little girl, I say to you, get up!'). Immediately the girl stood up and walked around (she was twelve years old). At this they were completely astonished. He gave strict orders not to let anyone know about this, and told them to give her something to eat."

Luke 7:11-17

"Soon afterward, Jesus went to a town called Nain, and his disciples and a large crowd went along with him. As he approached the town gate, a dead person was being carried out—the only son of his mother, and she was a widow. And a large crowd from the town was with her. When the Lord saw her, his heart went out to her and he said, 'Don't cry.' Then he went up and touched the coffin, and those carrying it stood still. He said, 'Young man, I say to you, get up!' The dead man sat up and began to talk, and Jesus gave him back to his mother. They were all filled with awe and praised God. 'A great prophet has appeared among us,' they said. 'God has come to help his people.' This news about Jesus spread throughout Judea and the surrounding country."

As you look at the preceding stories, what questions or thoughts come to mind? How does our view of death affect the way that we live? What do your friends and family think and believe about death and the resurrection?

> Have the students read the statement below that summarizes what the Seventh-day Adventist Church believes about death and the resurrection. Then have them read each verse and write what they think it means as they chain-reference the verses in their Bibles.
>
> Have the students share this passage with their partners and ask each other, "How are the people in the time of Christ like people today? How are they different?"
>
> "At this time the systems of heathenism were losing their hold upon the people. Men were weary of pageant and fable. They longed for a religion that could satisfy the heart. While the light of truth seemed to have departed from among men, there were souls who were looking for light, and who were filled with perplexity and sorrow. They were thirsting for a knowledge of the living God, for some assurance of a life beyond the grave" (*The Desire of Ages*, p. 32).

We Believe

Death and Resurrection

"The wages of sin is death. But God, who alone is immortal, will grant eternal life to His redeemed. Until that day death is an unconscious state for all people. When Christ, who is our life, appears, the resurrected righteous and the living righteous will be glorified and caught up to meet their Lord. The second resurrection, the resurrection of the unrighteous, will take place a thousand years later." [20]

a. Romans 6:23
b. 1 Timothy 6:15, 16
c. Ecclesiastes 9:5, 6
d. Psalm 146:3, 4
e. John 11:11-14
f. Colossians 3:4
g. 1 Corinthians 15:51-54
h. 1 Thessalonians 4:13-17
i. John 5:28, 29
j. Revelation 20:1-10

Which passages speak the most to you about God's promise about the hereafter?

Way to Pray

Which passages of Scripture most help you deal with the prospect of death? In your prayers to God, talk openly to Him about your life, your future, and the resurrection day.

More Than Words

Interview: Find someone who has lost a loved one in the past year or so and ask them to share with you what passages or stories from Scripture have brought them the most comfort. Ask them:

How does your view of death and resurrection affect the way you live each day?

In the Mirror

Think about what you would want people to say about you at your funeral. Not to be morbid, but what do you want your funeral to be like and why? How does what we know about death and the resurrection help us live in a world in which people die?

Lesson 14
The Second Coming

Ask the students: "How was your interview helpful for you personally? What insights did you gain?"

Objective: Students will understand the attributes of the second coming of Christ and experience the personal assurance that believers enjoy as they watch and work for the approaching day.

The opening material grows out of a reaction to a fearful, anxious approach to the time of the Second Coming. For whatever reason, some people think that knowing the time of the coming of Christ enables them to be ready. In the story, the important thing is not what happens at the appointed time, but how believers live until then.

Opening Story

One night I was eating dinner with one of my classmates in high school and we were talking about the second coming of Christ. As a teenager I had many questions about this topic. And so did Joey. "We do not have all the answers," his father said, "but we do have all we need to know. The best way to prepare for the Second Coming is simply to live each day as if it were your last."

"I tried that once," Joey told him, "and you grounded me for a month."

Obviously, the answer, "Just live each day as if it were your last," rarely works for us today and probably didn't work any better for the disciples when Jesus mentioned the fact that He would leave—and then come back again.

"There is a story about a man in a large city who was on his way to an interview for a new job with a highly successful company. Well groomed, wearing a nice suit smelling of expensive cologne, the man made his way to the corporate headquarters. As he was waiting for the elevator, an elderly janitor walked by, slipped on the wet floor, and fell down awkwardly. The young man chuckled to himself at the Three Stooges-like humor, unconcerned that the older man might have been hurt. He actually stepped over the fallen janitor, boarded the elevator, went up to the twenty-ninth floor, and entered the reception area of the firm. Soon his name was called, and he was ushered into a beautiful executive office. He was greeted by the woman that was going to conduct the interview. She was the company president. Immediately, she said, 'By the way, on your way up to see me, did you see anyone who needed help?' 'Yes,' he replied, 'an elderly janitor fell down right in front of me as I was waiting for the elevator.' 'Did you stop to help him?' she asked. 'Well, no, because I believe in promptness, and I didn't want to be late for this very important interview.' 'Of course,' said the company president, 'but you see, that was the interview!'"[21]

The time of the Second Coming is not for us to know, but rather what Christ has for us to do while we wait is our business. Christ seeks to divert our anxious hearts from the time of His coming and to focus them on the Holy Spirit's work in our lives as we wait.

This popular phrase from Jesus in John 14, "Don't let your hearts be troubled. . . . I will come again and receive you to myself that where I am you will be also," is more meaningful when you realize the next two chapters are about how Jesus never really leaves us. He remains with us through the Holy Spirit. The seamless ministry continues through the Holy Spirit working through us until the coming of Christ.

Life of Christ

John 14:1-20

" 'Do not let your hearts be troubled. Trust in God; trust also in me. In my Father's house are many rooms; if it were not so, I would have told you. I am going there to prepare a place for you. And if I go and prepare a place for you, I will come back and take you to be with me that you also may be where I am. You know the way to the place where I am going.' Thomas said to him, 'Lord, we don't know where you are going, so how can we know the way?' Jesus answered, 'I am the way and the truth and the life. No one comes to the Father except through me. If you really knew me, you would know my Father as well. From now on, you do know him and have seen him.' Philip said, 'Lord, show us the Father and that will be enough for us.' Jesus answered: 'Don't you know me, Philip, even after I have been among you such a long time? Anyone who has seen me has seen the Father. How can you say, "Show us the Father"? Don't you believe that I am in the Father, and that the Father is in me? The words I say to you are not just my own. Rather, it is the Father, living in me, who is doing his work. Believe me when I say that I am in the Father and the Father is in me; or at least believe on the evidence of the miracles themselves. I tell you the truth, anyone who has faith in me will do what I have been doing. He will do even greater things than these, because I am going to the Father. And I will do whatever you ask in my name, so that the Son may bring glory to the Father. You may ask me for anything in my name, and I will do it. If you love me, you will obey what I command. And I will ask the Father, and he will give you another Counselor to be with you forever—the Spirit of truth. The world cannot accept him, because it neither sees him nor knows him. But you know him, for he lives with you and will be in you. I will not leave you as orphans; I will come to you. Before long, the world will not see me anymore, but you will see me. Because I live, you also will live. On that day you will realize that I am in my Father, and you are in me, and I am in you.' "

What do you wonder about the second coming of Jesus? Make a short list of the big questions you have personally and the kind of answers you hope to glean from this study.

Have the students read the statement below that summarizes what the Seventh-day Adventist Church believes about the second coming of Jesus. Then have them read each verse and write what they think it means as they chain-reference the verses in their Bibles.

Although we have emphasized not being preoccupied with the time and timing of the Second Coming, the verses that construct this teaching are still mostly about the timing, the desperate scenes of hate and wrongdoing, and the physical way in which Christ will return. The world is earnestly waiting for a clear message about the end, and the Seventh-day Adventist Church has a beauty of a story to tell. To have these passages clearly marked in your Bible and fitted in your mind is necessary as we approach the Advent.

We Believe

The Second Coming

"The second coming of Christ is the blessed hope of the church, the grand climax of the gospel. The Saviour's coming will be literal, personal, visible, and worldwide. When He returns, the righteous dead will be resurrected, and together with the righteous living will be glorified and taken to heaven, but the unrighteous will die. The almost complete fulfillment of most lines of prophecy, together with the present condition of the world, indicates that Christ's coming is imminent. The time of that event has not been revealed, and we are therefore exhorted to be ready at all times."[22]

a. Revelation 1:7
b. Matthew 24:43, 44
c. 1 Thessalonians 4:13-18
d. 1 Corinthians 15:51-54
e. 2 Thessalonians 1:7-10; 2:8
f. Revelation 14:14-20
g. Revelation 19:11-21
h. Matthew 24
i. 2 Timothy 3:1-5
j. 1 Thessalonians 5:1-6

Way to Pray

Write a prayer to God about your expectations of His soon return. Think about the attitudes you want to foster in your own heart about "the end."

More Than Words

Choose a day during the coming week to practice living as though Jesus would arrive that day. What things do you think you will spend your time doing? What interruptions will you allow to change your schedule? Go about your daily tasks as though Jesus might appear any moment while also realizing what He has called you to do and be. (In other words—you can't skip school, work, the dentist, etc. . . .) Partner up with a friend and seek to live with an attitude of expectation.

In the Mirror

Describe in detail the coming of Christ as you see it in your imagination. Include the sounds, the smells, the scenes, and describe how you perceive Jesus and His face as He arrives.

Lesson 15
The Millennium and the End of Sin

Before you begin the study on the millennium, have the students take a few minutes to share what they appreciated most in the last study.

Objective: Students will see the compassion and justice of God as He finally removes sin.

The **Opening Story** builds on the sense of justice that still exists even in sinful humans. Things "ought" to be different. Philosophers spoke of this inherent emotion as it relates to injustice. It was clear to the child that the pain he felt was not the way things were meant to be. Why? How? As God deals with the sin problem we long for things to be different.

Opening Story

"I hate this!" my son cried as he looked up at me with tears streaming down his cheeks. "It's not fair! I hate owies!" The cut on his knee bled enough to scare him, and the pain from the surrounding scratches infuriated my 4-year-old boy so much that in between the crying he erupted into shouts of anger. "I want this to stop! When will it stop hurting, Daddy?"

I could have mentioned to him that the pain-free life he thought he was entitled to did not exist, that his suffering was not an attack on him, but the reality of living in a sin-filled world. In short, I could have said, "Get used to it!"

Before you turn me in to the authorities, know that I would never wish those thoughts on anyone, much less say them to my 4-year-old. Why? Because our Father in heaven has something else in mind for us to "get used to."

As the effects of sin increase around us, the response for believers is not to ignore it, excuse it, evade it, or accept it. God will put an end to the suffering, and He will invite everyone who trusts in His grace to "get used to" a new way—a new way to live, breathe, and grow. The old way will go away. God will make sure of that. But in getting rid of the old way we will need to get used to life the new way.

Jesus describes a time of judgment that will expose sin for what it is and also reveal God's grace in all its fullness as well. He warns people to get serious about sin and about the great plan God has for eliminating it forever.

> The students should consider two aspects as we look at the millennium and how God ultimately deals with sin:
> **1.** "Fear him who, after the killing of the body, has power to throw you into hell." In other words, whatever you do, do not become one of the people who lose not only their lives but also their souls.
> **2.** "Are not five sparrows sold for two pennies? Yet not one of them is forgotten by God. Indeed, the very hairs of your head are all numbered. Don't be afraid; you are worth more than many sparrows." Those whose eternal life rests in the Savior need have no fear. Sin and death cannot touch them.

Life of Christ

Luke 12:1-10

"Meanwhile, when a crowd of many thousands had gathered, so that they were trampling on one another, Jesus began to speak first to his disciples, saying: 'Be on your guard against the yeast of the Pharisees, which is hypocrisy. There is nothing concealed that will not be disclosed, or hidden that will not be made known. What you have said in the dark will be heard in the daylight, and what you have whispered in the ear in the inner rooms will be proclaimed from the roofs. I tell you, my friends, do not be afraid of those who kill the body and after that can do no more. But I will show you whom you should fear: Fear him who, after the killing of the body, has power to throw you into hell. Yes, I tell you, fear him. Are not five sparrows sold for two pennies? Yet not one of them is forgotten by God. Indeed, the very hairs of your head are all numbered. Don't be afraid; you are worth more than many sparrows. I tell you, whoever acknowledges me before men, the Son of Man will also acknowledge him before the angels of God. But he who disowns me before men will be disowned before the angels of God. And everyone who speaks a word against the Son of Man will be forgiven, but anyone who blasphemes against the Holy Spirit will not be forgiven.'"

> Have the students read the statement below that summarizes what the Seventh-day Adventist Church believes about the millennium and the end of sin. Then have them read each verse and write what they think it means as they chain-reference the verses in their Bibles.
>
> While many have questions as to what we will do during the millennium, my answer is that it will be whatever it takes to prevent any possibility of sin again. The issue the universe faces is about God's character. Is He harsh or too demanding? Did people really have a fair chance to be saved? In the end, we will have no question, no doubt, no fear of God or His ways, only an eternally abiding love for His relentless desire to save people. When the destruction of the wicked comes, we will not only agree with what God does, but it will make sense to us.

We Believe

The Millennium and the End of Sin

"The millennium is the thousand-year reign of Christ with His saints in heaven between the first and second resurrections. During this time the wicked dead will be judged; the earth will be utterly desolate, without living human inhabitants, but occupied by Satan and his angels. At its close Christ with His saints and the Holy City will descend from heaven to earth. The unrighteous dead will then be resurrected, and with Satan and his angels will surround the city; but fire from God will consume them and cleanse the earth. The universe will thus be freed of sin and sinners forever."[23]

   a. Revelation 20

b. 1 Corinthians 6:2, 3
c. Jeremiah 4:23-26
d. Revelation 21:1-5
e. Malachi 4:1
f. Ezekiel 28:18, 19

Way to Pray

As you pray, make a list of all the things that you want to talk to God about during the millennium. As God seeks to prepare you for heaven, what sin does He want to put an end to in your life today?

More Than Words

Discuss with someone this week what it might be like when sin will be no more. Try to encourage those who need the hope of a righteous end and then reflect on your experience with that person.

In the Mirror

Reflect on the beauty of the 1,000 years; also spend some time wondering about what it will be like to live without the effects of sin, and write your thoughts on paper.

Lesson 16
The New Earth

Have the students consider the previous lesson as you meet together. Do they still have some unanswered questions? unresolved wonderings?

Objective: Students will discover God's marvelous plan for restoring and re-creating the earth and will seek to create ways in which they can foster the reality of a place called Paradise.

The **Opening Story** examines our own assumptions about heaven. How do our views affect the way we see it? What is the difference between heaven and the new earth?

Opening Story

"Ahh. This is heaven," my friend said. But it was not heaven to me! We were in a small sailboat out on the ocean, and the only thing that remotely resembled anything lovely was the security of the life vest I clutched. I'm not much of a water person, but my friend could think of no other place on earth he'd rather be than *stranded out on the ocean with no wind, no food, no solid ground!*

Although I have never been to heaven, I was certain that this was not it. But what is heaven, and what will it really be like? The images of harps and clouds, of people with wings floating around like celestial butterflies, are not biblical—nor are they something we all would say "This is heaven" to. What will heaven be like? is a popular question but a dangerous one. The only way to even begin to try to give an answer is to make comparisons—or contradictions. The apostle John tells us what heaven will not be like. Revelation 21:4 describes heaven as having "no more death or mourning or crying or pain."

If you were to describe "heaven," how would you do it?

The new earth is a better way to see God's original hope for humanity. When we think of Paradise we don't imagine cloud-enshrined condos—we conjure up a real place. But how real is Paradise?

Ask the thief on the cross. Jesus gives him a personal invitation to the good life. Watch and see:

The truly good life is not simply the absence of badness. Can you imagine what might be going through the mind of the thief on the cross next to Jesus? Does he realize what he is asking for as he declares, "Remember me . . ."? When Jesus hands him the promise of eternal life in Paradise, do you think the thief is considering how great it will be to not have to endure all the bad things of this life? No, he is thinking, *I'm never going to let this Savior out of my sight.* The new earth is more than the absence of sin—it is the presence of Christ and the life He always wanted us to live.

Life of Christ

Luke 23:39-43

"One of the criminals who hung there hurled insults at him: 'Aren't you the Christ? Save yourself and us!' But the other criminal rebuked him. 'Don't you fear God,' he said, 'since you are under the same sentence? We are punished justly, for we are getting what our deeds deserve. But this man has done nothing wrong.' Then he said, 'Jesus, remember me when you come into your kingdom.' Jesus answered him, 'I tell you the truth, . . . you will be with me in paradise.'"

Have the students read the statement below that summarizes what the Seventh-day Adventist Church believes about the new earth. Then have them read each verse and write what they think it means as they chain-reference the verses in their Bibles.

Questions to ask them: How will life on the new earth be like life now? How will it be totally different?

We Believe

The New Earth

"On the new earth, in which righteousness dwells, God will provide an eternal home for the redeemed and a perfect environment for everlasting life, love, joy, and learning in His presence. For here God Himself will dwell with His people, and suffering and death will have passed away. The great controversy will be ended, and sin will be no more. All things, animate and inanimate, will declare that God is love, and He shall reign forever. Amen."[24]

   a. 2 Peter 3:13

   b. Isaiah 35

    c. Isaiah 65:17-25

    d. Matthew 5:5

    e. Revelation 21:1-7; 22:1-5; 11:15

Way to Pray

Meditate on the creative power of Christ and pray about the parts of your life that you want God to re-create. What do you want to be new in your heart today?

More Than Words

Isaiah tells us that in the new earth we will plant vineyards—that is, do normal, everyday stuff. It seems as though we can have some real, tangible ideas about how we will live in the new earth. Place a seed or put a flower in the yard or in your window as a symbol of your hope for the new earth. Not only does it remind you of the joy to come; it furthers your faith experience and hopefully deepens the reality of the new earth in your mind.

In the Mirror

Reflect on how the new earth relates to the plan of salvation.

Lesson 17
Stewardship

As the students meet together for this lesson, have them spend some time reflecting on and sharing the insights that came to them in their interviews.

Lessons 1 through 12 built on the foundation of our relationship to God and to each other.

Lessons 13 through 16 build on the big-picture events that frame God's plan of redemption throughout history.

Lessons 17 through 21 focus on the practical ways to live as believers as God's children.

Objective: Students will deepen their understanding of the way God calls believers to a complete surrender of their lives, resources, and hearts for the work and glory of His kingdom.

Ranking questions can help clarify a person's priorities. In this case, there is really no order that is better than another, only what reflects our current life situation. Have the students share with their partners their responses and why they answered the way they did.

Open Questions

Rank in order (1—the greatest sacrifice; 5—the least)
In my life the greatest sacrifice for me to give would be:

____ Money
____ Time for church work
____ Talents for service
____ My energy for good causes
____ Opinions and preconceived ideas

The **Opening Story** builds the foundation for true discipleship. God's greatest desire is for us to grow in ways that make us like Him. Of all the character qualities needed in humans, selflessness is at the top of the list. The choice to spend ourselves fully for the work of the church is not popular, but it is a powerful demonstration that we understand whom everything belongs to.

Opening Story

"A long time ago a very godly and generous businessman in London was asked for a donation for a charitable project. Very little was expected because the businessman had recently sustained a heavy loss from the shipwreck of some of his ships. To the amazement of the leaders of the charity, he gave about ten times as much as he was expected to give to the project. When asked how he was able to give so much in light of his business difficulties the businessman replied, 'It is quite true, I have sustained a heavy loss by these vessels being wrecked, but that is the very reason why I give you so much; for I must make better use than ever of my stewardship lest it should be entirely taken from me.'"[25]

While I'm not sure whether the man gave from fear of losing everything or from a real conviction that his stewardship could glorify God, the point is well made. Mark it down as a truth for eternity—God is the great giver and selfless sacrificer (if that can be considered a word), and He expects His children to follow suit. There are many ways to give, and Christians are challenged to be selfless in all of them, not just some. Money, time, talents, energy, passion, interests, relationships, possessions, reputation—they are all areas that can speak plainly of Christ's gracious and selfless love. Apparently, the woman at the Temple figured it out.

> The passage to focus on is the landmark moment when Jesus says: "I tell you the truth, this poor widow has put more into the treasury than all the others. They all gave out of their wealth; but she, out of her poverty, put in everything—all she had to live on." Have the students ask themselves if they are ready to give themselves the way the woman gave. What needs to happen in their hearts and lives for this kind of surrender to take place?

Life of Christ

Mark 12:41-44

"Jesus sat down opposite the place where the offerings were put and watched the crowd putting their money into the temple treasury. Many rich people threw in large amounts. But a poor widow came and put in two very small copper coins, worth only a fraction of a penny. Calling his disciples to him, Jesus said, 'I tell you the truth, this poor widow has put more into the treasury than all the others. They all gave out of their wealth; but she, out of her poverty, put in everything—all she had to live on.'"

Have the students read the statement below that summarizes what the Seventh-day Adventist Church believes about Christian stewardship. Then have them read each verse and write what they think it means as they chain-reference the verses in their Bibles.

Notice the word "ownership." As the students look together at the way God wants believers to live, have them discuss the role "ownership" plays in formulating our attitudes and perceptions about giving.

We Believe

Stewardship

"We are God's stewards, entrusted by Him with time and opportunities, abilities and possessions, and the blessings of the earth and its resources. We are responsible to Him for their proper use. We acknowledge God's ownership by faithful service to Him and our fellowmen, and by returning tithes and giving offerings for the proclamation of His gospel and the support and growth of His church. Stewardship is a privilege given to us by God for nurture in love and the victory over selfishness and covetousness. The steward rejoices in the blessings that come to others as a result of his faithfulness."[26]

- **a.** Genesis 1:26-28; 2:15
- **b.** 1 Chronicles 29:14
- **c.** Haggai 1:3-11
- **d.** Malachi 3:8-12
- **e.** 1 Corinthians 9:9-14
- **f.** Matthew 23:23
- **g.** 2 Corinthians 8:1-15
- **h.** Romans 15:26, 27

Way to Pray

As you pray this week, make a list of all the things that are precious to you and give them to God one by one for His service. Acknowledge the "what's mine is mine" attitudes you may have held and trust God with your whole life.

Consider a prayer that gives God your future: career, spouse, college, etc. . . .

More Than Words

Interview someone who has children in college or older children. Ask the following questions:

When in your life has God come through miraculously for you as a result of your faithful giving?

Why do you think it is hard for us to consider our things or even time as belonging to God and not to ourselves?

What words of wisdom do you have for someone my age about giving and working in the church?

In the Mirror

Reflect on and write about the things you would lay your life down for. What would you surrender the work of the gospel for?

Lesson 18
Christian Behavior

Before you move on to the study of Christian behavior, have the students look back at last week's lesson and share any insights they gained from the interviews, activities, or other exercises they completed.

Objective: Students will understand the importance of living their lives by the principles that God has given to His children.

The **Opening Story** exposes the reality of lifestyle by examining the mind-set of those who live under the city streets in New York. It seeks to develop the notion that two worlds exist that we can live in and for. Satan brings about things that nobody wants—yet many buy the products of his work. It seems mindless, especially in this story, but many are the ways that people try to avoid the truth that God's way brings life, joy, and meaning. Satan's way destroys, corrupts, and cripples those who embrace it.

Opening Story

Below New York City live people who have, for one reason or another, chosen to dwell in the sewers. The homeless, the mentally ill, the broken, the outcasts, the has-beens, the addicts, the mindless, the misfits—they huddle beneath the streets of one of the world's most famous cities.

Jennifer Toth, a reporter, studied those who dwelt in the tunnels. In her book *The Mole People* she cites an interchange with a man who let her interview him in exchange for a free lunch:

Flacko, a would-be leader underground, said, "If I was in charge I'd put up a big sign on a platform saying, 'C'mon down! Everyone welcome! Come live free—rent-free, tax-free, independent, free like Mandela!'"

"When he stops smiling, he turns earnest and leans over our table in the Chinese restaurant . . . 'If you write this book,' he says, 'you tell them the tunnels rob you of your life. No one should come down here . . . everyone down here knows it. They won't say it, but they know it.'"[27]

Sounds like the game of the deceiver, doesn't it? Jesus said, "The thief comes only to steal and kill and destroy; I have come that they may have life, and have it to the full" (John 10:10).

God's hope is that others will see His glory in us—the way we live, the way we work, and the way we play. But the question "How do we then live?" has not been a popular one lately, because many think that God's challenge to live holy lives contradicts the message of grace. That if salvation is free, we don't have to do anything in response to God's gift.

Look at the passages of Scripture that describe the kind of life God wants us to live. The underworld and the lies that promote a "better way" are loud and compelling, but Christ won't play that game. He won't seduce us into an addiction. Have you seen the bumper sticker that declares "Addicted to Jesus"? Wrong Jesus. Addictions are a form of slavery. They rob your will of its strength by making it seemingly impossible to choose otherwise. But that's not Jesus. Honesty, purity, faithfulness, wholeness, beauty, and joy are a few of the many life experiences that Christ calls every believer to experience. And another one is obedience. Can you imagine Christ—knowing how much you mean to Him—wanting anything less than the best for you? Not a chance.

Most people know it. Scripture makes the alternatives clear. Look in the Bible and see for yourself.

> The phrase to focus on is the last line: "Let your light shine before men, that they may see your good deeds and praise your Father in heaven." It is not enough to abstain from aspects of life that will destroy a person; one needs also to focus on doing deeds that make people praise God. Have the students take a few minutes to share what they think this might look like in real life.

Life of Christ

Matthew 5:13-15

"'You are the salt of the earth. But if the salt loses its saltiness, how can it be made salty again? It is no longer good for anything, except to be thrown out and trampled by men. You are the light of the world. A city on a hill cannot be hidden. Neither do people light a lamp and put it under a bowl. Instead they put it on its stand, and it gives light to everyone in the house. In the same way, let your light shine before men, that they may see your good deeds and praise your Father in heaven.'"

> Have the students read the statement below that summarizes what the Seventh-day Adventist Church believes about Christian behavior and the Christlike lifestyle. Then have them read each verse and write what they think it means as they chain-reference the verses in their Bibles.
>
> The topic of Christian standards has led to much discussion and even controversy among Christians in the Adventist Church because of the highly personal nature of the topic. Consider the principles that God has invited His children to live by.

We Believe

Christian Behavior

"We are called to be a godly people who think, feel, and act in harmony with the principles of heaven. For the Spirit to re-create in us the character of our Lord we involve ourselves only in those things which will produce Christlike purity, health, and joy in our lives. This means that our amusement and entertainment should meet the highest standards of Christian taste and beauty. While recognizing cultural differences, our dress is to be simple, modest, and neat, befitting those whose true beauty does not consist of outward adornment but in the imperishable ornament of a gentle and quiet spirit. It also means that because our bodies are the temple of the Holy Spirit, we are to care for them intelligently. Along with adequate exercise and rest, we are to adopt the most healthful diet possible and abstain from the unclean foods identified in the Scriptures. Since alcoholic beverages, tobacco, and the irresponsible use of drugs and narcotics are harmful to our bodies, we are to abstain from them as well. Instead, we are to engage in whatever brings our thoughts and bodies into the discipline of Christ, who desires our wholesomeness, joy, and goodness."[28]

a. Romans 12:1, 2

b. 1 John 2:6

c. Ephesians 5:16-26

d. Philippians 4:8

e. 1 Peter 3:1-4

f. 1 Corinthians 6:19, 20

g. Leviticus 11

h. 3 John 2

Way to Pray

Be honest with God in prayer about the parts of your life that do not seem to be what God would like for us. Talk openly with Him about the way you feel about the changes that you sense He's asking you to make.

More Than Words

Share the commitments or decisions you have made to live according to God's dreams for you with your partner or with a friend who will help you and remind you of your choice.

In the Mirror

Reflect on what you think this whole topic of living abundantly has to do with God's plan of salvation. How does living lives that are holy relate to what happened at Calvary?

Lesson 19
Marriage and Family

As you begin the study on marriage and God's plan for the family, have the students interact with their partners about some of the decisions they have made to glorify God with their lifestyle. What parts of the last study were most helpful in making such decisions?

Objective: Students will discuss God's original plan for the family and the reason for the brokenness that plagues families today. Also, they will set goals for their lives based on Scripture.

The **Opening Story** describes what has become common and often expected in many homes across the world—"People fall in and out of love." The idea doesn't match with the way that God has chosen to love His creation. Deep in the heart of God's love for humanity resides the one truth that has the potential to save any marriage on the brink of failure: humility. Humility isn't self-hate; it is self-forgetfulness.

Opening Story

The small round breakfast table sat trapped between the angry couple. Although only a few feet separated the two, it seemed as though they were looking at each other from the opposite ends of one of those long royal banquet tables where you can barely see the person at the other end. Gloria and Ron were seemingly at the end of their marriage. It had slowly eroded away for 23 years, and now all they had to talk about was the way each of them felt about their own needs and how they had not been met.

The failure and fall of many relationships have their roots in a preoccupation with self: my needs, my rights, my expectations, my feelings. The opposite is true in growing marriages: my responsibility is to fulfill the needs of my spouse—the needs I promised to meet. Robert Orben alludes to this principle:

"We begin marriage, hoping for fulfillment, but often find frustration. Our own immature neurotic traits are magnified by the fact that the marriage partner has another set of neurotic tendencies. Instead of seeking fulfillment for ourselves, the primary goal should be to fulfill the needs of one's partner. It is thus that our own needs are met."

While a marriage is more than just meeting the other person's needs (remember that

Christ alone can satisfy some of them), it seems that the breakdown of marriage begins with "self" becoming the priority. The opposite is also true: when the other person is primary to you, most of your own frustrations fade into the background.

Many have given up on this sacred union that began in Eden. It seems as though they look at marriage only tentatively or with a certain amount of resignation. How do you and I foster a sense of honor for this beautiful relationship? It starts when we are young. But most of all, it begins with the way we love God first. You see, to love another person with your own human, sinful problems makes for an incomplete experience—one that does not always end well. But to love God first and fully—that experience alone makes you a prize for marriage. To know Christ is the best preparation for marriage.

Ask Ron and Gloria. That is where they started after decades of growing apart. They began with Christ. As they looked upon the Savior their hearts turned from their inward focus to each other. They learned to love each other, not with the romantic fury of adolescent lovers, but with a new, real, Godlike love that has made a world of difference in their marriage.

As we consider marriage, notice that even in the day of Christ the struggle to maintain one was real. We find a lot of bickering and arguing over the rules of divorce and remarriage, and most of the arguments missed the mark of what they should have discussed—not how we should divorce, but how we can learn to love the way God intended.

> "'For this reason a man will leave his father and mother and be united to his wife, and the two will become one flesh.' So they are no longer two, but one. Therefore what God has joined together, let man not separate." Why is this kind of unity hard to sustain?

Life of Christ

Matthew 19:1-9

"When Jesus had finished saying these things, he left Galilee and went into the region of Judea to the other side of the Jordan. Large crowds followed him, and he healed them there. Some Pharisees came to him to test him. They asked, 'Is it lawful for a man to divorce his wife for any and every reason?' 'Haven't you read,' he replied, 'that at the beginning the Creator "made them male and female," and said, "For this reason a man will leave his father and mother and be united to his wife, and the two will become one flesh"? So they are no longer two, but one. Therefore what God has joined together, let man not separate.' 'Why then,' they asked, 'did Moses command that a man give his wife a certificate of divorce and send her away?' Jesus replied, 'Moses permitted you to divorce your wives because your hearts were hard. But it was not this way from the beginning. I tell you that anyone who divorces his wife, except for marital unfaithfulness, and marries another woman commits adultery.'"

> Have the students read the statement below that summarizes what the Seventh-day Adventist Church believes about marriage and the family. Then have them read each verse and write what they think it means as they chain-reference the verses in their Bibles.
>
> Like many of Christ's teachings, unity in the home is not difficult to comprehend, but it is hard to do. It seems that the secret of successful marriages lies in the selfless qualities practiced by a devoted couple.

We Believe

Marriage and Family

"Marriage was divinely established in Eden and affirmed by Jesus to be a lifelong union between a man and a woman in loving companionship. For the Christian, a marriage commitment is to God as well as to the spouse, and should be entered into only between partners who share a common faith. Mutual love, honor, respect, and responsibility are the fabric of this relationship, which is to reflect the love, sanctity, closeness, and permanence of the relationship between Christ and His church. Regarding divorce, Jesus taught that the person who divorces a spouse, except for fornication, and marries another, commits adultery. Although some family relationships may fall short of the ideal, marriage partners who fully commit themselves to each other in Christ may achieve loving unity through the guidance of the Spirit and the nurture of the church. God blesses the family and intends that its members shall assist each other toward complete maturity. Parents are to bring up their children to love and obey the Lord. By their example and their words they are to teach them that Christ is a loving disciplinarian, ever tender and caring, who wants them to become members of His body, the family of God. Increasing family closeness is one of the earmarks of the final gospel message." [29]

   a. Genesis 2:18-25
   b. Matthew 19:3-9
   c. 2 Corinthians 6:14
   d. Ephesians 5:21-33
   e. Matthew 5:31, 32
   f. Exodus 20:12

g. Ephesians 6:1-4

h. Proverbs 22:6

Way to Pray

Speak to God openly about your hopes and fears about marriage. Tell Him specifically about how you want Him to be involved in the choosing of a marriage partner. Make some decisions in prayer this week and commit them to God, then share them with your study partner.

More Than Words

Write a letter to your mate (you don't have to have a name yet, or a real person). Describe what you want your marriage to be like and what you are willing to commit yourself to. You might include in your letter your commitment to purity from now until that time. Perhaps you would like to reveal your deepest hopes for your relationship. Such a letter is not a waste of time. Keep the letter—let it remind you of the promises you make to honor God and your future spouse—even though you don't know who he or she is yet.

In the Mirror

Reflect on how the marriage relationship relates to the whole plan of salvation. How does marriage show us God's desire to relate to us?

Lesson 20
Christ's Ministry in the Heavenly Sanctuary

Before you look at the beautiful message of the sanctuary, have the students share what they learned from their interviews and how the lesson on marriage and the family spoke personally to them. What specific decisions did they make now about their futures?

Objective: Students will survey the meaning and purpose of the sanctuary (on earth and in heaven) and discover the incredible significance of the events that mark the beginning of the Adventist movement.

The **Opening Story** addresses the issues of justice and righteousness. Someone has to pay. Forgiveness alone does not make anyone righteous. If someone steals and they ask forgiveness, they are still only forgiven. The work of the sanctuary, from the beginning of time, has been to demonstrate God's way of restoring humanity.

Opening Story

"I said I was sorry!"

"That's great, Troy. Now all you have to do is find a way to pay for the damage."

"Pay for the damage! I don't have that kind of money. How can I pay for the damage? I said I was sorry—isn't that enough?"

"Actually, no. In this case 'sorry' isn't enough. 'Sorry' and $68 is enough, however, and I'm wondering if you have thought about what you might do to raise the money."

How could they be that heartless? My father and the next-door neighbor were being completely unreasonable—and, I might add, downright unchristian. Where was their compassion? Where was their grace and forgiveness? Whatever happened to "forgive and forget"? Instead, it felt more like "forgiveness when you pay the debt!" Does that sound very biblical?

Think about these scenarios:

A jury finds a man guilty of raping and murdering six teenage girls. In court he announces, "I admit to doing these awful crimes, and I'm very, very sorry. I promise to never do it again."

"The court recognizes your guilt and your admission," the judge declares, "and as long as you promise never to do it again, you may go."

How does that sound? Does it seem like grace to you? No? Why do you so desperately want justice? Isn't forgiveness enough?

If it is, then why did Jesus have to die on the cross? Why couldn't God just pardon us all? Calvary is a very clear example that God does not tolerate sin. He does not simply wave His hand and make the bad stuff go away. The hard truth of it is that in God's world, if you choose to sin, someone has to pay. But it's a good thing that it's God's world, otherwise that someone would have been you and me.

This is not a New Testament concept—it is as old as sin and as real as the skin on your bones. Yet just as old as the problem is the solution. God, in the ministry of the Old Testament sanctuary, taught the children of Israel what grace really is. It was about blood, payment, death, cleansing, judging, forgiving, changing, healing, trusting, and accepting the grim but wonderful reality that someday a Savior would come—no more lambs—and would pay for our sin.

The grand moment arrived at Calvary. Watch—because as Jesus is fully condemned and put to death for our sin, the curtain of the sanctuary is torn. God judges Jesus as though He were you and me, and He judges you and me as though we were Him.

> The passage to focus on: "And when Jesus had cried out again in a loud voice, he gave up his spirit. At that moment the curtain of the temple was torn in two from top to bottom." Why is this significant to our study of the sanctuary?

Life of Christ

Matthew 27:45-54

"From the sixth hour until the ninth hour darkness came over all the land. About the ninth hour Jesus cried out in a loud voice, 'Eloi, Eloi, lama sabachthani?'—which means, 'My God, my God, why have you forsaken me?' When some of those standing there heard this, they said, 'He's calling Elijah.' Immediately one of them ran and got a sponge. He filled it with wine vinegar, put it on a stick, and offered it to Jesus to drink. The rest said, 'Now leave him alone. Let's see if Elijah comes to save him.' And when Jesus had cried out again in a loud voice, he gave up his spirit. At that moment the curtain of the temple was torn in two from top to bottom. The earth shook and the rocks split. The tombs broke open and the bodies of many holy people who had died were raised to life. They came out of the tombs, and after Jesus' resurrection they went into the holy city and appeared to many people. When the centurion and those with him who were guarding

Jesus saw the earthquake and all that had happened, they were terrified, and exclaimed, 'Surely he was the Son of God!'"

> Have the students read the statement below that summarizes what the Seventh-day Adventist Church believes about the heavenly sanctuary. Then have them read each verse and write what they think it means as they chain-reference the verses in their Bibles.

We Believe

Christ's Ministry in the Heavenly Sanctuary

"There is a sanctuary in heaven, the true tabernacle which the Lord set up and not man. In it Christ ministers on our behalf, making available to believers the benefits of His atoning sacrifice offered once for all on the cross. He was inaugurated as our great High Priest and began His intercessory ministry at the time of His ascension. In 1844, at the end of the prophetic period of 2300 days, He entered the second and last phase of His atoning ministry. It is a work of investigative judgment, which is part of the ultimate disposition of all sin, typified by the cleansing of the ancient Hebrew sanctuary on the Day of Atonement. In that typical service the sanctuary was cleansed with the blood of animal sacrifices, but the heavenly things are purified with the perfect sacrifice of the blood of Jesus. The investigative judgment reveals to heavenly intelligences who among the dead are asleep in Christ and therefore, in Him, are deemed worthy to have part in the first resurrection. It also makes manifest who among the living are abiding in Christ, keeping the commandments of God and the faith of Jesus, and in Him, therefore, are ready for translation into His everlasting kingdom. This judgment vindicates the justice of God in saving those who believe in Jesus. It declares that those who have remained loyal to God shall receive the kingdom. The completion of this ministry of Christ will mark the close of human probation before the Second Advent."[30]

The elements of the sanctuary outline Christ's ministry to us, not only at Calvary, but today in heaven. Ultimately, the sanctuary was then, and still is, about Jesus.

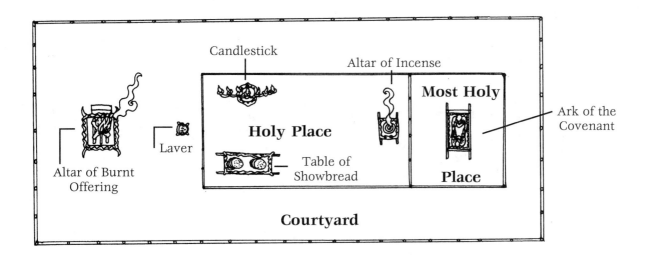

What is the sanctuary?

The courtyard contained the altar of burnt offering and the laver.

The tent of the sanctuary consisted of two parts: the holy place and the Most Holy Place. The holy place housed the seven-branched candlestick (lampstand), the table of showbread, and the altar of incense. The Most Holy Place held the ark of the covenant, which housed the Ten Commandments, which God had written on two tables of stone. Two golden cherubim stood facing each other, and in the middle of the covering was the mercy seat.

What happened?

As a sinner, you would bring a sacrifice (usually a lamb) and place your hands on the innocent animal. The animal was killed as you confessed your sins, in a way taking the sins and placing them on the victim. The priest sprinkled the blood of the animal on the altar of burnt offering or in the holy place. Called the "daily sacrifice," the ritual transferred the sin to the sanctuary. Those who confessed their sins thus walked away forgiven.

Because the sanctuary now contained the sins of the sinner, the high priest would need to cleanse it once a year on the Day of Atonement. On it God judged everyone who had confessed their sins throughout the year. This day was a time of awe and solemn reverence. The high priest chose two goats on the Day of Atonement. One of them he would sacrifice—this was called "the Lord's goat." The other was the scapegoat. The high priest sacrificed the Lord's goat and took its blood into the Most Holy Place. The high priest entered this room only once a year on this special day. He sprinkled the blood on the mercy seat, then returned to the holy place and sprinkled blood on the altar of incense. Finally he moved into the courtyard, where he sprinkled the blood on the altar of burnt offering.

After he finished this, the high priest placed his hands on the head of the other goat (the scapegoat) and confessed the sins of all the people of Israel for the past year and symbolically transferred them to the scapegoat. A Levite took the scapegoat into the wilderness for it to wander around until it died, still bearing the sins of Israel.

What does it mean?

God showed Moses the sanctuary in heaven, and the one Israel's leader then built was a model of the heavenly one. The various parts of the sanctuary have tremendous meaning and purpose. The sanctuary service demonstrates the two parts of Christ's ministry (the work of intercession and the work of judgment).

The First Part (the Courtyard and the Holy Place)

When people confessed their sin over the lamb and it was killed and placed on the altar, it symbolized the sacrifice of Christ as He died on Calvary. (Remember, John the Baptist said, "Behold the Lamb of God who takes away the sins of the world.")

The laver, filled with water, illustrates baptism and the forgiveness of sins as the water washes away the old person of sin.

In the holy place the table of showbread depicts Christ, who is the bread of life (John 6:35). The candlesticks symbolize that Jesus was the light of the world (John 8:12). And the altar of incense stands for the way Christ intercedes for sinners (John 17).

The Second Part (the Most Holy Place)

The ministry of the second compartment involves judgment. The truth about sin is that even though God provides forgiveness for sin, justice demands that someone has to pay. The ark of the covenant is a timeless symbol of God's unchanging law of righteousness. It is important to remember that what makes the sacrifice and the blood and death necessary is God's law. Sin (transgression of the law) brings death. The ark represents God's throne, where His justice calls for an answer to the sin problem.

The scapegoat depicts Satan, whom God banishes from the sanctuary. He bears responsibility for the sins of the people. Justice is served. Sin, death, and shame die with the one who initiated them.

The sanctuary is not a sick ritual of an angry God who wants blood. No, quite the opposite, it lets us witness a loving but just God who deals with the sin problem by becoming the payment for sin. While many stories of God's love are warm and fuzzy, the sanctuary service is not—it is God's love conquering the cold, cruel effects of sin. Although not pretty, it saves.

As you read the passages that describe the heavenly sanctuary and God's plan of salvation, also turn to chapters 23 and 24 in *The Great Controversy* for a more thorough explanation on the work of the sanctuary and Christ's ministry in the sanctuary.

a. Hebrews 8:1-5; 4:14-16

b. Daniel 7:9-27; 8:13, 14; 9:24-27
c. Numbers 14:34
d. Ezekiel 4:6
e. Leviticus 16
f. Revelation 14:6, 7; 20:12; 14:12; 22:12

Way to Pray

In a prayer to God, respond to the truths about your guilt and sin and confidently accept His judgment of you.

More Than Words

This week, not only find a way to forgive someone who has wronged you, but treat them as though they had never wronged you before. It is not forgetting their misdeed, but remembering with mercy.

In the Mirror

Consider how the sanctuary must have helped the children of Israel to understand grace. Also, what are the drawbacks of such a system? Think about how we relate to justice and how and when we demand it. What can you learn from this topic about God's mysterious character?

Lesson 21
The Remnant and the
Mission of the Church

Before you study the last lesson in this series, have the students share with their partners what they found most helpful in their study of the sanctuary.

Objective: Students will discover the wonderful and sacred responsibility of inviting people to know the Savior and unite together to communicate the truth of the gospel to the world.

The **Opening Story** simply describes the awkward, sometimes strange, responsibility of being the one to bear a message.

Opening Story

"You tell him."

"I don't want to tell him—you tell him."

The argument continued as the two boys tried to decide who would break the news to their father that they had broken the key to the car door in the door lock itself.

I had been sitting in my car waiting for my wife to pick up a few things at the store as I watched the boys race from the front of the store through the parking lot toward the car parked right next to mine.

Although the biggest boy (probably a year or so older) was in the lead, the smaller boy was gaining on him as they made the last few strides to the green station wagon with wood-grained paneled sides. Both obviously trying to get into the front seat, they laughed as they wrestled for position. I couldn't see what happened, but knew the moment that it did. They both stopped and stared at the lock of the driver's side, then glanced at each other. The key had snapped off cleanly in the lock. Now they had to decide who would tell their father about the broken key.

Who will bring the message back to those who need to hear? I have always remembered that experience because of the many times I have had to be the one to bring news. Good news such as "Your mom is out of surgery and is going to be fine," "You passed your class!" or "You have been chosen to be one of our employees!" Then there were times when the news was more than disappointing. "You didn't make the team," or, equally as devastating, "She just wants to be friends." (Who wants to be the bearer of that kind of news?) "I'm sorry, but your brother did not survive the accident."

God's people have never been a majority. Throughout history whole herds of people have rejected God's word, His plan, and His heart's desire. It is often hard to imagine so many people being so utterly oblivious to God's truth. It reminds one of a certain college cross-country race. "At an NCAA cross-country championship held several years ago, the athletes were running along a prescribed route when they stumbled on a perplexing choice. There were apparently two directions that looked reasonable. Unsure of which way to go, the crowded pack began to follow the front runners, who had made their choice. All, that is, except Mike Delcavo. He knew they were going the wrong way, and he tried to convince them of it. As he started running in the opposite direction, and urging the rest to follow him, the majority of the runners ignored him, while others laughed at him. Only four other runners followed Delcavo, while the other 123 runners ran the other way. Out of 128 runners, only Mike and four other runners chose the right direction."[31]

The remnant is a group of people given the responsibility of bringing a message. Its character and content come from God. The chosen people are the instruments by which God delivers that message. The children of Israel had the privilege of declaring the glory and wonder of God to the nations who didn't know of the divine Creator. The role of being a messenger is simple: know what the message is and deliver it.

Jesus stood before His disciples and gave them a similar command. He had a message, and they were to deliver it.

Life of Christ

Matthew 28:19, 20

"Therefore go and make disciples of all nations, baptizing them in the name of the Father and of the Son and of the Holy Spirit, and teaching them to obey everything I have commanded you. And surely I am with you always, to the very end of the age."

How do you think the disciples felt about such a challenge?

With all the trouble the disciples had had before about who was going to be first, with what attitude do you imagine they approached this task? Why?

How would you characterize the special work of the disciples at the end of Jesus' ministry? How would you describe our special task in our world today?

> Have the students read the statement below that summarizes what the Seventh-day Adventist Church believes about the remnant and the mission of the church. Then have them read each verse and write what they think it means as they chain-reference the verses in their Bibles.

Also have them discuss with their partners the different layers of "the church." What is unique or special about the Seventh-day Adventist Church in light of its mission?

We Believe

The Remnant and the Mission of the Church

"The universal church is composed of all who truly believe in Christ, but in the last days, a time of widespread apostasy, a remnant has been called out to keep the commandments of God and the faith of Jesus. This remnant announces the arrival of the judgment hour, proclaims salvation through Christ, and heralds the approach of His second advent. This proclamation is symbolized by the three angels of Revelation 14; it coincides with the work of judgment in heaven and results in a work of repentance and reform on earth. Every believer is called to have a personal part in this worldwide witness."[32]

a. Revelation 12:17; 14:6-12; 18:1-4
b. 2 Corinthians 5:10
c. Jude 3, 14
d. 1 Peter 1:16-19
e. 2 Peter 3:10-14
f. Revelation 21:1-14

Way to Pray

As you pray, what do you want to invite God to do in your life that will enable you to carry His message? What do you want Him to do *in* you, then *through* you?

More Than Words

Find someone you know or are acquainted with who from your viewpoint loves the Adventist Church's mission. Ask them what it is about the Adventist faith that is most meaningful to them. Why are they a Seventh-day Adventist? What is our role in the last days?

In the Mirror

How do you see your church carrying out its task until Jesus comes? What do you think we need to do more of and what do we need to do less of in order to finish our job?

[1] *Seventh-day Adventists Believe,* p. 4.

[2] *Ibid.,* p. 16.

[3] *Ibid.,* p. 28.

[4] *Ibid.,* p. 36.

[5] *Ibid.,* p. 58.

[6] *Ibid.,* p. 98.

[7] *Ibid.,* p. 118.

[8] Warren Wiersbe, *Being a Child of God,* p. 21.

[9] *Seventh-day Adventists Believe,* p. 180.

[10] *Ibid.,* p. 68.

[11] *Ibid.,* p. 232.

[12] *Ibid.,* p. 248.

[13] James S. Hewett, *Illustrations Unlimited,* pp. 68, 69.

[14] C. S. Lewis, *Mere Christianity,* pp. 40, 41.

[15] *Seventh-day Adventists Believe,* p. 106.

[16] *Ibid.,* p. 194.

[17] *Ibid.,* p. 206.

[18] *Ibid.,* p. 134.

[19] Michael Green, *1500 Illustrations for Biblical Preaching,* p. 96.

[20] *Seventh-day Adventists Believe,* p. 348.

[21] James W. Moore, *When You're a Christian, the Whole World Is From Missouri,* p. 139.

[22] *Seventh-day Adventists Believe,* p. 332.

[23] *Ibid.,* p. 362.

[24] *Ibid.,* p. 374.

[25] Green, pp. 162, 163.

[26] *Seventh-day Adventists Believe,* p. 268.

[27] Jennifer Toth, *The Mole People,* p. 233.

[28] *Seventh-day Adventists Believe,* p. 278.

[29] *Ibid.,* p. 294.

[30] *Ibid.,* p. 312.

[31] Daniel Schaeffer, *The Bush Won't Burn and I'm All Out of Matches,* p. 67.

[32] *Seventh-day Adventists Believe,* p. 152.

Appendix A
"What's in the Box?"

Spiritual Gifts Survey

Spiritual Gifts Questionnaire for Youth

"What's in the Box?" is a simple approach to finding and practicing our spiritual gifts. The task for the loving and mission-minded church is to ask, "What's in the Box?" In other words, "What is in our kids that can significantly shape and move our church forward—today?"

1. Indicate whether each statement is:

Almost Never	Rarely	Sometimes	Frequently	Almost Always
1	2	3	4	5

For example, a statement might declare "I get really frustrated when I hear people talking about doing something but not doing it."

If you "almost never" feel that way, then you would circle the 1 under "almost never." If you find that you frequently get upset about that, then you would circle number 4.

2. As you answer all the statements, put the number you chose for each question in the light gray area of the column to the right. You should have 10 numbers in each column. Add up the total for each column and write the score in the box at the bottom of the chart.

3. The higher scores are in the areas of the gift you might have. The way to know for sure is to practice using those gifts, and as you have success, you will become more certain about the way God has gifted you.

"We have different gifts, according to the grace given us. If a man's gift is prophesying, let him use it in proportion to his faith. If it is serving, let him serve; if it is teaching, let him teach; if it is encouraging, let him encourage; if it is contributing to the needs of others, let him give generously; if it is leadership, let him govern diligently; if it is showing mercy, let him do it cheerfully" (Romans 12:6-8).

The *ChristWise* approach to spiritual gifts is based on Romans 12:6-8. Some studies on spiritual gifts have up to 24 different spiritual gifts as part of their inventory. For young people, we use the passage in Romans because it simplifies the gifts into seven major categories, which are easier for kids to manage.

The following is a summary of the gifts with a short explanation and an example of what that might look like in a young person.

Prophesy

Speaking the wisdom of God

The term *prophesy* might scare people because it carries all kinds of ideas from calling fire down out of heaven to being able to see into the future. While those experiences may occur, the gift of prophecy has more to do with a person's ability to understand and speak wisely on behalf of God. Individuals who have this gift have the ability to be "in tune" with God in a special way. They tend to be willing to speak up, speak out, and go against the flow of peer pressure. You might see it in the way a young person tries to get people to "do the right thing." We don't want to avoid the possibility that they might see "dreams and visions," but mostly the gift involves courage and character and being really perceptive.

Server

Those who just want to get things done have tremendous value to the church. When God lives in such individuals, great things happen for Him. While some may just want to make plans, helpers make lists of the things to do and get started. They feel best when they are working, and even if the details seem menial, they see how the little parts can fit into the big picture. You can see it in children who always have to be helping, constantly volunteering, and can't sit still for very long.

Teacher/Learner

We combine the gift of teacher/learner because most good teachers love learning. Rarely are teachers effective if they are not teachable themselves. In the church, they like to study and discover truth and also enjoy finding the best ways to communicate it. Such kids not only love it when they understand but they enjoy the way they discovered it and seem to be willing to help others learn.

Builder

Builders have the ability to challenge and strengthen others with their words and deeds. Often called the gift of encouragement, it comes from the idea of building a house. We construct a house step by step, piece by piece. It is obvious as well that while it takes time to build a house, it requires only one stick of dynamite or one earthquake or tornado to utterly destroy it. The same is true with our words and actions. Negative words and actions can destroy quickly, but positive affirmation builds gradually. The builder has a special ability to say the right thing at the right time. Desiring to move people forward with their words and actions, they tend to be positive, proactive people.

Giver

Those who joyfully spend their time, talents, service, and resources for good works we call givers. They don't have to have a lot of money to have this gift—most young people don't. But their sacrificial spirit and generosity tend to stick out. What drives them is not the appearance of being a generous person, but that they just feel so good about helping other people that they are free with their time, their stuff, and their energy.

Leader

People have many different ideas about what really makes someone a leader. The word literally means "to stand before," or "to preside." Some think it is the person who is the loudest. One of the best definitions for leadership is "the ability to influence others." This could go both ways (positive or negative). Have you heard some of the stories great leaders tell about their childhood—all the trouble that they caused? Somehow, though, they were able to influence others. The best leaders are ones who tend to get others involved instead of being the one who does everything themselves. A leader who has to do everything is usually a server in the wrong job.

Compassion

The gift of compassion is the natural inclination to show mercy and to bring help and healing to another person. If someone is lonely, hungry, or hurting, the gift of compassion moves people deep within. Such individuals have to do something about a problem. You can see it in those who react to injustice or unfairness. When there is an opportunity to make a difference, they become a part of the healing. The difference between someone with the gift of compassion and someone who is a server is that compassion sees someone in pain sooner than others.

Questions	Answers					Gifts							
	Almost Never	Rarely	Sometimes	Frequently	Almost Always								
I'm very sensitive to what is good and what is not.	1	2	3	4	5	X							
I am the first person to jump in and help others.	1	2	3	4	5		X						
I like to be in charge of people.	1	2	3	4	5			X					
I can sense when others are hurting, and I reach out to them.	1	2	3	4	5				X				
I feel that it is my job to provide and continue to give resources to those less fortunate than myself.	1	2	3	4	5					X			
I want people to work together.	1	2	3	4	5							X	
I do not like games in which people can lose.	1	2	3	4	5								X
I see the Bible as the truth.	1	2	3	4	5	X							
I want to be appreciated for the tasks I do for others.	1	2	3	4	5		X						
I have a vision for the future.	1	2	3	4	5			X					
I don't like to focus on the bad in others.	1	2	3	4	5				X				
I trust that God will take care of me.	1	2	3	4	5					X			
I get many tasks done in time.	1	2	3	4	5						X		
Major decisions are hard for me to make.	1	2	3	4	5								X
I feel that God directly speaks to me.	1	2	3	4	5	X							
It is easier for me to do things for others than just to listen and talk to them.	1	2	3	4	5		X						
I like new goals and new pursuits.	1	2	3	4	5			X					
I want others to be happy.	1	2	3	4	5				X				
I don't like others to know how much I give of my resources.	1	2	3	4	5					X			
I have a real sense of respect for those older than I.	1	2	3	4	5						X		

Questions	Answers					Gifts						
	Almost Never	Rarely	Sometimes	Frequently	Almost Always							
I feel best when everyone else is happy.	1	2	3	4	5							☐
I want to tell others of what God has said to me.	1	2	3	4	5	☐						
I see the needs of others and act on that.	1	2	3	4	5		☐					
I respect those who are older than I and those who have more wisdom than I do.	1	2	3	4	5			☐				
I don't like to hurt others by my actions or words.	1	2	3	4	5				☐			
If I cannot give money or objects, I will give of my time.	1	2	3	4	5					☐		
I get along well with people regardless of their age.	1	2	3	4	5						☐	
When others are hurting I have a hard time thinking about anything else.	1	2	3	4	5							☐
I can be harsh and blunt when I talk to people.	1	2	3	4	5	☐						
I cannot leave a project until it is completed in the best possible way.	1	2	3	4	5		☐					
I want to work with a good group of people to accomplish a task.	1	2	3	4	5			☐				
I hurt when I see others in pain and sorrow.	1	2	3	4	5				☐			
I love to give of myself and my resources.	1	2	3	4	5					☐		
I feel as if I'm most helpful when I'm in charge.	1	2	3	4	5						☐	
I tend to believe what other people tell me.	1	2	3	4	5							☐
Sometimes I have a low self-esteem.	1	2	3	4	5	☐						
I prefer to be a follower.	1	2	3	4	5		☐					
I do not let others know when criticism has hurt me.	1	2	3	4	5			☐				
I don't want to be the center of attention.	1	2	3	4	5				☐			
I always give 10 percent of my earnings and then offerings on top of that.	1	2	3	4	5					☐		

Questions	Answers					Gifts
	Almost Never	Rarely	Sometimes	Frequently	Almost Always	
If people don't like me or what I have done, I don't let it upset me.	1	2	3	4	5	
I feel that I can help others by praying.	1	2	3	4	5	
I do not like to be wrong in the opinions I hold.	1	2	3	4	5	
It is easier for me to do a job than find someone to do it.	1	2	3	4	5	
I am good at networking and finding people to help the cause.	1	2	3	4	5	
I enjoy reaching out to those who are sick, or to those who seem upset.	1	2	3	4	5	
I like to cheer people up by what I donate to others.	1	2	3	4	5	
I do not really like to do detailed work.	1	2	3	4	5	
I can't stand it when people fight or are hateful to each other.	1	2	3	4	5	
I want to see others grow deeper in their relationship with Christ.	1	2	3	4	5	
Sometimes I help so much that I don't focus on the spiritual needs of others.	1	2	3	4	5	
I like my life to be organized.	1	2	3	4	5	
I don't want people to feel left out or alone.	1	2	3	4	5	
My biggest desire is to share with others what Jesus did for them on the cross.	1	2	3	4	5	
Letting others know how I feel comes pretty easy for me.	1	2	3	4	5	
I notice quickly when others feel left out.	1	2	3	4	5	
I know when others speak if their words are from God.	1	2	3	4	5	
I enjoy being hospitable to others.	1	2	3	4	5	

Questions	Answers					Gifts						
	Almost Never	Rarely	Sometimes	Frequently	Almost Always							
I tend to be a workaholic.	1	2	3	4	5			▢				
I would enjoy going to a poverty-stricken society to reach out to others.	1	2	3	4	5				▢			
I am happy to do without things so that others can live a better life.	1	2	3	4	5					▢		
I like to dream of better ways to get things done.	1	2	3	4	5						▢	
I tend to think of the other person's feelings.	1	2	3	4	5							▢
I want to be instrumental in sharing the gospel and changing people's lives.	1	2	3	4	5	▢						
I am the first to offer my help in a task that needs to be accomplished.	1	2	3	4	5		▢					
I put my heart and soul into the job and organization that I am a part of.	1	2	3	4	5			▢				
I communicate with people on a one-on-one level, not in large groups.	1	2	3	4	5				▢			
I manage money well.	1	2	3	4	5					▢		
I feel as if I have to win when playing a game.	1	2	3	4	5						▢	
I can sense when people are lying to me.	1	2	3	4	5							▢
TOTALS												
						P	S	T	B	G	L	C

P = Prophesy   T = Teacher   G = Giver   C = Compassion

S = Server   B = Builder   L = Leader

Appendix B
Small Group Study Questions
for the "Life of Christ" Sections

Lesson 1

John 20:24-31

1. After three years of ministry Christ's message seemingly had not gotten through to people—not just to Thomas, but to many others. While Christ did many wonderful acts of kindness, many of His closest followers still had many questions as to who He was. Why do you suppose that is true?
2. Why do you think Thomas was "not with the disciples" when they first saw Jesus after His resurrection?
3. How long was it before Thomas eventually saw Jesus? Why do you think it took so long for Thomas and Jesus to meet together?
4. What evidence did Thomas and the other disciples have to really know Jesus? Do you think just seeing Christ is enough to know and believe?
5. Do you see yourself as a trusting person or as more skeptical?
6. In John 20:30, 31, what do we have in the way of knowledge about Jesus and what do we not have? According to John, is that enough? Why?

Lesson 2

Matthew 28:18-20

1. What words would you use to describe your human father or mother? Describe one of your parents in 25 words or less.
2. Is this description true? Is it accurate? Is it complete? In what ways is our understanding of God complete/incomplete?
3. How do we live in service to a God we don't know completely?
4. Where do we see evidence of the Trinity throughout the life of Christ? throughout the Bible?
5. How do the "three who are one" relate to Each Other? Are They separate? Do They have different roles and abilities?
6. In your own words, describe what you believe to be true about the Trinity.

Lesson 3

Luke 4:1-13

Mark 8:27-33

Mark 14:32-38

Matthew 27:39-43

1. Why do you think Jesus went into the wilderness? What was His motivation?
2. What is significant about His being there for 40 days?
3. When Satan tempts Jesus, he begins by saying, "If you are the Son of God . . ." Why does he do this, and what is his master plan?
4. What was tempting to Jesus about the three tests? What is the "real" temptation for Jesus? How are these temptations different from what we face? How are they alike?
5. What is significant about the way Jesus responds to the temptations?
6. What other times was Jesus tempted like this?
7. What is the war between good and evil about? What is the temptation Satan constantly throws at Jesus?
8. How would you describe Jesus' response to these dilemmas? With what attitude does He react?
9. In a sentence or two, describe what was God's will as opposed to the will of Jesus in the garden. (When Jesus said, "Not My will, but Yours . . .")
10. What do you think it will take for us (you) to be able to pray that prayer under any circumstance? What circumstance is most difficult for you to surrender your will to God's?

Lesson 4

Mark 1:40-45

1. Whom do you know—or know of—who seems almost unreachable?
2. Who do you think is harder for God to save, those whose sinful lives keep them far away or those who don't think they are that far away from God at all?
3. Describe what you know about lepers in the time of Christ.
4. What is significant about the leper's statement "If you are willing, you can make me clean"? Discuss the leper's attitude about his condition and his confidence in Jesus' abilities.

5. What is the difference between pity, sympathy, and empathy? How does compassion fit into these three words?

6. What do you think is significant about the fact that Jesus "touched" him and said, "I am willing"?

7. Have you considered what that moment of healing must have been like? Share among each other how you envision this miracle occurring.

8. Why do you think Jesus told him to show himself to the priest and go through the ritual of cleansing? Read Leviticus 14:1-9 and see if you can make any connection between this ritual and the meaning of Christ's work on the cross. Is there a connection? Of the two birds, which represents the leper? What does the other bird symbolize?

9. How did the leper's testimony impact the ministry of Christ? Share with your group a time when someone's personal story of conversion had a big effect on your relationship with God.

10. In what ways are we all like the leper, and how does this story reflect Christ's attitudes toward sinners?

11. How is the leper's experience with leprosy and healing like our experience with sin and salvation?

Lesson 5

John 1:10-13

1. Read John 3:1-12. "You are a great teacher from God, and God is with you." How does Nicodemus's understanding of who Jesus is affect the way he talks to Jesus? What if that is all Jesus is: "a teacher sent from God"? Does that change the way he relates to Christ? In what way?

2. Discuss what you think is going on in Nicodemus's heart as he waits until night before visiting Jesus. What kind of person do you think he might be?

3. What role do miraculous signs play in authenticating Jesus' ministry? Do His miracles dispel any doubts about His being Messiah?

4. How would you define the kingdom of God? What is a kingdom?

5. What do you think it means to be born again? As you look at Nicodemus's response, why do you think he is having such trouble understanding what Jesus is talking about?

6. Consider the statement "Spiritual things are spiritually discerned" (see 1 Corinthians 2:14).

7. What do you think Jesus is referring to when He says, "Born of water and the Spirit" (John 3:5)?

8. Why is the "wind blowing" a good metaphor for the work of the Holy Spirit in a person's life? Share a moment from your own experience when the Spirit quietly spoke to you and worked with you in a private, personal way.

9. After reading John 1:10-13, discuss the basic steps to becoming born of God, or born again.

10. Think of a time in your relationship with God that you became new. What prompted your surrender? How did you respond?

11. "Born, not of human will or human decision, but born of God." When you think of the word "adoption," how does this concept fit in with the new-birth experience? In what way is baptism a rebirth experience that is different from normal birth?

Lesson 6

John 1:1-14

1. When have you called out to someone in public, only to find out the individual was not who you thought he or she was? What happened?

2. What is significant about the fact that Jesus was the active agent at Creation (Colossians 1:13-16; Hebrews 1:1, 2)?

3. Why do you think John starts his Gospel the way he does? Compare his opening statement with the opening statements of the other Gospels. Next, look at the beginnings of 1 John and the book of Revelation and see what you discover.

4. The phrase "In him was life" (John 1:4) is powerful. How do we see this idea played out in the life of Jesus? Give a few examples of how you believe Jesus demonstrated this phrase.

5. The phrase "that life was the light of men" (verse 4) is also powerful. How was Christ's life a light for people in those days? How is their darkness like ours today?

6. Explain the meaning of the statement "The Word became flesh and made his dwelling among us. We have seen his glory" (verse 14). How does it relate to the creation of the world? Also explain this statement in light of the sanctuary of the Old Testament (Exodus 29:45, 46; 24:16; 40:34).

7. How do you see the two attributes "grace and truth" demonstrated in Jesus' life?

Lesson 7

Matthew 22:34-40

1. Share a time in your life when someone asked you a "loaded question." How did you respond?
2. How would you have answered the question that the expert in law posed to Jesus? Which commandment would you have chosen? Why?
3. Whom do you know who seems to love God "with all their heart, all their soul, and all their mind"? How has their life influenced yours?
4. Why do you think Jesus quoted Deuteronomy 6:4-6 instead of one of the Ten Commandments? What does His response tell us about how to relate to God's law?
5. When have you had a moment in which you felt as if you "loved God with all your heart, soul, and strength"? Describe what was happening in your life at that time.
6. How does Jesus completely avoid the meaningless question and answer the meaningful one?
7. "All the Law and the Prophets hang on these two commandments" basically says that the entire Old Testament is God's law. Brainstorm about some of the famous stories and passages of the Old Testament and put them under the category of one of the two commandments.

Lesson 8

Luke 13:10-16

1. Can you think of a time in your life when another's hypocrisy infuriated you?
2. When have you ever "majored in minors" or focused on the unimportant rather than the most important?
3. Discuss what this woman's condition might look like today.
4. What do you think people thought would be the source of her illness?
5. When Jesus saw her, He set her free. For 18 years she was in misery. What is significant about the way Jesus "sees" people and "frees" them? How does the Sabbath fit with this idea?
6. When the leaders were "indignant" because Jesus healed on the Sabbath, what thoughts went through your head as you read their words? How did you feel?
7. Do you think Jesus considered healing "work"? Even if He did, do you think it would have changed His response? Why/Why not?
8. How does the analogy of the ox/donkey and the "daughter of Abraham" explore the motives of the religious leaders?

9. If, for Jesus, Sabbath is about seeing and freeing people, how would your Sabbaths change if you were to follow that example?

Lesson 9

Read the passage or passages (as a group or in pairs, each pair having one passage).

Matthew 9:11-13

Matthew 20:20-28

Luke 19:5-10

Matthew 5:17, 18

Reflect on the following questions:

1. What is happening in each passage that prompts Jesus to make a statement?
2. What does Jesus say He came to do/be?
3. How do you see this fulfilled in specific moments of His life and ministry?
4. Read John 20:30, 31 and 21:24, 25. What does this say about the stories from the life of Christ we have? And what does it say about the many stories we don't have? What is the purpose of the stories about His life?
5. C. S. Lewis said, "A man who was merely a man and said the sort of things Jesus said wouldn't be a great moral teacher. He'd either be a lunatic—on the level with a man who says he's a poached egg—or else he'd be the devil of hell. You must make your choice. Either this man was, and is, the Son of God, or else a madman or something worse." How do you respond to this statement? On what basis is this statement true?

Lesson 10

Mark 14:17-26

1. What holiday most reminds you of what God intended the day to celebrate? What aspect seems to have become obscured the most?
2. Describe the most memorable Communion service you have ever attended and participated in.
3. When Jesus announced the betrayal of one of the disciples, how do you think it changed the mood of everyone present? Why do you think betrayal receives such a stern rebuke: "It would be better if they were never born"?
4. What is the meaning given to the emblems (bread and the wine) in the Last Supper?

5. When Jesus promises that He will wait until He comes again to eat and drink this meal with us, how does this statement make the Communion service more sacred?

6. How can you experience the blessings of God's grace at Communion both personally and as a church? What are some ways you can deepen the importance and meaning of this experience in your church?

Lesson 11

Luke 10:1-20

1. When have others asked you to do something you thought you were unqualified or untrained to do? Share your experience.

2. How would you characterize the type of work Christ calls His followers to do? Describe the degree or level of difficulty of the tasks that Jesus challenged the disciples with.

3. What preparation did they have? What skills did they need the most for this task?

4. Why do you think Jesus sent them out two by two?

5. When Jesus says, "He who rejects you rejects me," what does this say about the nature of the ministry He calls disciples to? How do you relate to rejection?

6. When the disciples returned from their work they shared all their experiences with joy. Did you think they all succeeded? What stories did they tell?

7. "Christ calls us to be faithful, not successful." How does this phrase relate to the above story? How much of our behavior as Christians depends on the reactions of others?

Lesson 12

Matthew 16:13-18

1. Who is a person in your church who would be sorely missed if they should leave? Why? (Don't use pastors as an example.)

2. What metaphor or symbol would you use to describe your church? Why did you choose the symbol you selected?

3. What do you think Jesus was trying to teach with such questions about His identity?

4. "Who do you say I am?" Is this a question for the disciples or just Peter? Why?

5. How much do you think the disciples really knew about who Jesus was?

6. How do you think God revealed this knowledge to Peter?

7. "You are Peter, and on this rock I will build my church." The statement has started a lot of arguments in the past. We can interpret it in several ways. Think about which one makes the most sense to you: (1) The rock Jesus refers to is Himself—not Peter. Jesus is simply saying, "You are Peter [a little stone]" but on "this rock," pointing to Himself, "I will build my church." (2) The rock is Peter's confession of Jesus as Lord, signifying that on the testimonies of believers the foundation is built. (3) The rock is Peter, and here begins the reign of papal supremacy. (4) The rock is Peter, and Jesus is simply saying that the church is going to be built on people, people who testify to "who I am."

8. Look at Acts 2:44-47 and imagine your church living like this. What would happen to your community if your church began to do such things? What would it take to cause this kind of revolution? Is that something you are interested in?

Lesson 13

Read the passage or passages (as a group or in pairs, each pair having one passage).

John 11:1-44

Mark 5:35-43

Luke 7:11-17

1. When in your life has the fear of death been very real to you? How did you resolve your fear?
2. With what attitude does Jesus approach the scene of death? How does He behave toward the loved ones and the deceased?
3. What does it mean that with one word, one breath, one touch Jesus overcomes death? How does this kind of Savior draw people?
4. Why do you think the Gospels include these three stories? What do they say about God, death, resurrection, and hope that is not mentioned in the other stories?
5. How does the one who trusts in Christ respond to death? Even though we believe, do we not still have fears? How do we then live?

Lesson 14

John 14:1-20

1. When in your life has someone promised you something you thought was impossible to deliver?
2. How well do you think the disciples understood the mission of Jesus? What are some of the parts of His life and ministry that they might have found hard to believe?

3. The disciples are obviously anxious and troubled about the way Jesus is talking. Why do you think they became uncomfortable when He mentioned leaving?

4. "I will come again and receive you to Myself." Even in light of passages that speak of a deep abiding relationship, why does the second coming of Jesus strike a certain amount of fear even in the minds of believers?

5. Note the verses that describe the role of the Holy Spirit in our lives while we work and wait for His return. What does the work of the Holy Spirit have to do with the second coming of Christ?

6. How does our attitude about the Second Coming differ from that of the disciples who heard these words straight from the lips of Jesus?

7. Consider the message of the second coming of Christ. How foreign is it to the world we live in? Do you think people today are interested or willing to hear about such things? Why or why not?

8. Practice the presence of the Holy Spirit this week. What are some practical ways to be mindful of God's Spirit in your life?

Lesson 15

Luke 12:1-10

1. When have you thought that someone's motives were pure, only to find out that they had deceived you? How did you feel? Do such experiences make us skeptical or suspicious?

2. Why do you think it is so difficult to discern another person's motivation?

3. Spend a few minutes talking about what is happening around this passage, as well as the circumstances of Jesus' words to His disciples. How does the frantic scene add to the hard things Jesus says in this story?

4. What verses or phrases seem to speak to you about the authenticity and the sincerity of people's hearts?

5. Discuss the serious way in which Jesus warns the disciples of the issues of deception, judgment, and loyalty. Where do you see these themes discussed in this passage (deception, judgment, loyalty), and what does Jesus say about them?

6. How do you explain the harsh nature of Christ (verses 4 and 5) and in the same breath words of comfort, hope, and affirmation (verses 6 and 7)?

7. To Christ, how important is our public confession of Him? How does our confession of Christ now affect His relationship to us?

8. People are complex beings. When Christ finally ends sin, sinners, and Satan by fire, how will we know God was true, just, and right in His punishment?

Lesson 16

Luke 23:39-43

1. "First impressions aren't always correct." How has this been true for you? When have you had to change your mind about someone after learning more about them?

2. As the two thieves are crucified with Jesus, is their initial hostility toward Christ something you might expect? How does the statement "Aren't you the Christ? Save yourself and us!" contradict the very purpose of Christ dying on Calvary?

3. How would you characterize the request of the converted thief? Bold? Presumptuous? A shot in the dark? Explain.

4. In what ways is our experience similar to that of the thief on the cross? How is it different?

5. Paradise—do you think that when the thief hears these words he is thinking about trees and waterfalls, with bunnies hopping freely around in a cool green meadow? What do you think "Paradise" means to this man who has just been handed this gift?

6. What does Paradise mean for us?

Lesson 17

Mark 12:41-44

1. What is your favorite place to go just to watch people? Why?

2. Have you ever caught someone doing an act of kindness who thought they were not being watched? What happened?

3. Think about your state of mind when you give at church. How would you describe your attitude?

4. Compare the givers in this story. In Christ's mind, what would it take for the rich to give as much as the widow?

5. Think about the different ways people can be tremendously wealthy as well as poverty-stricken. In what ways are you wealthy, and in what ways are you poor? How is an awareness of the two helpful in your walk with God?

6. Whom do you know who is a "giver" like this widow (not necessarily in money, but in time, talents, energy, love)?

7. Why do you think the Gospels include this story? What truths do you think it teaches?

8. How do you think you will be different because of your study of this passage?

Lesson 18

Matthew 5:13-15

1. Who would you say has had the most influence on you as a Christian? Why?
2. Why are lifestyle and personal choices such a hot debate in Christian churches?
3. Why is salt a powerful metaphor for Christian living? What attributes of salt make it useful for others?
4. Why is light a powerful metaphor for Christian living? What attributes of light make it useful for others?
5. What would change in your lifestyle if you used the ideas "salt" and "light" to gauge every decision you made? "Am I a light to this world when I . . . ?"
6. Get specific with your partner or group about how you can apply the concepts of salt and light to your lifestyle. Set some goals for this week to be "salt" and "light" in specific scenarios.

Lesson 19

Matthew 19:1-9

1. Think of three married couples you admire (at least one with children). Why did you choose those three? In one word, describe each marriage.
2. Here again, the Pharisees ask an insincere question. How does Jesus turn their trick question into a teachable moment?
3. Jesus clearly states that marriage is about two people becoming one. Talk about the different ways this applies to the marriage relationship (two becoming one).
4. What is significant about the statement "What God has joined together . . ."?
5. How is the reason that God permitted divorce in the Old Testament because of "the hardness of their hearts" the same today? In what way is it different?
6. What should be the Christian response to marriages that fall apart? How should people be a source of help? What should the church do?
7. What are some personal goals you have as you prepare yourself to be a godly partner for marriage?

Lesson 20

Matthew 27:45-54

1. When in your life have you felt that God was far away?
2. When in your life have you sensed His closeness the most?
3. When Jesus cried out, "Why have you forsaken me?" was it true that God had left Him? If so, why? Or did Jesus just feel abandoned even though God still remained close by? What does this heart-wrenching plea signify for Jesus as well as for us?
4. What do you think the Temple curtain being torn in two really means?
5. What do you think made the difference for the centurion in his attitude toward Christ? What caused him to change his mind about who Jesus was?
6. Read Matthew 1:23; 18:20; and 28:20. What phrase or idea seems to repeat itself throughout the book of Matthew? How does the life of Christ demonstrate the purpose of God's plan to build a sanctuary (Exodus 29:45, 46)?

Lesson 21

Matthew 28:19, 20

1. How do you think the disciples felt about such a challenge?
2. With all the trouble the disciples had had before about who was going to be first, with what attitude do you imagine they approached this task? Why?
3. How would you characterize the special work of the disciples at the end of Jesus' ministry?
4. How would we describe our special work in our world today?
5. What specific ministries and projects do you think you can do that will contribute to finishing God's mission on earth?